# AGORAPHOBIA
## Nature and Treatment

# AGORAPHOBIA

## Nature and Treatment

**ANDREW M. MATHEWS**
*University of London*

**MICHAEL G. GELDER**
*University of Oxford*

**DEREK W. JOHNSTON**
*University of Oxford*

NEW YORK UNIVERSITY PRESS
Washington Square, New York

© 1981 The Guilford Press, New York

First published in hardcover by The Guilford Press. First paperback edition published in 1986 by NEW YORK UNIVERSITY PRESS, Washington Square, New York, N.Y. 10003

Printed in the United States of America

**Library of Congress Cataloging-in-Publication Data**

Mathews, Andrew M.
  Agoraphobia, nature and treatment.

  Bibliography: p.
  Includes indexes.
  1. Agoraphobia.   I. Gelder, Michael Graham.
II. Johnston, Derek W.   III. Title.
[RC552.A44M38   1986]        616.85'225        85-32081
ISBN 0-8147-5426-0

**TO PHYLLIS SHAW**

# AGORAPHOBIA
## Nature and Treatment

# Preface

This book is the outcome of more than a decade of intensive clinical research into a single problem: agoraphobia. Agoraphobia remains at once the most disabling of phobias and the most difficult to treat. We have attempted not only to summarize our own findings but, by drawing on the work of others, to review the current state of knowledge about the origins and treatment of this distressing condition.

However, we also have a practical aim. In the latter half of the book, we attempt to give professional readers a means of helping their agoraphobic clients. To meet this aim, we have incorporated appendixes that, in conjunction with Chapter 10, provide a complete description of a self-help treatment method. Furthermore, we have shown this method to be effective and economical. Appendixes 1 and 2 are intended to be given to clients and relatives, and since we regard their use as an essential part of treatment, both are available as separate offprints through clinicians.

Finally, we acknowledge gratefully the many people who have generously provided help, encouragement, and active collaboration over many years. The Medical Research Council, U.K., has supported most of the research work that is reported here. The book itself could not have been written without the willing secretarial help of Beverley Haggis, Betty Merry, and Margaret Reuben.

The early part of the research, from which the rest has developed, was carried out by one of us (M.G.) in collaboration with Dr. Isaac Marks. The ideas developed at this time owe much to him. Subsequent work has been carried out by a team whose members over the years have included Pepe Catalan, Dennis Gath, Leila Jannoun, Meredith Lancashire, John Teasdale, and Paul Walsh, and—throughout the program of research—Mary Munby, to whom we are particularly grateful.

Until her death, Phyllis Shaw was also a member of the group. Her contribution to the research and to the team as a whole was very great. This book is dedicated to her.

*Andrew M. Mathews*
*Michael G. Gelder*
*Derek W. Johnston*

# Contents

## 11. FUTURE DIRECTIONS IN THEORY AND RESEARCH ON AGORAPHOBIA

# AGORAPHOBIA
## Nature and Treatment

# 1. The Nature of Agoraphobia

IT IS OVER a hundred years since Westphal first wrote about agoraphobia. Since then the condition that bears this name has been shown to be widespread and to cause much suffering, especially among young women, whom it affects most often. Many attempts have been made to treat agoraphobia; drugs, psychotherapy, behavioral treatment have all been advocated, but until recently little progress has been made. In the last few years, as a result of clinical and experimental research, great strides have been made in devising behavioral treatments for agoraphobia. This monograph describes this research and gives an account of the treatment methods and of the results that can be obtained. However, treatment cannot be discussed without an understanding of the nature of the condition and of the factors that have been thought to cause it. This first chapter deals with the nature of agoraphobia, and it can begin in no better place than with Westphal's original account.

## THE ORIGINAL CONCEPT OF AGORAPHOBIA

Westphal (1871) suggested the name *agoraphobia* for a condition in which the most striking symptom was anxiety that appeared when one was walking across open spaces or through empty streets. Westphal was not the only person to have noticed the condition at that time, for there is an earlier description by Benedikt (1870) in the previous year. However, Benedikt thought that the central feature was dizziness rather than anxiety, and he accordingly suggested the name *Platzschwindel* ("dizziness in public places"), which has not survived.

It is interesting to compare these original descriptions with the condition that we now call *agoraphobia*. The similarities are clear enough. The essential situational element in the symptoms was prominent: anxiety was present only in quite specific and predictable circumstances—crossing an open square, walking along an empty street, or in church, at the theater, or in other large rooms in which many people were gathered. This anxiety was alleviated by the presence of a companion, especially when the patient's attention was distracted by conversation. One of Westphal's patients was less anxious when he carried a stick or an umbrella—something that patients commonly report today. Alcohol also relieved the symptoms.

Westphal identified the symptoms as those of anxiety, in this way correcting Benedikt, who thought that dizziness was the central complaint and that it was caused by a disorder of the eye muscles. Westphal described palpitations, sensations of heat, blushing, and trembling—all symptoms that agoraphobic patients experience in the 1980s just as they did in 1870. He also recorded anticipatory anxiety and the associated fears of dying, as well as the patients' apprehension that they may attract unwanted attention. In view of the interest that has been expressed subsequently in the relationship between temporal lobe disorders and agoraphobia (see p. 11), it is interesting that two of Westphal's patients had experienced epilepsy earlier in life and that he devoted a large part of his paper to a discussion of the relationship between epilepsy and neurotic symptoms. With all these similarities between Westphal's cases and the many series of agoraphobic patients described since, it is surprising to find that his much-quoted (though little-read) paper was based on only three patients.

There are some minor but important differences between Westphal's description and the patients we see today. All three of his cases were men, but we now see agoraphobia much more often among women. He emphasized open spaces and empty streets, but nowadays, although patients describe these same phobic situations, there is often more emphasis on crowds.

A contemporary article by Cordes (1871) describes similar cases and makes the important observation that anxiety is based on the ideas in the patient's mind and is not provoked in an entirely automatic way by the stimuli in the environment. Cordes therefore grasped the importance of what are now called *cognitive factors*. His description includes the common physical symptoms of palpitations, nausea, headache, pressure in the chest, and breathlessness. He also pointed out that fear is often provoked by crowds, which indicates that Westphal's failure to note this point probably relates to the selection of his three patients but does not reflect any real change in the clinical picture over the years.

Before we leave these early accounts of the condition, it is appropriate to refer to the clear description of the clinical picture given by Legrand du Saule in 1885. It is notable that although he described the clinical picture in a female patient, he commented that she was uncommon and that the disorder was more usually seen in men. Perhaps changing social roles may explain why more women now seek help for a condition that disables those who wish to leave home, to travel, and to enter public places. It is difficult otherwise to understand why these 19th-century doctors described the condition predominantly among men.

## THE CLINICAL PICTURE TODAY

Agoraphobia usually begins between the ages of 18 and 35 (mean age about 28; Marks & Herst, 1970), but since untreated cases often persist for many years, patients are often seen who are older. Some authors have reported two peak ages of onset, at about 20 and 30–35 (Marks, 1970; Bowen, 1979). About two-thirds of patients are women (Marks, 1970; Terhune, 1949). The central symptom is phobic anxiety, that is, anxiety that appears only in clearly defined situations. In agoraphobia, the situations that provoke anxiety share certain common themes, usually distance from home or another safe place, crowds, and confinement. Within these themes, specific examples include buses and trains, theaters and stores (particularly stores in which the customer must wait in line before paying), and other places that are difficult to leave immediately, for example, the hairdresser's or dentist's chair. Table 1.1 shows the anxiety-provoking situations most frequently reported by the agoraphobic people who responded to a mail survey carried out by Burns and Thorpe (1977a). We shall see later that this grouping of fears, originally identified by clinicians, has been confirmed by cluster analysis of questionnaires and ratings (Marks, 1970; Hallam & Hafner, 1978). Finally, we must note that symptoms are often increased by general stress, such as arguments between marital partners, and this is also evident from Table 1.1. Just as anxiety appears because of or is made worse by certain predictable situations, so it is relieved by circumstances that also have common themes that are shared by different patients. The most striking of these is that anxiety is nearly always less in the presence of a trusted companion. For some, only an adult person will do;

TABLE 1.1. Percentage of agoraphobic people reporting certain situations that provoke anxiety[a]

| Situation | % |
| --- | --- |
| Joining a line in a store | 96 |
| A definite appointment | 91 |
| Feeling trapped at hairdresser, etc. | 89 |
| Increasing distance from home | 87 |
| Particular places in neighborhood | 66 |
| Thinking about my problems | 82 |
| Domestic arguments and stress | 87 |

[a]Modified from Burns and Thorpe (1977a).

for others the presence of a child, a dog, or even an inanimate object such as an umbrella or a shopping basket decreases the symptoms (see Table 1.2).

Phobic anxiety is usually accompanied by some degree of avoidance. The patient stays away from the situations that provoke the most fear, and life becomes more and more restricted. Relatives or friends are persuaded to take over the shopping or to accompany the children to school, while visits to the homes of friends and relations are gradually given up. From the beginning, fear is not only felt when the patient has entered the situation; it begins as soon as the situation is anticipated. Thus, a housewife will start to feel anxious as soon as she prepares to go shopping, and as the condition progresses, anxiety starts from the moment of waking on the day on which it is necessary to go out. This anticipatory anxiety may be worse than the anxiety that the patient experiences in the situation itself, and patients often report that once they have gone out, they feel less frightened than expected. This is an important point, which, as we shall see later, has some bearing on treatment.

As in all anxiety states, the symptoms are physical as well as mental. The physical symptoms are no different from those of any other anxiety state, but the mental symptoms are rather more specific to agoraphobia. The physical symptoms include dry mouth, sweating (especially of the palms of the hands and the axillae), awareness of forceful and rapid action of the heart, a feeling of being about to faint, dizziness, and, indeed, the whole variety of physical sensations that can accompany anxious mood. Hyperventilation—and the symptoms consequent upon it, such as tingling of the fingers—can occur, and Tucker (1956) reported that they occur frequently, though we do not have this impression. Hysterical behavior is seen in a number of patients, often when anxiety is intense, but this is not a constant feature of the condition.

The mental symptoms include, as well as the well-known feeling of fearful anticipation, a number of characteristic thoughts. These include the "fear of fear," which is reported by anxious patients of all kinds, together with certain specific cognitions. *Fear of fear* refers to the anticipation of anxiety and thoughts that the mental and physical symptoms of anxiety will lead to worse consequences—a thought that in turn generates more anxiety. For example, mounting feelings of anxiety often make the patient anticipate that he/she will lose control and behave in a disinhibited way, or even become insane; while rapid heart action may lead the patient to expect a cardiac arrest or coronary thrombosis. The other thoughts, which are characteristic of agoraphobia, center on the patients' expectation that they may faint if they become very anxious and may come round to find themselves surrounded by unsympathetic onlookers. The frequency with which this and other fears are reported is shown in Table 1.3.

Agoraphobic patients do not complain of phobic anxiety symptoms alone. Generalized anxiety, depersonalization, depression, obsessional symptoms, and poor psychosexual function may all be part of the disorder.

TABLE 1.2. Percentage of agoraphobic people reporting certain situations that relieve anxiety[a]

| Situation | % |
| --- | --- |
| Being accompanied by spouse | 85 |
| Sitting near the door in a hall or restaurant | 76 |
| Focusing my mind on something else | 63 |
| Taking dog, baby carriage, etc. | 62 |
| Being accompanied by a friend | 60 |
| Talking problems over with my doctor | 62 |
| Talking problems over with a friend | 62 |
| "Talking sense to myself" | 52 |

[a]Modified from Burns and Thorpe (1977a).

TABLE 1.3. Cognitions in agoraphobia[a]

|  | First fear | Second fear |
| --- | --- | --- |
| Fainting/collapsing | 37.9% | 15.8% |
| Death | 13.2% | 19.7% |
| Other personal illness | 10.4% | 9.7% |
| Losing control (e.g., be-coming hysterical) | 7.4% | 6.7% |
| Causing a scene | 6.2% | 25.8% |
| Inability to get home to place of safety | 5.9% | 8.5% |
| Becoming mentally ill | 5.8% | 7.0% |
| Heart attack | 4.1% | 4.0% |
| Other | 8.9% | 3.0% |

[a]Modified from Burns and Thorpe (1977a).

Most agoraphobic patients describe some generalized anxiety, which is present as a background to the more severe anxiety that they experience in phobic situations, and occasionally this background anxiety mounts up into a severe state, which is often called a *panic attack*. The frequency of depersonalization is difficult to determine because the symptom is not clearly defined and patients' reports about it are particularly likely to be affected by the style of questioning. Roth and his colleagues (e.g., Roth, 1959) have suggested that patients who have prominent symptoms of depersonalization are suffering from a separate condition, but this view is not generally accepted. The depressive symptoms that are commonly present appear usually to be an understandable psychological reaction to the distress and disability caused by the phobic anxiety, although in a few cases, depression seems to have arisen without such obvious cause. This finding has led to the suggestion that agoraphobia is primarily an affective disorder—and this is a matter that we shall discuss later in this chapter. The obsessional symptoms that occur in agoraphobia shade into the intrusive anxious cognitions that have been described already, although a few patients also describe obsessional thoughts with a different content.

Buglass, Clarke, Henderson, Kreitman, and Presley (1977) also examined the frequency of these symptoms in agoraphobics and controls. Table 1.4 shows their findings (presented in a slightly different way from that adopted in the original publication).

Poor psychosexual functioning is common among agoraphobic patients (Marks & Gelder, 1965; Roberts, 1964), as it is among patients with severe anxiety (Winokur & Holeman, 1963). Because sexual enjoyment and performance usually increase when phobic anxiety subsides, whether spontaneously or as a result of treatment, it seems likely that it is secondary to the anxiety symptoms. This view is supported by the findings of the survey by Buglass *et al.* (1977), who found that sexual problems usually started with or after the anxiety symptoms and not before. The sexual problems that we have just considered pose further problems for husband and wife, and it is a common assumption that major marital difficulties are commonly present when one partner is agoraphobic. However, Buglass *et al.* (1977) found that marital problems were no more frequent among a group of 30 agoraphobic patients, drawn from general practice, than they were in 30 healthy controls from the same practice. Our experience of seeing a large number of agoraphobic patients in the course of clinical investigations agrees with these findings, and it seems likely that the widely held impression to the contrary derives from a relatively small number of striking cases in which prominent marital problems cause so much difficulty in treatment that they are remembered long after less complicated cases are forgotten.

We have already noted some of the effects of agoraphobia on social functioning. As a woman finds it harder to go out, her husband and her older children become more and more involved in her problems. Family holidays are often restricted, and the help of neighbors may be enlisted to take younger children to school. Family outings for pleasure are progressively

TABLE 1.4. Frequency of symptoms other than phobias in agoraphobics compared with healthy controls[a]

| | % | |
| --- | --- | --- |
| | Agoraphobics ($n = 30$) | Controls ($n = 30$) |
| General anxiety | 80 | 17 |
| Depression | 30 | 3 |
| Obsessional symptoms | 10 | 3 |
| Depersonalization | 37 | 13 |
| Loss of libido | 53 | 3 |

[a]Modified from Buglass, Clarke, Henderson, Kreitman, and Presley (1977), using their numbers for symptoms "clearly present."

curtailed. Burns and Thorpe (1977b) carried out a mail survey of 963 agoraphobic patients identified through publicity in local and national newspapers and on television and radio. The percentages who chose each of the following consequences of the disorder as the most important are shown in brackets: lack of social contact (28%), personal psychological effect (21%), inability to work (17%), effect on marital relationships (13%), travel restrictions (10%), and guilt regarding children (5%). The relatively small importance attached to travel restrictions is interesting.

There is no agreement about the personality of agoraphobic patients, partly because descriptions pay varying amounts of attention to the personality before the onset of the disorder and to the personal qualities of the patient once the condition has become established. Previous personality is considered further in Chapter 3; here we shall be concerned with observations made after the patient has developed the disorder. There is rather general agreement with a picture that has been well described by Ey, Bernard, and Brisset (1974), who emphasized a constant state of alertness, a passive and dependent attitude, and a tendency toward sexual inhibition. Terhune (1949) and Tucker (1956) have also remarked on the passive and dependent qualities of agoraphobic patients. Shafar (1976) viewed three-quarters of patients as having abnormalities of personality, though not all were regarded by her as abnormally dependent.

Finally, among the problems that may arise in the course of agoraphobia, mention must be made of the abuse of alcohol and anxiolytic drugs. Dependence on drugs is less common now that barbiturates have been almost wholly replaced by benzodiazepines. However, although physical dependence is less common with these preparations, psychological dependence is common and often encouraged by overprescribing. The frequency of alcoholism among agoraphobic patients is difficult to determine since the only systematic data in the literature (Mullaney & Trippett, 1979) approached the problem from the other direction by looking for phobic states among patients referred to an alcohol treatment unit. Mullaney and Trippett reported the surprising finding that one-third had disabling agoraphobia or social phobias, while a further third had "less disabling phobic symptoms." Such high figures cast doubt on the selection of their patients and on their definition of disabling symptoms. Clinical experience is more in keeping with the figure of Quitkin, Rifkin, Kaplan, and Klein (1972) of 5–10% of alcohol and drug abuse combined. Alcohol abuse is probably more common among people with social phobias than among those with agoraphobia, and it is probably more common among men than among women in both conditions. Clearly, it is important to inquire thoroughly about the use and abuse of drugs and alcohol in all agoraphobic patients.

Since people who have agoraphobic symptoms do not always consult doctors or psychologists, it is interesting to know how these differ from the group we have described. Marks and Herst (1970) found that those who did not consult professionals had phobias and other symptoms no less severe than those of the rest, but they differed significantly on measures of ability to confide in other people. They were, somewhat surprisingly, as likely to consult their doctors about physical symptoms as were the rest. Only a few said that they had not sought help from their doctor because they could not travel to his/her office.

## DOES THE AGORAPHOBIC SYNDROME REALLY EXIST?

This account of an agoraphobic syndrome will have suggested several questions to the reader. Is agoraphobia a discrete syndrome or merely the extreme end of a continuum of fears that are widely distributed in the population? If the symptoms cluster together as a syndrome when patients are first seen, do they continue to do so? Is the condition really separate from anxiety neurosis (in which there is "free-floating" but no phobic anxiety) and from depressive disorders? There is now a substantial amount of evidence that is relevant to these questions and that, in our view, makes it possible to give reasonably confident answers.

The first question is whether the phobic symptoms that we have identified as typical of agoraphobia are really closely associated with one another and separate from other phobic complaints. Evidence about this question comes from studies in which questionnaires about fears have been given to populations of patients and the results subjected to factor analysis or a similar technique (Dixon, de Monchaux, & Sandler, 1957; Hallam & Hafner, 1978; Marks, 1967; Shapira, Kerr, & Roth, 1970). These studies agree in finding a substantial factor loading with agoraphobic symptoms. Moreover, studies of normal subjects show that agoraphobic complaints are the least common forms of fear reported (Snaith, 1968; Agras, Sylvester, & Oliveau, 1969); indeed, they do not appear at all in the study of Hersen (1973). It appears, therefore, that there is a group of agoraphobic symptoms that are associated with one another and that they are probably not merely a more severe form of fears that are common in the population.

The next problem concerns the relationship between agoraphobia and affective disorders, that is, depressive illness and states of generalized anxiety. Statistical inquiries confirm that mild agoraphobic symptoms are common in states of anxiety and depression (Roth, Garside, & Kerr, 1972), and no clear separation of anxiety and phobic states has been achieved by these methods. Equally, depressive symptoms are common among agoraphobic patients (Bowen, 1979). Hallam (1978) has concluded from this kind of evidence that "agoraphobia is not a central feature of a phobic syndrome, but a variable feature of patients with neurotic anxieties." In making this statement, he failed to take account of another criterion that has been employed (since the days of Kraepelin) in deciding whether a group of symptoms can be regarded as cohering together sufficiently to constitute a syndrome. This decision requires a study of the condition over many years and not merely an analysis of the information available at the time when the diagnosis is made.

There are, unfortunately, rather few long-term prospective follow-up studies of agoraphobic patients who have been diagnosed reliably. Those that are available are discussed more fully in Chapter 10. Here we need only note that they are in agreement on this important question. Marks (1971) reported a four-year follow-up, while our own group has followed patients for up to nine years (Munby & Johnston, 1980). In neither investigation was there any evidence that patients who fulfilled the criteria of the agoraphobic syndrome when first seen developed the clinical picture of a generalized anxiety state or a depressive illness during the subsequent years. Thus, whatever the relation of anxiety states and agoraphobia at the time of onset, it appears that once agoraphobia has developed, it remains the same condition.

A variant of the view that agoraphobia is merely an atypical form of an affective disorder has been suggested by Mendel and Klein (1969). They appear to regard the disorder as separate from generalized anxiety states; however, they believe that it is not the avoidance that makes the distinction but the panic attacks that arise in the absence of phobic situations. They base their argument mainly on response to drug treatment—always rather insecure grounds in psychiatry, where few drugs have specific effects. Unfortunately Klein and his colleagues have never formulated a definition of *panic attacks* that allows them to be distinguished clearly from acute anxiety experienced in response to phobic stimuli. Klein's ideas gain a little indirect support from the findings by Bowen (1979) of a high incidence of affective disorders and episodic alcoholism (which he regards as symptomatic of affective disorder) in the relatives of agoraphobics.

We can conclude that although there is good evidence that agoraphobia is a syndrome separate from other phobic disorders and from depressive illness, its relation to other anxiety states is rather less clear. This point will be considered further in Chapter 3.

## THE PHOBIC-ANXIETY DEPERSONALIZATION SYNDROME

Before we leave the subject of the relationship of agoraphobia to other psychiatric disorders, it is appropriate to refer briefly to a syndrome that Roth and his colleagues claimed to have isolated. They suggested that agoraphobic patients who report depersonalization make up a separate group, and that the disorder in these patients characteristically starts after a particularly severe stress (hence the alternative name of *calamity syndrome*). That the syndrome is otherwise very similar to agoraphobia is shown by the following extract from the paper by Harper and Roth (1962, p. 132):

> Two-thirds of the consecutive series of 300 patients studied in hospital were women and the commonest ages of onset were late in the third and fourth decade. Patients are prone to become panic stricken when unaccompanied in the street, in crowds, buses, shops and particularly when inactive or compelled to wait, as in cinemas or queues. In these situations the feelings of depersonalisation are usually intensified. Variable depressive, obsessional, hysterical and hypochondriacal symptoms are common in addition to the central features of the syndrome.

However, these authors went on to describe other features that they supposed to be characteristic of the syndrome:

> In some 40% of cases features reminiscent of temporal lobe dysfunction, other than depersonalisation, are present; these include déjà vu experiences, perceptual disorders such as olfactory or visual hallucinations and micropsia. In 60% of cases the state of chronic tension is punctuated by abrupt attacks of acute panic often with fears of impending death.

Harper and Roth described certain similarities between phobic-anxiety depersonalization syndrome and temporal lobe epilepsy. We have not been impressed with the validity of this syndrome, and we describe it here only to complete the account.

## EPIDEMIOLOGY

Before we consider the epidemiology of the agoraphobic syndrome, it is appropriate to examine what is known about the frequency in the community of all kinds of phobias. The most informative survey was carried out by

Agras *et al.* (1969) who inquired specifically into the epidemiology of phobias among the population of one small North American town. They found a total prevalence of 77 per 1,000 population, but their figures must be interpreted with caution because they reported equal rates in men and women, which is contrary to general experience. Of these phobias, agoraphobia constituted 8%, that is, 6 per 1,000. A much higher estimate—260 per 1,000—was obtained by Langer and Michael (1963) but this ratio must be viewed against the low threshold that was set for symptoms in this study; it is probably an overestimate. Of the two, the figure obtained by Agras *et al.* is probably the more realistic.

The incidence of phobic disorders (i.e., phobias that are sufficiently severe to cause definite disability) was 2.2 per 1,000 in the first of these two studies, *disability* being defined as absence from work or inability to perform household duties. This ratio is somewhat higher than the .5 per 1,000 reported by Hollingshead and Redlich (1958) and by Lemkau, Tietze, and Cooper (1942), presumably because different thresholds were accepted for disability. For our purposes, we require to know what proportion of these phobic disorders are agoraphobia. Agras *et al.* reported that of the phobias being treated (2.2 per 1,000), agoraphobia constituted half. Marks (1969) also reported that about half the phobics seen by psychiatrists are agoraphobics, and the same proportion was found by Burns and Thorpe (1977a) in a survey of readers of a women's magazine who were asked to report phobic disorders. Finally, the proportion of psychiatric patients who are diagnosed phobic is about 2–3% (Terhune, 1949; Errera & Coleman, 1963; Marks, 1969), and of these, the majority are agoraphobic.

It is generally agreed that agoraphobia is very uncommon in childhood (see, for example, Rutter, Tizard, & Whitmore, 1968).

## MODE OF ONSET

Agoraphobia usually begins in early adult life. In this way, it contrasts with the childhood origin of most simple phobias and the onset in late adolescence of the majority of social phobias (Marks & Gelder, 1966). There is reasonable agreement about the mean age of onset in different reported series: 24 years (Marks & Gelder, 1965), 28 years (Burns & Thorpe, 1977a), 29 years (Marks & Herst, 1970), and 31 years (Buglass *et al.*, 1977). However, there is a wide range around this mean: Marks and Gelder reported a standard deviation of nearly 10 years. Burns and Thorpe are unusual in reporting that nearly 10% started before the age of 15 and 13% after the age of 40. Marks and Gelder found a suggestion of a bimodal distribution of age of onset, with one peak in late adolescence and the second around the age of 30.

Patients usually say that the disorder began suddenly with an unexpected attack of panic experienced in one of the situations that they later came to fear and avoid. In Snaith's (1968) study, two-thirds of the patients described this type of sudden onset, and in such cases, it is usually said that the panic occurred at a bus stop, in a large store, or on public transport. It is unusual for patients to remember any single stressful event that immediately preceded this first attack of panic. However, on closer inquiry, it is often found that the attack occurred at a time when the patient was under some stress of a less acute kind, such as the illness of a child, marital conflict, or some other common family problem. Investigations that have attempted to test these common clinical impressions are discussed in Chapter 3. A few cases begin after childbirth or operations, but these minority do not appear to justify the speculations that have been made about the role of endocrine imbalance. As Marks (1969) has pointed out, the presence and the nature of a precipitating factor seem to have no obvious relationship to the subsequent course of the disorder.

Following this first attack of anxiety, most patients experience anxiety only when they return to the same or to a closely similar surrounding. From these beginnings, the condition progresses more-or-less quickly so that other situations become associated with fear, and at the same time, the fear encountered in the original situation grows worse. In a few cases, the onset is so acute that the patient returns home from the first attack of panic, stays indoors—sometimes in bed—for days, and thereafter has great difficulty in leaving the house.


## NATURAL HISTORY

The natural history of agoraphobia is difficult to determine because reports vary in the criteria for improvement and the length of follow-up. Moreover treatment of various kinds has been carried out with nearly all patients, and the effects of these different treatments on the natural course are difficult to determine. Clinical experience suggests that there are many short-lived episodes that are underrepresented in the series reported by psychiatrists. It is against this background that we must assess the following reports, from which we have excluded those of patients who have received behavior therapy. Terhune (1949) studied 86 phobic outpatients, most of whom presented with agoraphobia and were followed up for several years.

Permanent relief of phobias was reported in 67%, and a further 24% experienced substantial improvement in social functioning. Friedman's (1950) study of travel phobia concerned a group of patients who were mainly agoraphobic, but the follow-up varied from 3 days to 32 years, so that few useful conclusions can be drawn from the author's report that 46% had recovered. Roberts's (1964) study of 38 married women, all housebound by phobic anxiety, is also difficult to assess because of the wide variation in the length of follow-up—in this case, from 1½ years to 16 years. Of these severely disabled women, only 24% were able at follow-up to leave their homes unaccompanied without experiencing phobic anxiety. Although 53% could go out even though they experienced the same symptoms, their going out was often limited, and 24% were still housebound. We include this report here because although all the patients had received firm encouragement to go out, none received formal behavior therapy.

In the study reported by Errera and Coleman (1963), the length of follow-up was less variable—an average of 23 years and a range of 22–24 years. However, the 19 patients reported came from an original group of 47, the rest being lost to follow-up for one reason or another. Agras, Chapin, Jackson, and Oliveau (1972) followed up 16 adult phobics prospectively for five years. Six were agoraphobic. These untreated phobics showed no reduction in their phobias over that time. Symptoms had persisted more-or-less unchanged in 15 and were still present in a mixed form in another 3. Follow-up studies by Tucker (1956) and Sim and Houghton (1966) are also difficult to interpret. In the face of this incomplete evidence, it is difficult to improve on Marks's (1969) conclusion that many cases of agoraphobia are short-lived but that phobias that have persisted for a year are unlikely to remit over the next several years if untreated. Nevertheless, every clinician has seen patients who experienced quite long periods of partial remission. In the absence of clear evidence about the prognosis of untreated anxiety states of similar severity, it is difficult to compare anxiety states with agoraphobia, but the clinical impression is that the presence of agoraphobic symptoms, and particularly of the avoidance that goes with them, results in a worse prognosis. This impression is supported by studies showing that of patients with anxiety states, about one-half had recovered on follow-up, irrespective of treatment (Greer, 1969).

As well as long-term variations in severity, short-term fluctuations in

severity of agoraphobic symptoms have been reported. Thus Buglass *et al.*
(1977) found that a third of their patients reported that symptoms could
vary within the space of a month from their being housebound to their being able to travel with some discomfort, while Burns and Thorpe (1979b)
reported similar observations from their group of 963 agoraphobics, nearly
90% of whom described marked fluctuations from day to day. However,
we have not found such wide variations where diary records of actual day-
to-day achievements have been collected. This is an important issue that
merits further investigation.

## SOCIAL AND FAMILY ASSOCIATIONS

Agoraphobia, if it is at all severe, invariably affects routines in some
way. Patients who cannot shop, travel to work, collect their children from
school, or travel to see their friends invariably involve other people in their
problems. They ask friends and relatives to accompany them or to under-
take tasks for them. They may refuse invitations, or leave social gatherings
before they end. Moreover, Burns and Thorpe (1977a) reported that 1 in 5
of their respondents regarded their agoraphobia as imposing some strain
on their marriage. The extent to which patients ask others to take over their
domestic and social responsibilities may be related to personality differences. Thus Marks and Herst (1970) reported that agoraphobic patients
who continued working were more likely to have outgoing personality traits
than were those who were not at work. These considerations make it self-
evident that agoraphobia has social consequences; the problem is whether
it also has social causes. It is a question for Chapter 3, on etiology, but here
we need to decide whether there is evidence for association between agoraphobia and problems in the family.

Many of the reports that suggest that marital problems are common
among agoraphobic patients originate from psychotherapists. It must be
asked, therefore, whether the marital problems were among the reasons
that these particular agoraphobic patients sought and obtained psychotherapy—rather than being the cause of their agoraphobia in the first
place. In the study of Buglass *et al.* (1977), to which we have already re-
referred, 30 married agoraphobic women referred were compared with
matched controls chosen from general practice records and screened for the
absence of psychiatric symptoms. The groups were matched for age, sex,
social class, and marital status. Despite the most careful inquiry, no differ-

ences were found between the groups, either on measures of attitudes and behaviors or on ratings of domestic organization and marital interaction. Nonetheless, the husbands of the agoraphobic patients complained that they were adversely affected by their wives' condition, an observation that may explain some of the findings of other investigations, which have not included a control group. The husbands thought of themselves as increasingly sympathetic as time went on, and at the time of interview, nearly 60% regarded themselves as sympathetic. However, the patients saw things somewhat differently. About half agreed that their husbands were generally concerned and sympathetic, but about 10% were reported as remote, silent, and perplexed.

Buglass *et al.* did not find that the spouses of female agoraphobic patients were more neurotic than those of the controls, a finding that confirms those of Agulnik (1970), who examined both men and women patients, and Hafner (1977a), who studied only women. That there may be differences in this regard between men and women is suggested by the work of Hagnell and Kreitman (1974), who found that when it is the wife who is the neurotic patient, the husband is not put at greater risk of developing neurotic symptoms, but that when the husband is the patient, the wife's risk of becoming neurotic is increased. This risk rises with the length of time the neurosis has been present, suggesting that it is a consequence, not a cause, of the condition. Hafner (1977b) has suggested that the interaction may be even more complex. He found some evidence that women agoraphobics who scored highest on tests for hostility and extrapunitiveness were married to intrapunitive men with low hostility scores; and the converse was found for hostile and extrapunitive men and intrapunitive wives who had low hostility. These findings were based on small numbers and, for this and other reasons, require replication before any definite inferences can be drawn from them.

Many agoraphobic women are concerned that their condition will affect the development of their children. However, there was no evidence in the study of Buglass *et al.* of any greater morbidity in the children of agoraphobic patients than in those of control women. This was true whether individual symptoms were examined or the number of disturbed children was counted in each group. Moreover the number of children with childhood phobias was the same in the two groups: 18% among the children of the agoraphobic mothers; 25% among the controls. The type of phobia—specific fears of animals and insects—was similar in the two groups.

We can conclude that, at least when the patient is the wife, there is no good evidence for any substantial detrimental effect of agoraphobia on family life, if we exclude those routines, such as shopping, that are directly affected by the patient's avoidance behavior. And it must be said that progress will be more rapid if further studies of these problems include properly chosen control groups.

# 2. Assessment Methods in Agoraphobia

IN THE FIRST chapter, we described the clinical features of agoraphobia. To go deeper into the nature and treatment of the condition requires measurement as well as description, and in this chapter, we shall describe how measurement has been attempted. We shall be concerned with the main techniques that have been used in the assessment of agoraphobic fear and avoidance, including the response of agoraphobic patients to treatment. Clearly, in many situations the researcher or the therapist may wish to measure other aspects of the patient's behavior and psychological state. However, such measures raise few special problems in agoraphobia. Readers unfamiliar with behavioral assessment techniques in general will find the necessary information in one of the many excellent texts, such as that edited by Hersen and Bellack (1976).

In a highly influential analysis of emotion, Lang (1971) suggested that fear and anxiety consist of three loosely connected components, which he has termed the "verbal–cognitive, the motor and physiological." This is to say, fear is composed of what people say, feel, and think; what they do; and how they respond physiologically. In agoraphobia, these three components of fear and conglomerates of them have been measured in a variety of ways, which include ratings of the patient's state by a skilled interviewer, self-ratings by the patient, objective testing of the patient's preparedness to enter a feared situation, diaries of time spent out of the house, and physiological responses to real or surrogate versions of phobic situations.

## PSYCHIATRIC RATING SCALES

The most widely used method of assessing agoraphobia has been a numerical rating of the patient's state following a psychiatric interview.

This technique was introduced by Gelder and Marks (1966). A skilled psychiatrist, using an unstructured interview, attempted to discover the extent of the patients' agoraphobic difficulties by asking detailed questions about their current activities, their reasons for avoiding specific situations, their feelings—both subjective and somatic—when in fearful situations, and their beliefs about what they would do if they were not fearful. In Marks and Gelder's original use of this method, the patients were then rated on a scale of 1 to 5 (5 being maximal severity) with respect to a series of specific situations, one being characterized as the main phobic situation and up to four that were characterized as lesser phobic situations. For example, the main situation might be traveling on buses and the lesser situations walking down busy streets, entering supermarkets, going to the movies, and going to the hairdresser. The reliability of such ratings was assessed by correlating the ratings by independent assessors with ratings by the patients' therapists. The reliability coefficients were all about .8, which is reasonably satisfactory.

These rating scales predated Lang's three-system model of fear and, in fact, attempt to integrate the different aspects of fear into one composite score. Watson and Marks (1971) sought to improve upon a composite score by obtaining separate ratings of fear and avoidance after a similar psychiatric interview. In addition, they recognized the reluctance of many raters to restrict themselves to a scale of 1 to 5 and modified the scale to run from 0 to 8. The reliability of these ratings was again about .8 when assessors' ratings were compared with those of patients' therapists. These ratings have been used extensively in subsequent studies, and it has been found that fear and avoidance ratings correlate very highly indeed. For this reason, many users have recombined the scales to give one score for fear and avoidance; see for example, Hand, Lamontagne, and Marks (1974) and Teasdale, Walsh, Lancashire, and Mathews (1977). Another modification was introduced by Mathews, Johnston, Lancashire, Munby, Shaw, and Gelder (1976), who altered the scales of Gelder and Marks to disability ratings that reflect the degree to which the patients' phobias interfered with their lives, but these scales were not tied to any specific phobia. We have recently assessed the reliability of this form of rating (Munby & Johnston, 1980) in a group of 13 agoraphobic women assessed independently by two raters. Again the reliability was above .8.

Since some of the studies that we shall review in subsequent chapters used the 1–5 scales and others adopted the 0–8 scales, it is important to know how these relate to one another. Teasdale *et al.* (1977) compared the Wat-

son and Marks 8-point fear and avoidance scales with the Mathews *et al.*
5-point disability rating in a group of 18 agoraphobics treated with a form
of group exposure. In general, the two scales correlated highly, but the
Watson and Marks scales changed rather more than the Mathews *et al.*
scale, even when the latter was prorated to adjust for its limited range. This
difference is not surprising since the Watson and Marks scales are very
much more specific. Thus, if the main fear was of traveling in buses and
treatment was directed toward that fear, sizable reductions would be expected in a rating of fear and of avoidance of buses. However, if the same
patient had other fears, such as a fear of supermarkets or movie theaters,
and these were not treated, then the reduction in overall disability might be
quite modest. For this reason, it appears reasonable to suggest that both
methods of rating have value. When one is assessing the effectiveness of
treatment, specific ratings of particular aspects of the patient's phobia are
more likely to be sensitive to the changes produced by treatment. However,
these ratings tell us little about the impact of the phobia on the patient's
life. This lack can be remedied by the use of the disability ratings, and we
suggest that both forms of rating should be used routinely. This double
rating is done in the patient self-rating scale published by Marks and
Mathews (1979) and described later.

Psychiatric rating scales have much to commend them. They are easy to
use, take little time, and are reliable. They are also sensitive to the effects of
treatment, and as we will see later in the chapter, they correlate at a satisfactory level with other more objective measures of agoraphobic behavior.
In addition, they allow a complex concept, such as the disability produced
by agoraphobia, to be turned into a useful numerical value. However,
rating scales cannot really be used as valid measures of specific aspects of
fear such as avoidance or subjective or somatic anxiety, for it is likely that
such measures will interact when the same rater is making a series of
judgments about the patient. Therefore, while excellent for some purposes,
rating scales of this kind are not necessarily adequate measures of all
aspects of the degree or amount of change in fears.

## PATIENT SELF-RATINGS

In many of the studies of agoraphobia to be described in Chapter 6, patients rated their own phobic behavior and disabilities on scales similar to
those used by the independent assessors, and their ratings invariably cor-

related highly with those of the independent assessor. An alternative exists in the several fear questionnaires that have been developed (e.g., by Wolpe & Lang, 1964; Marks & Herst, 1970) and that attempt to measure patients' fear in many different situations. Marks and Mathews (1979) pooled their extensive experience of this type of measure to produce the fear questionnaire shown in Appendix 4. On this measure, patients rate on a 0–8 scale their avoidance of their own most important phobic situation and of the 15 situations specified in the questionnaire. These latter were derived primarily from Hallam and Hafner's (1978) factor-analytic study of fear questionnaires, and it gives measures of agoraphobia and fear of injury and of social situations. The questionnaire also measures a composite of anxiety and depression and gives an overall rating of the disability caused by the phobia. Marks and Mathews reported that this questionnaire obtains reliability coefficients of at least .8 when the interval between test and retest is one week, and that it is sensitive to changes following behavioral treatment. For example, agoraphobics show a larger reduction on the agoraphobia score than on the social phobia score after treatment, and the opposite holds for social phobics. In a sample of 63 agoraphobics seen for follow-up and rated some years after behavioral treatment, the agoraphobia score for this scale correlated .87 with a research worker's rating of their disability on the 1–5 scale, confirming the high reliability of the self-report measure.

## BEHAVIORAL TESTING

None of the measures we have discussed are direct measures of patients' behavior or feelings when in a phobic situation. Instead they are estimates made by the patients and raters and based on the patients' expectations and recollections. It is unlikely that these are as satisfactory as a direct measure of the patients' behavior when in the feared situations, as has long been recognized in analogue research on specific fears, in which the use of a behavioral avoidance test (BAT) is now de rigueur. The most popular BAT is that in which the subject attempts to ascend a hierarchy of increasingly fearful situations involving more and more intimate contact with a feared object. For example, the subject may be asked to stand some feet from a snake, then to stand beside a tank containing a snake, then to touch a snake with a heavily gloved hand, and through various intermediate stages, to end with a snake loose on his/her person. It is usually possible to produce a Guttman scaling of such a hierarchy in which all subjects who can complete a given item on the hierarchy can complete all nominally easier items. In this way, it is possible to record the number of items completed before and after treatment and to obtain a direct measure of phobic behavior. In addition, measures of subjective state and physiological arousal can be taken during the behavioral test so that all three components of fear can be measured before and after treatment and changes can be assessed.

Most of the major research groups investigating agoraphobia have attempted some form of behavioral testing, but no entirely satisfactory method has been devised. Agoraphobics' fears do not lie along a universal dimension amenable to Guttman scaling. Patients are frightened of different things, and even if they fear a common set of situations, they may not agree on the ordering of these situations with respect to fearfulness. Moreover, the situations that agoraphobics fear are complex and cannot easily be controlled, so that the testing of such fears is time-consuming and prone to error.

Several approaches have been tried. Emmelkamp and his colleagues based their behavioral measure on the time that patients spend away from a place of safety (e.g., Emmelkamp & Wessels, 1975; Emmelkamp & Emmelkamp-Benner, 1975; Emmelkamp, Kuipers, & Eggeraat, 1978). They required the patient to remain outside his/her home or the hospital for as long as he/she feels comfortable and lacking in tension. This time is taken as the measure of fear. The measure has proved sensitive to the effects of treatment in the studies that this group has carried out (see Chapter 6 and 7). However, the measure has at least two disadvantages: first, time spent away from home is not the essence of agoraphobia; it is only correlated with the patient's problem. In general, the longer patients are away from home, the further they can be expected to have traveled from there and the more likely they are to be entering difficult and demanding situations. However, this need not always be so. The second disadvantage in this form of testing is that the patient is instructed to "stay outside until he begins to feel uncomfortable or tense and then he has to come back straight away" (Emmelkamp & Wessels, 1975, p. 10). These instructions are deceptively simple. It is very likely that many patients are tense and uncomfortable for much of the time, and they are certainly likely to be so before they leave home on a behavioral test. Therefore they inevitably must make a decision as to the level of tension or discomfort that is acceptable to themselves and to the therapist. It is not simply a question of the presence or absence of tension. Such a judgment must surely be altered easily by the demand characteristics of the situation, and for this reason, any changes observed after treatment could reflect not only reductions in phobic avoidance but also alterations in the patients' judgment of what they are prepared to tolerate before they label their feelings as tension. It should also be noted that this type of behavioral test does not allow any measure of alterations in patient's subjective state since anxiety is absent throughout—or at least the patient is obliged to claim that it is.

Some of these problems are avoided in the behavioral testing we favor. The procedure that we adopted (Gelder, Bancroft, Gath, Johnston, Mathews, & Shaw, 1973; Mathews, Johnston, Lancashire, Munby, Shaw, & Gelder, 1976; Mathews, Teasdale, Munby, Johnston, & Shaw, 1977) is as follows. Prior to treatment, we obtained a hierarchy of phobic situations for each patient. This hierarchy attempted to sample the whole range of phobic situations from very easy to exceedingly difficult, and it was then used as the basis of an individual behavioral test. The hierarchy was constructed by our first asking each patient to describe two situations in one of which he/she felt totally relaxed while the other was the most difficult situation that he/she could imagine. The patient was then required to bisect the interval between these two situations and describe a third that occupied this central position on the dimension of fear. He/she then provided two further situations approximately central within the top and bottom half of the original dimension, and so on until a 15-item hierarchy was produced. The patient then confirmed that the 15 items so produced were in an ascending order of difficulty and that no significant aspects of his/her fear had been omitted. If they had been, an attempt was made to substitute for one of the existing items a new item that was of similar difficulty but measured another aspect of the phobia. An attempt was also made to ensure that before treatment began, the patient could carry out three or four of the items on the hierarchy, thereby allowing room for significant deterioration as well as for improvement. (A typical hierarchy is shown in Table 2.1.) This hierarchy was then used as the basis for an actual behavioral test in the situations described by the patient.

Since these situations are often complex and testing may be time consuming, it was not practical to test every item on the hierarchy until the patient reached one which he failed. Instead, the patient was asked to name the most difficult item on the hierarchy that he or she felt able to attempt at the time. This item was then attempted; if successfully, the patient was encouraged to try a harder item; if unsuccessfully, then the next item below was attempted. The test was terminated when the patient either failed an

TABLE 2.1 An agoraphobic's behavioral test hierarchy

---

1. At home with children doing housework.
2. Walking to the nearest shopping center to buy something at a quiet time and returning.
3. Catching a bus alone for three stops and walking back.
4. Going alone by bus into central Oxford and returning by bus (about 2 miles each way).
5. Walking to the nearest shopping center to buy something at a busy time and having to wait in the check-out line.
6. Going alone by bus into central Oxford, shopping alone in Woolworth's and another big store for ½ hour and return (about 2 miles each way).
7. Going up one floor in an elevator (with solid doors).
8. Going up five floors in an elevator (with solid doors).
9. Going alone by bus to visit friends in Banbury and being driven home (about 25 miles each way).
10. Going with somebody else to the movies (or the theater) and sitting in the middle of a row.
11. Going alone by train from Oxford to Didcot and being met at Didcot station (about 10 miles).
12. Going alone by bus to Oxford station, then by train to Didcot, and returning alone (about 10 miles each way).
13. Train trip to London with the children (about 60 miles).
14. Going up in the elevator of the Post Office Tower.[a]
15. Flying with the family for a vacation.

---

[a] A very high building in London.

item, having completed the next below or, and this was more common, refused to attempt a higher one. Immediately on leaving the situation, the patient also rated, on a 0–10 scale, the anxiety experienced. After treatment, the patient was retested and the item attempted before treatment was repeated so that any alterations in subjective state in a constant but difficult situation could be assessed. The most difficult item possible was determined then in the same way as before. For example, before treatment, the patient whose hierarchy is shown in Table 2.1 was able to achieve Item 6 with an anxiety rating of 4. The patient then received 16 weeks of flooding in imagination and *in vivo* exposure (see Chapter 6). The behavioral assessment was repeated after 8 weeks and at the end of the 16 weeks. After 8 weeks, the patient carried out the initial test item with an anxiety score of 0 and was able to ascend the hierarchy to Item 13, also with an anxiety score of 0. At the end of the 16 weeks of treatment, she could again carry out Item

6 with an anxiety rating of 0, and in addition, she carried out Item 14 with an anxiety rating of 5.

The most satisfactory method of scoring such a behavioral test appears to be a simple count of the number of items that the patient can carry out, even though this method ignores the hierarchy position of the items achieved. We consider this method best since true Guttman scaling is not always achieved even on carefully constructed individualized hierarchies, and after treatment, patients are often able to achieve items that are nominally higher than others that they still find impossible. This result may be due to inaccurate hierarchy construction in the first place, or, more probably, it may come about because treatment has not been equally effective with all aspects of the patient's fear.

The advantage of this form of behavioral test is that it measures several aspects of the patient's problem and does so in as realistic a way as possible. It is not a test of a correlate of agoraphobia but a direct test of what the patients can or cannot do and what they feel when in the phobic situations. The most important disadvantage of this form of testing is that with such idiographic measures it is difficult to compare the results of different subjects. Moreover, the validity of the measure is wholly dependent on the adequacy of the initial hierarchy determination. The sampling of the patient's phobic behavior is inevitably subjective, and if the chosen items are not spaced evenly as in an equal-interval scale, the effects of treatment may be seriously distorted. However, it has been our experience that careful construction does lead to hierarchies that give an accurate indication of patients' progress and that behavioral tests based on these hierarchies correlate quite highly with other forms of measurement of phobic behavior.

All the behavioral tests that we have described measure what the patient can do. It is equally important to measure what the patient actually does from day to day, since a treatment that enables a patient to produce occasional heroic performances but does not affect daily life is of limited value. A reasonably representative measure can be obtained by requiring patients to complete diaries of their daily comings and goings. We describe results from such diaries in Chapter 9, while an example of the diaries we use is shown in Table 2.2. Rather surprisingly, such simple measures have not been used routinely in the study of agoraphobia, and so there is little general experience of what patients might be expected to do. Nor is it agreed how best to derive numerical data from such diaries. We have found that time spent away from home is a satisfactory measure. The validity of this measure may be improved if time spent at work or on social visits is ex-

TABLE 2.2 Three days' activities of a patient being treated for agoraphobia

| Date | Time | | Valium (if used) | Anxiety (0-10) | Destination and/or purpose of trip (with approximate distance from home) | Transport | | | | | | |
| | Out | Back | | | | Accomp'd | Met | Alone | Walk | Car | Bus | Other |
|---|---|---|---|---|---|---|---|---|---|---|---|---|
| February 2, 1976 | 11:40 AM | 12:05 PM | — | 4 | Bicycled to Cowley Road stores. Left bicycle and visited three stores. Long line in one—no hassle. | | | | | | | Bicycle |
| | 12:10 PM | 12:30 PM | — | 4 | Bicycled to store in Magdalen Road. Long wait in line. | | | ✓ | ✓ | | | Bicycle |
| | 2:30 PM | 4:15 PM | — | 3 | Walked with bicycle to allotment.[a] | | | ✓ | ✓ | | | |
| | 7:20 PM | 11:30 PM | Ativan (2.5 mg) | 4 | My husband drove us to the home of friends in Milan Road for dinner. I felt very apprehensive beforehand but soon settled down. He drove home. | ✓ | | | ✓ | ✓ | | |

| Date | Start | End | | Miles | Description | | | | | | Bicycle |
|---|---|---|---|---|---|---|---|---|---|---|---|
| February 29, 1976 | 2:00 PM | 3:00 PM | — | 5 | Went for a drive around Kidlington and Woodstock. | ✓ | | | | | |
| | 7:05 PM | 8:05 PM | — | 5 | Drove alone to laundromat on Cowley Road. | | | ✓ | ✓ | ✓ | |
| | 9:00 PM | 10:15 PM | — | — | Went to a local bar. | ✓ | ✓ | ✓ | ✓ | ✓ | |
| March 1, 1976 | 11:00 AM | 11:40 AM | — | 2 | Bicycled to Cowley Road. Left bicycle. Visited four stores. Bicycled home. | | | | | | |
| | 8:10 PM | 9:30 PM | — | 4 | Drove alone to see friends in Marsh Road. | | ✓ | ✓ | ✓ | | |
| | 9:50 PM | 10:40 PM | — | — | Went to local bar. | ✓ | ✓ | ✓ | ✓ | ✓ | |

aCommunity vegetable garden.

cluded on the grounds that the latter are often less frightening to the patient
and therefore may not be valid measures of agoraphobia. When the diary
information shown in Table 2.2 is scored, it can be seen that the patient
spent a total of 14 hr 10 min out of her home, of which 5 hr 30 min was spent
in social visits and 8 hr 40 min was spent in other activities. It will be apparent that this method of scoring is not entirely satisfactory in this case
because the time spent visiting was not a neutral period for this patient (her
anxiety ratings were quite high when visiting), while the time in the local
bar was neutral. Clearly the criticisms we have applied to Emmelkamp's
behavioral test also apply to this type of measure. However, although time
out of the house is only a correlate of the patient's central problems, it frequently represents a reasonable measure of agoraphobia. Moreover, as our
own studies have shown, treatments that decrease the fear and avoidance
of agoraphobics also increase the time spent out of the home. It can be seen
from Table 2.2 that the diaries contain much more detailed information
about the journeys than is represented in the scores we derive. We recommend that this information be gathered even though it cannot be scored,
since it is useful in guiding treatment and allows the researcher to assess the
validity of the measures derived from the diaries.

## PSYCHOPHYSIOLOGICAL MEASUREMENT

Psychophysiological methods of assessment have been used in many
studies of "analogue fears." The techniques and results have been outlined
by Epstein (1976). In general, it is found that subjects with specific fears
show increased physiological arousal when exposed to the feared object
and that the degree of arousal relates positively to the fearfulness of the object. It seems that these findings are also true of agoraphobia even though
the relevant methods of assessment have only rarely been used in clinical
studies. Most investigations have used exposure to phobic images or, less
often, verbal descriptions of phobic situations. By the use of such techniques, it has been shown that in phobic patients, including those with agoraphobia, exposure to phobic images leads to an increase in heart rate
(Marks, Marset, Boulougouris, & Huson, 1971; Gelder *et al.*, 1973;
Mathews *et al.*, 1976; Watson & Marks, 1971); an increase in skin conductance fluctuations (Marks, Boulougouris, & Marset, 1971; Watson &
Marks, 1971); larger skin conductance deflections (Marks, Marset,
Boulougouris, & Huson, 1971; Gelder *et al.*, 1973); and increased skin con-

ductance level (Gelder *et al.*, 1973; Mathews *et al.*, 1976). Only the study by Mathews *et al.* (1976) was restricted to agoraphobic patients, but it appears likely that the results of the other studies can be generalized to agoraphobia since they contained a high proportion of agoraphobic patients. There is, therefore, convincing evidence that increased autonomic arousal is associated with phobic imagery in agoraphobic patients, and it is reasonable to assume that such increased arousal would also be found in the actual phobic situation, as the very limited study by Stern and Marks (1973) suggests.

Psychophysiological arousal has proved less satisfactory as a means of assessing outcome. Marks, Boulougouris, and Marset (1971) showed that flooding, in comparison with desensitization, led to reduced autonomic responsiveness as assessed by heart rate, skin conductance fluctuations, and skin conductance deflections. In their comparison of two behavior therapies and a control treatment, Gelder *et al.* (1973) could find no difference in the effect on physiological responsiveness of the two procedures, even though other nonphysiological measures suggested that the behavioral treatments were more effective. However, resting heart rate was lower in the patients who had received behavior therapy. Equally, Mathews *et al.* (1976) could show no differential effect of various behavioral treatments on physiological responsiveness, but in this investigation, the treatments were equally effective on a wide variety of nonphysiological measures. It appears, therefore, that only one study has shown that changes in physiological responsiveness are sensitive to the differential effects of treatment. Nearly all studies show that responsiveness to phobic imagery is reduced after treatment, but it cannot be concluded that this reduction is an effect of treatment as distinct from the effect of repeated testing or even the passage of time. If it were found that behavioral treatments fail to affect one aspect of fear, this finding would be important and worthy of further study. However, before such inquiries are undertaken, it is important to recall the limitations in the assessments of physiological responsiveness that have been carried out. Nearly all the studies have concentrated on physiological responsiveness to imaginal versions of the phobic situation. Such responsiveness may have only very limited validity as a measure of true physiological responsiveness to the actual phobic situations, and it may be affected by treatments that do not affect responsiveness to the real situations. For example, treatments, such as desensitization, that concentrate on the presentation of imaginal stimuli during treatment may lead to a reduction in responsiveness to imaginal stimuli but not to real ones. In addition, these psychophysiological assessments require costly apparatus, are time-consuming, and make many patients anxious. For these reasons, we believe that psychophysiological assessments of this kind need not be given high priority in assessing patients. This does not mean that psychophysiological assessments with better techniques, particularly those using the ambulatory monitoring systems that are now available, might not prove to be of value in the future.

## CONCLUSIONS

The many elaborate and different systems used to measure agoraphobia can be justified if they contribute independent information on the patient's initial state or on the outcome of treatment. We have found that many of the measures are highly correlated and therefore unlikely to contribute independent information to the assessment of outcome, even though their combined use may increase the reliability of the assessment (Mathews *et al.*, 1976). In the Mathews *et al.* study, the only direct measure of agoraphobia that was independent of psychiatric ratings and the behavioral test (which correlated highly, $r = +.74$), was the physiological assessment, and this, as we have seen, has a rather limited validity as a measure of agoraphobia. In the 28 patients studied by Jannoun, Munby, Catalan, and Gelder (1980), the assessors' ratings of agoraphobic disability on the 0–8 scale was virtually independent of the total time out of the house as calculated from the patients' diaries ($r = -.30$). In addition, change in the diary measure after treatment was independent of change on the assessors' ratings ($r = -.15$). Since this measure has been shown to be sensitive to the effect of treatment, it would seem to be a useful independent measure of the patient's behavior.

What measures should be made in a particular study or in the treatment of a particular patient must, of course, be determined primarily by the aims of the study or the goals of the clinician. However, we suggest that for outcome research on agoraphobia, a minimal, but satisfactory, battery of tests would consist of independent raters' assessment of the patient on rating scales of specific phobic behavior and also a global disability rating; the patient's self-ratings and especially the form described by Marks and Mathews (Appendix 4); and measures derived from a diary of the patient's daily activities. In everyday clinical practice, the independent assessment can usually be dispensed with or replaced by similar ratings by the therapist. Since a direct behavioral test is difficult and expensive to organize, and because we have found that it correlates highly with other measures, we do not think it necessary for routine clinical practice and are of the opinion that it may also be unnecessary for most outcome investigations.

# 3. Theories of Agoraphobia

AS IN MANY other disorders of behavior, the theoretical explanations for agoraphobia range from the neurological to the sociological, and the various theories are usually presented as if they were mutually exclusive. In response to a similar diversity of views concerning the etiology of depression, Akiskal and McKinney (1973) have attempted to show that some of the disagreements may be more apparent than real, since the different theories often describe different stages of the same process or the same phenomena from different points of view. Although it is not our intention to claim that there is no real disagreement, it is possible to put forward an integrated theory that successfully accommodates most of the existing evidence. Before describing the alternative views and considering the extent to which an integrated theory is possible, it is necessary to evaluate the extent and status of this evidence.

## BIOLOGICAL FACTORS

In the absence of sufficient numbers of identical twins, studies of genetic influences have generally been confined to noting the incidence of similar problems among the relatives of agoraphobic probands. Harper and Roth (1962) reported an overall incidence of 33% of neurosis in the families of phobics, while Burns and Thorpe (1977b) found comparable rates for both siblings (35%) and mothers (28%), but a lower figure for fathers (13%). This difference was also reported by Solyom, Beck, Solyom, and Hugel (1974), who found neurosis of any kind in 55% of mothers but 24% of fathers, in contrast with 13% and 9%, respectively, in a control group of volunteers. The incidence of actual phobias among the parents of agoraphobic patients was found to be somewhat less, with 31% among the mothers and only 6% among the fathers (the corresponding figures for the control group were 11% and 2%). Buglass *et al.* (1977) gave considerably lower figures, finding that only 28% of mothers and 17% of fathers had neurotic disorders of any kind. The small number of parents reporting phobias is even more striking: only 4 among the total of 60 parents (7%), compared with 1 control parent (2%). These authors concluded that there is no evidence for an increased prevalence of phobic or other psychiatric illness among the parents of agoraphobics, since no significant differences were found between the patient groups and their carefully matched controls. Indeed, only one relevant finding reached significance: the number of brothers having a history of any psychiatric disorder—which reached 17% (controls 2%). These data lend no support to the case for any strong genetic influence in agoraphobia, and the findings that reach significance seem, if anything, more amenable to an environmental explanation.

As suggested earlier, a comparison of monozygotic (MZ) and dizygotic (DZ) twins is the most widely accepted method of evaluating the extent of genetic influences. The largest study of this kind at the time of writing (Torgersen, 1979) included only 11 twin pairs (with one of each pair presenting a clear phobic disorder) among the 99 MZ and DZ twin pairs who were studied. Torgersen factor-analyzed fear questionnaire scores from this group and was able to extract factors clearly corresponding to agoraphobic fears (trips, stores, crowds, etc.); fears of small animals; fears of injury or of social situations; and fears of "natural dangers" (e.g., fire, heights). If genetic influences are important, correlations between factor scores within MZ twin pairs should be greater than between those within DZ pairs. In fact, the correlations were significantly greater in the case of MZ pairs for all fear scores *except* those on the agoraphobic factor. On this factor, the differences were in the direction expected (MZ: $r = +.69$; DZ: $r = +.39$), but the evidence for direct genetic determination of agoraphobia remains weak.

There is another line of evidence that suggests an indirect genetic influence mediated by general personality factors such as neuroticism. On this dimension, agoraphobics appear to have higher scores than do patients with specific phobias of animals (Marks, 1969). Also, neuroticism scores derived from the Eysenck Personality Inventory are more highly correlated in MZ than in DZ twins (Slater & Shields, 1969). To reconcile these findings with the apparent lack of evidence for direct transmission, it might be supposed that neuroticism or high trait anxiety represents a general vulnerability factor, which is not related specifically to agoraphobia.

If this is true, we must look elsewhere for the reasons that some vulnerable individuals develop agoraphobia and others do not.

The high levels of neuroticism and general anxiety found in agoraphobic patients are related to similarly high levels of autonomic activity. In both frequency of spontaneous fluctuations in skin conductance and rate of habituation of the GSR, agoraphobics seem closer to patients with generalized anxiety states than to those with specific fears (Marks, 1969). These common factors of autonomic overactivity and the tendency to develop acute anxiety might indicate that anxiety neurosis and agoraphobia have a common biological etiology. Klein, Zitrin, and Woerner (1978) claimed that the effects in agoraphobia of tricyclic antidepressants (see Chapter 4) are due to specific action on "spontaneous" panic attacks—as distinct from generalized anxiety—and they suggested that this effect may indicate a separate etiology. In a recent review of this diagnostic question, Hallam (1978) concluded in favor of classifying agoraphobia with anxiety states rather than phobias, albeit on descriptive rather than etiological grounds. He pointed to evidence from two sources in addition to the psychophysiological findings mentioned above: (1) failure to find mild forms of agoraphobia distributed in the population in a manner similar to specific fears and (2) overlap between symptoms of general anxiety and those of agoraphobia in a population of patients. As we pointed out in Chapter 1, this conclusion does not take into account the natural history of the agoraphobic syndrome. Agoraphobia is frequently accompanied or preceded by generalized anxiety, but once phobic avoidance has developed, it does not appear to revert to a generalized anxiety state. Perhaps the two conditions have some common antecedents, but other factors then determine whether or not a stable pattern of phobic avoidance emerges.

## PERSONALITY DIMENSIONS

Except for the well-established findings of high trait anxiety and neuroticism among agoraphobic patients, research into personality dimensions has been disappointing. Agoraphobics have been found to be more "field-dependent" than other phobics on an embedded-figures test (Rock & Goldberger, 1978), but until the mechanisms involved in field dependence are understood more clearly, this is not a particularly helpful finding. A potentially more useful correlation has been reported between "external locus of control" and phobic anxiety scores among agoraphobics (Emmelkamp & Cohen-Kettenis, 1975). This correlation suggests the possibility that some individuals react to acute anxiety by external attribution and consequent avoidance, while others, who make internal attributions, do not become agoraphobic. However, any such conclusion must remain speculative until locus-of-control scores can be shown to be a cause rather than an effect of agoraphobia.

By far the most popular hypothesis about the personality of agoraphobics is that they show two general behavioral dispositions: dependence on others and a tendency to use avoidance as a method of coping with difficult situations (cf. Andrews, 1966). Unfortunately, while Andrews recognized the necessity to investigate these dispositions objectively, he could not cite any convincing support for the idea beyond the fact that most clinicians share the same view. For example, Wolpe (1958) is quoted as describing an agoraphobic in the following terms:

> An only child, during her childhood and adolescence she had been incredibly over-protected by her mother who insisted on standing perpetually in attendance on her. She was permitted to do almost nothing for herself, forbidden to play games lest she get hurt, and even in her final year at high school was daily escorted over the few hundred yards to and from school by her mother, who carried her school books for her. (p. 4)

Andrews suggested that because of this degree of overprotection, the person learns a pattern of dependence on others that leaves her/him predisposed to develop phobic avoidance later. This idea suggests the questions of how many people receive the same degree of overprotection but do not develop a dependent style or subsequent phobias and of whether it is possible to compare objectively these variables in agoraphobic and control groups. Several studies that have attempted this difficult task are summarized in Table 3.1.

In the earliest of these, Webster (1953) compared the case notes of phobic (predominantly agoraphobic) patients with those of patients with anxiety neurosis or conversion hysteria. "Dominant overprotection" was said to have occurred in 96% of phobics, compared with 44% in the other two groups. Snaith (1968) contrasted agoraphobics with other phobic patients and found no difference between them on ratings of "overprotection" or "rejection." Shafar (1976), using undefined ratings, concluded that dependency problems were present in 38% of her agoraphobic patients. In all these studies, the lack of an appropriate control group or of objective measuring instruments makes it hazardous to draw definite conclusions.

TABLE 3.1. Overprotection, dependency, and stability of family background: Summary of seven studies

| Source | Subject groups | Measures | Results |
|---|---|---|---|
| Webster (1953) | Agoraphobics; anxiety neurotics; conversion hysterics | Ratings taken from therapy case notes | Higher proportion of agoraphobics judged as overprotected and as having unstable fathers. |
| Snaith (1968) | Agoraphobics; other phobics | Standard ratings by interview | Higher proportion of agoraphobics with unstable families; no difference in overprotection. |
| Shafar (1976) | Agoraphobics; other phobics | Subjective ratings (unspecified) | No difference in frequency of unhappy, disrupted childhood; more dependency in general. |
| Solyom et al. (1974) | Mixed phobics; volunteer subjects | Ratings and questionnaires | Tendency for agoraphobics to report greater maternal overprotection. |
| Solyom et al. (1976) | Mothers of agoraphobics; overprotective mothers | Standardized self-report questionnaires | Mothers of agoraphobics more overprotective than validation group. |
| Buglass et al. (1977) | Agoraphobics; matched controls | Structured interview | Agoraphobics come from more "anomalous home situations"; no objective evidence of dependency; but agoraphobics feel more dependent and ambivalent. |
| Parker (1979) | Agoraphobics; social phobics; matched controls | Standardized questionnaire by mail | Agoraphobics report less maternal care; no difference from controls in overprotection. |

Solyom *et al.* (1974, 1976) have made two attempts to examine the same question. In the first, the authors reported that maternal overprotection was noted in interviews with agoraphobic patients more frequently than in interviews with control volunteer subjects. However, this difference (44% vs. 28%) did not reach an acceptable level of statistical significance. In the subsequent paper, the authors validated an overprotection questionnaire by giving it to two groups of mothers, one rated overprotective, the other not protective, before giving it to the mothers of 21 agoraphobic patients. This last group scored significantly higher than either validation group, specifically on the subscales supposedly measuring excessive contact and maternal concern. However, Buglass *et al.* (1977) failed to find differences between their agoraphobic and control groups on a number of possible objective indexes of dependency, namely, a history of separation anxiety, difficulty in school, unusual conformity, and freedom to choose clothes. Nevertheless, subjective ratings showed that 27% of the patients in this study (but none of the controls) reported the simultaneous awareness of dependency and resentment about it. Finally, Parker (1979) reported on the results of a mail questionnaire survey of agoraphobics, social phobics, and a control group drawn from a general practice. Overall, the phobic patients reported that their patients had been both less caring and more overprotective. In the agoraphobic group alone, only the maternal care scores significantly distinguished the phobics from controls. This negative finding was reinforced by low negative correlations between agoraphobic severity and both maternal care and overprotection scores. Thus the more severe agoraphobics reported less maternal care but relatively less overprotection. The direction of these correlations in the socially phobic group were in the opposite direction.

Can any conclusion be drawn from these apparently confused and contradictory results? At least some of the contradictions may be attributable to the use of different measuring instruments, many of which are of dubious validity. Further, the practice of obtaining retrospective ratings after the development of the agoraphobia has obvious dangers, particularly since phobic avoidance can itself be interpreted as evidence of a dependent personality. A first step toward resolving the confusion might be to determine whether "dependency" is a general personality trait and "overprotection" a unitary parental characteristic. As Mischel (1968) has pointed out, many so-called personality characteristics may well involve a great deal of situational specificity. Our understanding of agoraphobic patients would be considerably advanced if it could be established that (for example) they have been reinforced for using avoidance as an anxiety-relieving device in specific situations. Until more precise formulations of this type are made and tested, the question must remain unanswered, despite the suggestive evidence that dependence is a relevant variable.


## FAMILY ENVIRONMENT

Although maternal overprotection has been considered in the preceding section, there are other features of the patient's family of origin, or later marital family, that have been examined for their possible etiological importance. In the study by Webster (1953), the fathers of agoraphobics were said to be more frequently absent from the parental home than were the fathers of the other patient groups; and the husbands of female agoraphobics were more likely to be judged as unstable. Although the reliability of these ratings was high, they were derived from case notes and may simply reflect the preconceptions of the therapist. As will be seen later, others have reported evidence of relatively unstable home backgrounds among agoraphobic patients, but the suggestion that many of the husbands of agoraphobic women are abnormal has not been confirmed. Thus Snaith (1968), using a standard rating scale, found more unstable family backgrounds among agoraphobics than among other phobics (33% vs. 10%). Moreover, a compatible conclusion was reached by Buglass *et al.* (1977), for although they found no excessive parental loss or conflict, a significantly greater number of the patients' families included step- or adopted relatives. This last study also included a careful evaluation of the present marital and family situation. The husbands viewed their agoraphobic wives as less "active" and less "potent," and the couple held rather more divided opinions about joint concerns. However, the scores and ratings for factors such as self-assertion and mutual affection were similar for the patient and control groups, as was the pattern of joint activities. There was no evidence of "assortative mating"; indeed, control partners actually resembled each other more closely than did partners in the phobic group. The authors concluded that the family setting of the two groups was strikingly similar and found no support for the suggestion that there is a distinctive "agoraphobic marriage."

This last conclusion is of some importance because there is a common clinical impression that agoraphobic symptoms may be produced or maintained by features in the marital relationship. This point of view seems to have been adopted by Hafner (1977a) and Milton and Hafner (1979), who appear to believe that since marital dissatisfaction before treatment is related to a poorer therapeutic response, a causal relationship must exist between marital state and agoraphobia. Obviously, even if such data are confirmed, they are open to alternative explanations, for example, that both marital dissatisfaction and treatment response are causally related to a third variable, such as high levels of neuroticism or general anxiety. And even if a direct link were to be shown between marital conflict and agoraphobia, the causal direction could as well be the reverse, namely, that the more severe the agoraphobic disturbance, the more disruptive are its effects on the marriage. This is not to argue that complex interactions may not exist between marital relationship and the cause of agoraphobia but simply to point out that the existing evidence is inadequate to support a definite conclusion.

## LIFE EVENTS AND LIFE STRESS

Most agoraphobics report a sudden onset to their symptoms, usually in the form of an acute episode of anxiety or a panic attack. Thereafter the severity of the symptoms often fluctuates, and it has often been suggested that both onset and fluctuations are causally related to changes in interpersonal relationships or to environmental stress (cf. Snaith, 1968). One analysis of the type of event or stress experienced at the time of onset showed that relative to control subjects with specific fears, agoraphobics reported a significant excess of serious illness or death of relative or friend, and of domestic crises or other conflicts (Solyom *et al.*, 1974). While there appears to be some agreement that there is an association between stressful experiences of a general kind and the onset of agoraphobia, these authors reported less success in obtaining reports of traumatic or frightening events occurring in situations that subsequently became associated with fear. In view of their theoretical importance for a conditioning explanation of phobias, Buglass *et al.* (1977) made a deliberate search for such "specific" events; for example, a patient who, while out walking with her small son, saw him almost run over by a truck, was classified in this way. Of the 30 patients studied, only 7 could recall frightening events at about the time of onset, and only two of these events took place in the subsequently phobic situations. Obviously this negative evidence needs to be treated with caution, since patients were being asked to recall events that might have taken place many years before (the mean duration of the phobias at the time of the interview was eight years). Nevertheless, as in earlier studies, patients could apparently recall nonspecific or background stressors at the time of onset; thus, of the 30 patients, 15 could identify clearly one or more such stressors, and only 8 could report neither background stress nor stressful events. Unfortunately, the methodology of this study did not allow a comparison with an equivalent period in the lives of control subjects, so that unequivocal conclusions are not possible. We may conclude on balance, however, that the role of nonspecific background stress is rather strongly supported by the consistency in the data.

## ETIOLOGICAL MODELS

### PSYCHODYNAMIC THEORY

Psychoanalysts were the first to attempt a complete theoretical account of phobias, and in essentials the views advanced by Freud remain the basis of these ideas. In his "Analysis of a Phobia in a 5-Year-Old Boy" (1909/1925), Freud described how "little Hans" saw a horse fall and subsequently developed a fear that all horses would fall down and would bite him. In Freud's view, however, horses had nothing to do with the little boy's real fears, which arose through a process of displacement. Horses, he suggested, symbolized Hans's father, and their bite symbolized the threat of castration. This rather extraordinary account has already attracted such a barrage of attacks and counterattacks that any discussion of its supposed insights on the one hand or its scientific deficiencies on the other would seem redundant. The essential feature of this influential theory is the idea that the original source of fear has been replaced in a phobia by an alternative object that represents the original source symbolically but allows the patient to avoid recognizing that fact. Thus phobic avoidance serves the patient's psychological needs, while the real motive remains unconscious because of the mechanisms of displacement and repression. In the case of agoraphobia, popular candidates for the underlying motives are sexual, aggressive, and dependency needs, associated with regression to an earlier stage of development. Fenichel (cited by Andrews, 1966) described a case in the following way:

> The anxiety attacks of a female patient with agoraphobia and crowd phobia had the unconscious and definite purpose of making her appear weak and helpless to all passers-by. Analysis showed that the unconscious motive of

her exhibitionism was a deep hostility, originally directed towards her mother, then deflected onto herself. "Everybody look!" her anxiety seemed to proclaim, "my mother let me come into the world in this helpless condition, without a penis." (p. 458)

One cannot help feeling that only another psychoanalyst would have heard this proclamation so clearly!

Subsequent theorizing has considerably broadened the type of symbolism put forward, while retaining the idea that agoraphobic symptoms represent something else. To quote Friedman and Goldstein (1974):

The agoraphobic symptom may have a variety of remote meanings, including the idea of an open street as an opportunity for sexual adventure; the idea of leaving home; the idea that on an open street one may be seen and caught; the idea that some other person (usually a parent or sibling) may die while one is away from home; or the idea of being born. (p. 116)

Another influential writer, Arieti (1979), expressed a similar theme in suggesting that phobias do not arise just through displacement but are a way of making concrete the patient's vague and intangible anxieties. Typically, he argued, the development of a phobia involves a transition from interpersonal anxieties—for example, that the individual will be disappointed by others—into fears of specific situations such as crowds or bridges. Thus a global anxiety is reduced to a definite concrete fear and thereby transformed into something that is threatening in a physical rather than a psychological way and that can be avoided. Arieti's exposition illustrates the continuing reliance of psychodynamic theorists on clinical anecdote, since he cited no new evidence other than one long case history. Even if it is accepted that phobic symptoms do have other meanings and associations for some patients, these may just as well be secondary events—reactions or ideas that individuals have about the phobic anxiety they experience. Psychodynamic writers seldom consider such alternative explanations and this omission, combined with a failure to see the need for objective public evidence, makes it difficult to relate their theories to the research reviewed earlier. In general, support can only be found for the most broad generalizations, common to theories other than the psychodynamic, for example, that relationship conflicts may exacerbate or precipitate phobic avoidance. Rather than assume that the phobia represents some aspect of these conflicts, it seems more plausible that anxiety from various sources can summate to provoke an acute anxiety attack.

Despite the many failings of psychodynamic theories, which have in some ways retarded our understanding of etiology, Freud must be given full credit for being the first to describe some of the crucial features of agoraphobia. In particular he noted that "we often find the recollection of a state of panic; and what the patient actually fears is a repetition of such an attack under those special conditions in which he believes he cannot escape it" (Freud, 1919/1924a, p. 136).

The view that people suffering from agoraphobia are really suffering from something wrong in their marriage, discussed by a number of recent authors (e.g., Milton & Hafner, 1979), seems to represent a variation on the theme of unconscious motivation. In this view, agoraphobic behavior is a means of expressing or coping with aspects of an unsatisfactory marital relationship. For example, one patient is described by Milton and Hafner in the following terms:

> We believe that before treatment with us, this patient partly compensated for the lack of harmony and affection within the marriage and her fear of marital breakdown by the development of agoraphobia, thereby becoming very dependent on her husband, who felt compelled to help and support her. This increased help and support allowed the patient to feel that the marriage was relatively secure. But once the patient's agoraphobic and dependent behaviour lessened, the "compulsory" basis for the marriage was weakened, and the husband left for a more satisfactory partner. (p. 810)

Evidence concerning the association between treatment response and marital relationship has already been discussed, and it has been suggested that alternative explanations are possible. For example, the anxiety caused by marital conflict may increase the probability of panic attacks, and high neuroticism may lead both to conflict in marriage and to poor response in treatment. The idea that in some direct way agoraphobia is manufactured in order to meet the needs of a disordered marriage seems unnecessary and implausible. On the other hand, it is entirely possible that once phobic anxiety has started, its course will be influenced for better or worse by people close to the patient. Thus, if the husband of an agoraphobic woman is quite content that his wife should be housebound, he may be uninterested in or even obstructive to attempts at treatment that threaten to disturb his domestic calm. It remains to be shown, however, whether such situations are common or, as we believe, unusual and atypical.

LEARNING THEORY

Partly as a reaction against the unsatisfactory aspects of psychoanalytic formulations, alternative explanations based on conditioning have been advanced (e.g., Eysenck & Rachman, 1965). In these, phobias are considered examples of conditioned avoidance reactions, and no particular distinctions are made among specific fears, social phobias, and agoraphobia. Put simply, the fortuitous combination of environmental stimuli with either the evocation of intense fear, or the repeated evocation of mild fear is said to produce a classically conditioned fear reaction to the previously neutral environmental stimuli. By analogy with the learning of active avoidance responding in animals, which is resistant to extinction, subsequent phobic avoidance would be expected to preserve a high level of conditioned fear. Although this two-factor theory of avoidance has come under attack (e.g., by Herrnstein, 1969, and Seligman & Johnston, 1973), and questions are raised because phobias seem more resistant to extinction that is learned avoidance, this view of phobias has continued to attract support. Recent work suggests that certain types of conditioned stimuli (e.g., a sequence of warning signals) may prolong fear extinction very considerably (Levis & Boyd, 1979). Moreover, Eysenck (1976) has pointed to the possibility that some other parameters (e.g., intense stimuli and delays between exposures) may even lead to *increases* in conditioned fear. And Öhman, Fredrikson, and Hagdahl (1978) have reported a series of experiments showing that organisms seem innately prepared to react to certain "biological" stimuli with fear, so that an autonomic reaction to these stimuli is easily acquired and is extinguished only with great difficulty.

Returning to the particular case of agoraphobia, it is difficult to see how the conditioning formulation, or any of these recent extensions, can be relevant to etiology. As we saw earlier, agoraphobics cannot as a rule recall either any event that provoked intense fear or any repeated fearful events that occurred in the circumstances that they subsequently came to avoid. Instead, they report that the first acute anxiety seemed to come "out of the blue." Although this objection is vulnerable to the argument that people are not always able correctly to attribute their behavior to the actual controlling stimuli (cf. Nisbett & Wilson, 1977), doubt must still be cast on the theory that classical conditioning is the primary etiological agent. Alternatives proposed by Rachman (1977), such as parental modeling and other forms of vicarious learning, seem equally inapplicable since there is no evidence that agoraphobics have been especially exposed to these influences. Thus estimates of the presence of fears (not just agoraphobia) among the parents of agoraphobics range from 1 in 3 to 1 in 15, and many patients seem never to have come across any other person with similar problems. However, the equivocal data on dependence keep open the possibility that a more general form of learning could be relevant, namely, that of a general strategy of avoidant and dependent behavior.

A further possibility suggested by several previous writers is that the experience of a panic attack, even if it arises from sources independent of the patient's immediate environment, can itself act as a traumatic conditioning stimulus. The phobic behavior that follows is then considered an attempt by the patient to avoid not just the environment in which the attack occurred but the possibility of another panic. This view is certainly consistent with what patients actually say (cf. Chapter 1), and while leaving much unexplained, it is in our opinion probably correct. By the same token, circumstances felt by the patient to protect against the possible occurrence or the consequences of panic, such as the presence of known and trusted people, become sources of reassurance.

BIOLOGICAL MODELS

The findings cited earlier, that agoraphobics shown an elevated level of autonomic arousal and an unusually slow rate of habituation, were used by Lader and Mathews (1968) to support a biological model. It was proposed that if, as a consequence of this psychophysiological state, there is insufficient time for the response to one stimulus to die away before the next stimulus arrives, an upward spiral of autonomic response could result. If we assume that such an upward spiral could cause a panic attack, it would seem that both agoraphobics and patients suffering from anxiety neurosis would be vulnerable. As to why anxiety attacks appear more often in crowds and stores or other public places, it was suggested that these situations are characterized by a relatively high intensity and complexity of social and other stimuli. These stimulus characteristics have in fact been proposed as being innately arousing and fear-provoking on the basis of other evidence (cf. Gray, 1971). Once the hypothetical threshold has been passed, and an upward spiral of arousal is experienced as panic, learning and cognitive factors might be expected to increase the risk of repetition if the same circumstances should occur.

In the absence of evidence of a primary biological defect, it is possible that the onset of abnormal psychophysiological arousal is secondary to highly stressful life events, in both agoraphobics and patients with anxiety neurosis. Given the similarity between these two groups of patients, the question arises whether they have similar causes, with the differences between them reflecting alternative strategies of responding to the experience of the acute anxiety attacks. These strategies may in turn depend on a variety of factors that have already been discussed, such as avoidance as a general coping device, dependence on others, and locus of control.

COGNITIVE THEORIES

Goldstein and Chambless (1978) have emphasized the possibility that the way patients view their own experience of anxiety is an important determinant of phobic avoidance. In their reanalysis of agoraphobia, these authors agreed that panic attacks are likely to follow increased background stress, but they added two other preconditions that they believed to be important. These are, first, that agoraphobics are nonassertive, generally fearful people who perceive themselves as being incapable of functioning independently; and, second, that they are typically unable to make accurate connections between their emotions and the events that cause them. If these preconditions really exist, interpersonal conflicts—such as, for example, wanting to leave a relationship but being afraid to do so—could lead to intense anxiety and precipitate a panic attack. Failure to recognize any connection between the anxiety experienced and the conflict causing it might lead the individual to interpret the attack as a sign of impending death, disease, insanity, or some other disaster. Additionally, the postulated dependence, lack of self-assertion, and fearfulness could lead the individual to turn to others for help and thereby to perpetuate the very relationship that caused the original anxiety. Thus a self-defeating feedback loop could be established, increasing the possibility of further attacks.

Although this model is ingenious, it can be criticized on a number of grounds. The assumed preconditions have not been firmly established by any research into the previous personality of agoraphobics; indeed, as was seen earlier, even the most popular candidate—dependency—has proved difficult to substantiate. Second, nothing is said to explain why agoraphobics should feel anxiety when going out and when entering public places, rather than when staying at home, where they are equally likely to be exposed to a conflicting relationship. The only suggestion put forward—that feeling trapped in a relationship may generalize semantically to feeling trapped in phobic situations—is no more than a vague speculation. Despite these problems, the model is not incompatible with other explanations and could help to transform some of the less precise psychodynamic speculations into testable form.

Another cognitive view, put forward by Beck and Rush (1975), is that while both phobic and anxiety neurotics experience repeated cognitions related to possible danger, the content of these cognitions determines the differences in their behavior. Anxiety neurotics are thought to experience cognitions about dangers that are less easily avoided, more internal in origin, and not directly related to particular situations (e.g., death, disease, and social rejection). Phobics, on the other hand, are supposed to have cognitions relating to more external and avoidable situations. Although Beck and Rush made no specific mention of agoraphobia, these patients seem to share most of the cognitions attributed by the authors to anxiety neurotics. However, a useful distinction is still possible, since agoraphobics seem to make a cognitive link between these ideas and the situations that they avoid. That is, they come to believe that they are more likely to experience panic or collapse or to suffer ridicule in the public places that they avoid. Unfortunately, there is an almost complete lack of evidence about whether such cognitions cause anxiety and phobic avoidance or whether they are secondary to patients' observation of their own emotions and behavior. It is difficult to see ways to test this distinction, other than by devising ways of changing the cognitions directly, and testing the methods as a treatment for agoraphobia. As will be seen later (Chapter 11), such cognitive techniques are still in the process of development and have not been fully evaluated, so that no real, convincing evidence of this sort is available. Nonetheless, Beck's observations concerning the cognitions of agoraphobic patients is consistent with our own experience and may prove to be relevant to a complete understanding of the etiology of the condition.

AN INTEGRATED MODEL

So far, the various models and theories have been discussed separately. Now the possibility of an integrated account, which was put forward in the introduction to this chapter, can be explored. The main findings arising from clinical research and observation that must be accommodated within such an integrated model can be summarized as follows:

1. There is no evidence that agoraphobia is inherited directly, although traits of fearfulness and anxiety-proneness (which are elevated in agoraphobia) may have a genetic basis.
2. No convincing evidence has been found of the sort of traumatic events required by conditioning theory, but agoraphobia often begins in the setting of background stress.
3. There is a marked similarity between agoraphobia and anxiety neurosis in terms of autonomic state and aspects of symptomatology.
4. On the other hand, generalized anxiety states and agoraphobia appear to diverge in a number of ways: (a) differences in the selectivity of the anxiety reactions; (b) behavioral differences in avoidance

and dependence on others; and (c) cognitive differences in attributions to external provoking stimuli.

5. Once established, agoraphobic avoidance persists despite some variation with mood, suggesting additional maintaining factors (e.g., social learning or other cognitive processes).

The first four conclusions listed above, which are concerned with the phase of onset of agoraphobia, are illustrated in a hypothetical flowchart (Figure 3.1). If we start at the left-hand side of the figure, it is assumed that at least three general vulnerability factors may play a part in predisposing individuals to develop agoraphobia. The first, early family environment, would appear to be most in doubt, since not all studies agree in finding any significant distinguishing features. It is possible, however, that instability, overprotection, or lack of parental care may increase the likelihood of subsequent dependent or avoidant behavior. A high genetic loading for trait anxiety is assumed on the basis of the questionnaire and the autonomic measures found in agoraphobic patients, although it remains possible that these are secondary to the condition rather than causal. In combination with this genetic loading, "nonspecific" background stress factors seem the most likely cause of the generalized anxiety state that is postulated to be the immediate forerunner of agoraphobia. The high incidence of anxiety symptoms preceding the development of agoraphobia would sup-

FIGURE 3.1. Hypothetical flowchart showing factors leading to onset of agoraphobia.

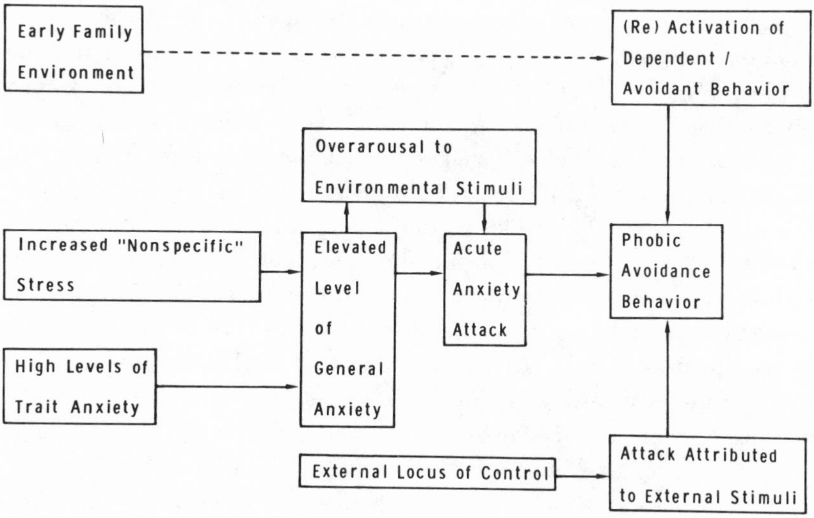

port the suggestion that at this stage, there is little or no distinction to be made between the natural history of agoraphobia and anxiety neuroses in general. The crucial event that is postulated to explain the development of phobic avoidance behavior, rather than another form of anxiety neurosis, is the occurrence while out of doors of an acute anxiety episode, experienced as a panic attack. This attack is supposed here to be the joint product of increased general anxiety and exposure to arousing environmental stimuli, which together provoke an upward spiral of autonomic responses. Obviously, alternative explanations for an initial panic attack are possible, including an as yet unrecognized physical pathology, cognitive processes such as anxiety-elevating thoughts, and the symbolic meaning of the patient's situation.

Whatever the cause of this first experience of acute anxiety, it seems to be crucial thereafter in directing patients toward an agoraphobic behavior pattern. Two additional factors are postulated as playing an important part at this stage, though they, too, must remain speculative in the absence of stronger evidence. The first concerns the patient's usual behavioral style in fearful situations, and particularly whether this is more consistently avoidance and dependence on others than active coping and self-reliance. To the extent that the evidence of early learning of a dependent style is considered adequate, it is thought plausible that this tendency could be activated by the experience of panic. Others have argued along similar lines that the dependent social role expected of women is consistent with the predominence of women among agoraphobics (Goldstein-Foder, 1974). Again, the absence of evidence does not allow an evaluation of this suggestion, but the present model does not provide any other explanation of the sex disparity. Yet some explanation is required because men and women are found more-or-less equally among patients with general anxiety states.

The second factor that, it is suggested, inclines patients toward a pattern of phobic avoidance is the extent to which the acute anxiety attack is attributed to external provoking stimuli (e.g., crowds and streets). Although in the present view this attribution would be partly correct, it is equally possible (and equally consistent with our model) for the person to attribute the attack to factors other than the immediate environment (e.g., worry and stress). If the latter attributions were made, it seems less likely that the physical setting of the attack would be avoided subsequently, although general anxiety would remain high. Unfortunately, the only evidence beyond clinical impressions that can be cited in support of this important idea is a statistical association between phobic severity and external locus of control.

The flowchart does not show the various additional factors that may come into play to maintain phobic behavior once it has begun, although these may be as important as—or even more important than—the events leading to its onset. For convenience in discussion, these may be divided into two factors: (1) aversive influences that discourage the patient from going out and facing feared situations and (2) other factors that positively reinforce avoidance or staying at home. In the first category, the crucial role played by fear of provoking a further attack of anxiety must impress any clinician who listens to what patients actually say about their problem. There can be no doubt that a severe panic attack, coming without any explanation or cause, is an extremely aversive experience. Whether or not thoughts of disaster play a part in etiology, following the experience of the first panic attack, thoughts that the attack may recur and fears of a worse attack, of loss of control in public, of possible physical disease, or even of death are frequent and distressing. Furthermore, it is at least possible that such fearful thoughts establish a type of feedback loop, in which anticipatory anxiety helps to provoke the very symptoms that are feared, and that in turn appear to confirm frightening thoughts. Additionally, it is probable that a secondary conditioning process ensures that incipient autonomic reactions will come to be elicited by places associated with previous panic attacks and are likely to be interpreted as danger signals to be avoided. Conversely, situations in which the patient has never experienced panic may come to serve as safety signals. As our understanding of such cognitive learning processes increases, it is to be hoped that explanations of the way in which phobic anxiety sometimes appears to spread out progressively and to restrict the patient's activities, while at the same time becoming more focused on external situations, will become more precise.

Factors that are assumed to play a role in positively reinforcing phobic behavior could also be part of such explanations. Patients may adopt a "sick role" and elicit sympathy and support from family and friends. Once such a pattern is established, the patient may well be caught in a "behavioral trap," whereby short-term gains from sympathy and exemption from anxiety-provoking tasks make it increasingly difficult to extricate him/herself from dependence on others. In the long run, the adjustment in lifestyle necessary to accommodate housebound patients may acquire an inertia of its own, so that the potential disruption involved in trying to return to a normal existence may lead to acceptance of the phobia by the patient's family. Indirect evidence of these postulated maintaining factors and the methods of reversing them are more properly the subject of later chapters on treatment methods.

# 4. Treatment with Drugs

DRUGS HAVE BEEN used to treat agoraphobia on their own and in combination with behavior therapy. In this chapter, we shall review the first of these uses, while reference to the joint use of drugs and behavior therapy will be found in Chapter 6. Although the main purpose of this chapter is to review the use of anxiolytic and antidepressant drugs, this is also a convenient place to consider the results of leukotomy, which has had a limited use for severe agoraphobia.

## ANXIOLYTIC DRUGS

Since anxiety is the most prominent symptom of agoraphobia, it is not surprising that anxiolytic drugs of various kinds have been used to treat the condition. It is surprising, however, that none has been evaluated thoroughly. In the past, barbiturates were used most often, but they have gradually been replaced by newer compounds that are less likely to cause drowsiness and to induce dependence. Nowadays it is the benzodiazepines that are used most widely in the treatment of agoraphobia. Many benzodiazepines are available, but although special claims have been made about individual compounds, there is no evidence that any one is more effective than the rest. For this reason, it is best to use one of the less expensive compounds, such as diazepam. This drug is usually given in the dose of 5 mg repeated up to a total of three times a day, although doses up to 30 mg a day are sometimes prescribed. Although many doctors still ask patients to take anxiolytic drugs at fixed times of the day, it is more rational, when one is treating phobic states, to instruct patients to take the drug shortly before the most severe anxiety is anticipated. This interval is usually about half an hour, but there is much variation from one person to another and patients should be encouraged to vary the interval until they find the one that suits best. Patients should also be told that it is important to restrict the use of drugs to situations that cause extreme anxiety, or to circumstances in which the drug is being taken to enable the patient to attempt something new, such as a longer trip from home.

Although anxiolytic drugs can give substantial temporary relief of symptoms, there is no evidence that they shorten the course of the disorder. They are palliative, not curative.

Against these short-term benefits must be set the fact that all anxiolytic drugs can give rise to dependence if taken for long periods. Although the benzodiazepines are less likely to do this than are the barbiturates, they must still be used with considerable care. And it is important to bear in mind that these drugs have been shown to impair performance on certain tasks, such as low-speed driving tests (Betts, Clayton, & Mackay, 1972). Whether they impair the actual automobile-driving performance of anxious patients is less certain because the overall effect may depend on initial level of anxiety, which can itself interfere with the skills required for driving. Furthermore, there is an accumulation of evidence that suggests that the therapeutic effects of the benzodiazepines decline after they have been used for more than about four months (see Committee on the Review of Medicines, 1980).

Recently, another group of drugs has been used to treat anxious patients. Beta-adrenergic blocking agents are capable of suppressing the peripheral autonomic symptoms of anxiety states, such as rapid pulse, palpitations, and tremor (Tyrer, 1976). The drugs produce some symptomatic relief in those agoraphobic patients whose most distressing symptoms are of this kind, but the majority describe prominent psychic anxiety and this is not treated effectively with these drugs. Although they have been evaluated in general anxiety states, the use of the drugs for agoraphobic patients has not been investigated thoroughly. However, Heiser and Defrancisco (1976) reported their experience with a group of 10 anxious patients, of whom 3 were agoraphobic; all 3 failed to respond.

If a beta-blocker is to be tried, propranolol is a suitable preparation. It is given by mouth in a dose of 10, 20, and occasionally 40 mg three times a day. It is important to start with a small dose and increase it gradually while monitoring pulse rate, which should not be allowed to drop below 55 beats per minute. Beta-blockers must be used with great caution in patients with bronchospasm or diabetes; after prolonged fasting; or when cardiac reserve is poor.

A special use of anxiolytic drugs has been described in the treatment of the phobic-anxiety depersonalization syndrome (we regard this as an artificial grouping of agoraphobic patients, whose symptoms of depersonalization are more severe than the rest). King and Little (1959) used intravenous thiopental (a short-acting barbiturate drug that is employed in anesthesia). A total of 10–12 slow intravenous injections of 2.5% of thiopental solution was given, the amount being sufficient to induce drowsiness but not anesthesia. No attempt was made to produce abreaction, any discussion with the patient being limited to simple explanation and reassurance. Treatment was usually given every other day. In these authors' controlled trial, patients were allocated randomly to treatment with thiopental, to placebo injections, or to brief psychotherapy. One month after treatment, 80% of the thiopental-treated patients were rated improved, compared with 50% of those in the control groups, while at three months' follow-up, the corresponding figures were 85% and 50%. However, complete recovery was seen in only one patient. These results have not been confirmed by other groups of workers, and the method has not gained general acceptance. We do not recommend it.

Finally, brief mention must be made of another treatment, which is directed to autonomic arousal and which enjoyed a brief vogue. Intravenous acetylcholine was introduced as a treatment for anxiety states by Lopez-Ibor (1952) and was studied also by Phillips and Hutchinson (1954). Its use in agoraphobia was reported by Sim and Houghton (1966). They carried out an uncontrolled investigation in which the use of acetylcholine injections was accompanied by a particularly vigorous program of rehabilitation in which patients were required to return to situations that they had avoided. It seems possible that the good results reported were due as much to these other measures as to the specific effects of the drug. The method has not been taken up by others, and we do not regard it as having a place in the treatment of agoraphobia.


## MONOAMINE OXIDASE INHIBITORS

Antidepressants of the monoamine oxidase inhibitor type were first recommended for the treatment of agoraphobia by Sargant and his colleagues in the 1960s. Sargant and Dally (1962) reported the treatment of 60 patients with anxiety states and claimed, on the basis of this clinical experience, that the monoamine oxidase series of antidepressant drugs, given alone or with a benzodiazepine, have potent effects in both general and phobic anxiety states. Before this claim is examined further, it is important to note some of the problems associated with the use of this group of drugs. If the patient eats foods such as cheese, broad beans, or yeast and meat extracts that have high concentrations of pressor amines, particularly tyramine, dangerous hypertension may occasionally occur because these substances are normally detoxified by monoamine oxidase enzymes. For this and other reasons, the drugs can also interact in a potentially dangerous way with other drugs, including opiates, meperidine, local anesthetics, sympathomimetic amines, methyldopa, and tricyclic antidepressants. These considerations make it obvious that monoamine oxidase inhibitors should be recommended for the treatment of agoraphobia only if they can be shown to be definitely superior to safer alternative drugs. In other words, their effects must be judged against those of the tricyclic antidepressants, which are considered in the next section.

With these cautions in mind, we can consider the evidence about the therapeutic effects of monoamine oxidase inhibitors on agoraphobia. Kelly, Guirguis, Frommer, Mitchell-Heggs, and Sargant (1970) carried out a retrospective study of 246 phobic patients who had been treated with a monoamine oxidase inhibitor given either alone or in combination with a benzodiazepine (usually chlordiazepoxide). A variety of monoamine oxidase inhibitors were used. Phenelzine (30–60 mg) and isocarboxazid (10–40 mg) were prescribed most often because they were regarded by the authors as being among the safest of these drugs and as having the lowest incidence of side effects. However, tranylcypromine (20–40 mg) or iproniazid (50–150 mg) were also used for some patients. The study was further complicated because a proportion of patients received a tricyclic antidepressant (amitriptyline or trimipramine) at night as well as the other drugs, and interpretation is made even more difficult because the investigation was retrospective and uncontrolled. For these reasons, there must be many reservations about the authors' conclusions, which were that monoamine oxidase inhibitors provide effective treatment for phobic states of all kinds, and that the results were not merely due to alleviation of concurrent depression because patients with depressive symptoms responded no differently from the rest.

In view of the claims about imipramine (which we discuss in the next section), it is noteworthy that Kelly *et al.* (1970) reported that monoamine oxidase inhibitors reduced the number and severity of panic attacks in their patients. However, they also stated that the presence of panic attacks before treatment did not affect the outcome of the phobic symptoms. Perhaps the most important and convincing finding of this study was that when the monoamine oxidase inhibitor was reduced or discontinued, about a third of the patients relapsed. Those who resumed treatment improved once more. In keeping with this finding, it has to be noted that many patients in the group continued the drugs for very long periods—some for five years or more. The part played by chlordiazepoxide in producing these results cannot be judged, since its use was not varied systematically. However, the authors stated that the withdrawal of chlordiazepoxide rarely led to the relapses that they observed when the monoamine oxidase drugs were discontinued.

Before turning to controlled investigations, we can note that King (1962) also reported uncontrolled observations of the effects of phenelzine in agoraphobic patients—though he diagnosed the group as having phobic-anxiety depersonalization syndromes. He described 84% of the patients reporting improvement in depersonalization, with a somewhat lower rate of improvement of symptoms. Unfortunately, his patients were followed for only three months.

More systematic inquiries into the effects of monoamine oxidase inhibitors in phobic patients have been carried out since these early studies. Tyrer, Candy, and Kelly (1973a, b) compared phenelzine and placebo in a double-blind controlled trial with patients who had long-standing agoraphobia and social phobias. Of the original 40 patients, 32 completed eight weeks of treatment in which phenelzine or placebo were taken in flexible dosage, which for phenelzine varied from 30 mg to 90 mg per day. After four weeks there were no significant differences between the groups, but after eight weeks, phenelzine was significantly superior to placebo. The pattern of changes recorded in symptoms led the authors to conclude that the drug was acting not as an antidepressant but against the phobic symptoms. However, the significant changes were recorded in secondary phobias and global ratings rather than in agoraphobia, panic attacks, or general anxiety. For this reason, it seems more appropriate to conclude that the drug has rather general effects and that any specific effects that it exerts on phobic symptoms must be rather small.

In another controlled trial, Mountjoy, Roth, Garside, and Leitch (1977) compared a combination of phenelzine and diazepam with placebo given with diazepam. They studied 117 neurotic patients, of whom 30 had phobic neuroses, 44 anxiety states, and 43 depressive neurosis. Phenelzine was given in doses up to 45 mg per day for the first two weeks and then increased to 75 mg per day for the second two weeks. Diazepam was prescribed in a flexible dosage according to the clinicians' judgment: the mean dosage turned out to be 18 mg for the group in which it was given with phenelzine and 15.6 mg for the group in which it was given with placebo. Among the agoraphobic patients, ratings of social phobias—rather than agoraphobia—fell more in the phenelzine group than in the other, but among the anxiety states, phenelzine was not superior to placebo. All but 11 of the 117 patients who were originally entered in the trial described side effects. Although the results of this study are rather complex, the most obvious conclusion is that if phenelzine has any effect on agoraphobic symptoms, it is not a large one.

Two other investigations have attempted to evaluate a monoamine oxidase inhibitor drug in the treatment of agoraphobia, and both compared the drug treatment with a behavioral treatment rather than with placebo. Lipsedge, Hajioff, Huggins, Napier, Pearce, Pike, and Rich (1973) studied 62 outpatients with severe agoraphobia. The design of their trial was rather complicated; six groups received methohexital-assisted systematic desensitization with iproniazid, methohexital-assisted systematic desensitization with placebo, "standard" desensitization with iproniazid, "standard" desensitization with placebo, iproniazid alone, and placebo alone. Whatever the treatment, the patients were encouraged to practice traveling alone for gradually increasing distances—whether or not they received formal behavior therapy. We shall see later that this can be a more potent procedure than the weekly sessions of desensitization. At the end of treatment, compared with placebo, the monoamine oxidase inhibitor led to a significant reduction of anxiety and a smaller, nonsignificant reduction in avoidance. Adding desensitization did not significantly increase the changes in patients receiving iproniazid, though desensitization did reduce anxiety and avoidance in patients who were taking placebo. Unfortunately, the subsequent course of the patients is difficult to interpret because although they were assessed at two months and two years after the end of treatment, many received further medication during the follow-up. The rest of the findings are also somewhat difficult to interpret, but they show no other convincing differences between any of the treatment combinations. Although the superiority of iproniazid over placebo was evident in a number of ratings, it is not apparent that its effect was large. A potentially important finding was that when iproniazid was stopped, the rate of relapse was high.

Solyom, Heseltine, McClure, Solyom, Ledwidge, and Steinberg (1973) also reported an experiment with a complicated design: 30 patients were assigned randomly to phenelzine with brief psychotherapy, placebo with brief psychotherapy, or behavior therapy. The most rapid improvement was observed in patients receiving phenelzine in combination with brief psychotherapy. The authors suggested that the sequence of changes began with a reduction in anxious anticipation, and that this was followed by reduction in the autonomic components of anxiety, with changes in avoidance behavior appearing last. However, the evidence is not very convincing. In contrast to the other groups, all the phenelzine-treated patients relapsed when the drug was stopped.

It is this finding about relapse that emerges most consistently from investigations of the phenelzine treatment of anxiety states. This is particularly clear in the one-year follow-up study by Tyrer and Steinberg (1975), who reported that three of the patients on phenelzine were still taking the drug at the time of follow-up despite efforts to stop the drug before assessment. On each occasion that the drug was reduced, the patients suffered an apparent relapse and the drug had to be continued. The authors concluded that the effect of phenelzine is mainly to suppress symptoms, and they also commented that they did not find after phenelzine treatment the improvement in social adjustment that has been observed after the behavioral treatment of phobias.

It must be concluded that attempts to confirm, in controlled trials, the claims that have been made for monoamine oxidase inhibitors on the basis of uncontrolled clinical experience have not produced strong evidence that these drugs have any specific effect on phobic symptoms. Indeed, the best evidence that they have any effect at all is the observation, which appears in several reports, that patients relapse when the drugs are stopped. If there is an effect, it does not appear to be mediated by relieving depression, and there are indications that the therapeutic effect appears only after about four weeks of treatment, long after the time at which the antidepressant effects of the drugs appear. The most economical explanation of all these findings is anxiolytic effect, which is slow to build up. However, if this is their mode of action in phobic states, it must be concluded that there are safer ways of bringing it about. Since there is some (rather weak) evidence that the effect may be more on anxiety than on avoidance, it is relevant to ask whether the effect is increased by behavioral treatment directed toward this avoidance behavior. Unfortunately, there is no study that can answer this question.

## TRICYCLIC ANTIDEPRESSANTS

Tricyclic antidepressants are safer than monoamine oxidase inhibitors, and since they, too, have anxiolytic as well as antidepressant properties, it is natural to inquire whether they have any place in the treatment of agoraphobia. There is surprisingly little information on this point except that provided by a single group of investigations led by Klein. Their observations are closely related to a theory proposed by Klein (1964) that the central symptoms of most agoraphobic states are the panic attacks that take place when the patient is away from phobic stimuli. In this view of agoraphobia, the phobic symptoms are regarded as secondary to this primary panic disorder, and it is Klein's belief that this central panic disorder responds to treatment with the tricyclic antidepressant imipramine. Mendel and Klein (1969) have also suggested that it is the failure to treat panic attacks that is responsible for relapses after behavior therapy. Klein and his collaborators have further suggested that behavior therapy deals only with anticipatory anxiety and avoidance, which have become secondarily attached to the primary panic disorder, and not with the central symptoms themselves (Zitrin, Klein, Lindemann, Tobak, Rock, Kaplan, & Ganz, 1976). It is a virtue of Klein's ideas that they lead to a testable hypothesis, namely, that patients with simple phobias, who seldom experience spontaneous panic attacks, should not benefit any more from imipramine than from placebo, while agoraphobic patients should improve more.

Unfortunately, the major investigation that Klein and his colleagues have carried out is complicated in its design and therefore difficult to interpret. Zitrin, Klein, and Woerner (1978) reported a comparison of 26 weekly sessions of behavior therapy given with imipramine, behavior therapy with placebo, and supportive psychotherapy with imipramine. The behavior therapy was itself rather complex, being a combination of desensitization in imagination, some "homework" tasks, and assertiveness training. The report is an interim one concerning 111 patients, and results are presented both as percentages of patients achieving marked or moderate overall improvement and as ratings of improvement at completion of treatment. Ratings were made of changes in agoraphobic symptoms, and global measures of improvement in several areas were also included. For agoraphobics, imipramine with behavior therapy was not more effective than imipramine with supportive therapy. However, there was no overall difference between behavior therapy and supportive treatment, and since other authors have found a difference (e.g., Gelder, Marks, & Wolff, 1967), doubt is cast on the efficacy of the behavior therapy in this investigation and the generalizations that can be made from it are thus limited. Looking at the results in another way, behavior therapy with imipramine was rather more effective than behavior therapy alone, but this difference was significant only in the patient's ratings, so that there is only weak support for another of Klein's ideas. Moreover, the authors presented no evidence on the effects of imipramine on what they claim to be the mediating variable for its therapeutic effects, namely, the frequency of panic attacks. Neither did they report changes in depression, although this is another possible mediator of the observed effects.

Among the agoraphobic patients, 30% relapsed when imipramine was discontinued, despite 26 weeks of treatment. For anyone considering the use of this treatment, some of the adverse effects of the drugs are important: 18% of agoraphobics complained that the drug induced insomnia, irritability, and jitteriness, and in these patients, a temporary reduction in dosage was required. Other patients also showed the well-known anticholinergic side effects of the drug. A number proved to be very sensitive to these effects and a few could tolerate only 10 mg per day of imipramine.

Zitrin, Klein, and Woerner (1980) reported a further investigation of imipramine in which 76 agoraphobic women were assigned randomly to imipramine or placebo. After four weeks of this treatment, all received "*in vivo* desensitization" for 10 weeks in group sessions that lasted from two to three hours. Imipramine was then continued for a further three months. Interpretation of the results is made difficult by the very high dropout rate (29%) in both groups: patients in the placebo group usually said they could not keep up with the group; patients taking imipramine usually dropped out because of side effects. At the end of the behavior therapy period, imipramine-treated patients had improved somewhat more than those taking placebo, and the difference was significant in the global improvement ratings made by patient, therapist, and assessor. During the subsequent three months of medication, the imipramine-treated patients continued to show greater improvement. The effects of discontinuing imipramine are not reported in detail, but Zitrin (1981) stated that more patients relapsed after imipramine than after placebo and confirmed that this is an important practical problem in the use of this form of treatment. She wrote that some patients "used the drug as a crutch and did not make a substantial effort to reorient themselves toward their phobias. Thus, when medication was withdrawn, if a panic occurred the avoidance behavior became re-established" (p. 170).

Of the many other tricyclic antidepressants, only clomipramine has so far been specifically claimed to have value in treating agoraphobia, although Zitrin (1981) mentioned that she has found that other tricyclic antidepressants have effects similar to imipramine. Beaumont (1977) reported an uncontrolled multicenter trial in which the drug was given to 765 phobic patients, in doses that were increased gradually to 150 mg per day. Of these, 285 withdrew from the study—139 because they were unable to tolerate the side effects of the drug. Among the 480 who completed 12 weeks of treatment, improvement in the region of 70–80% was reported in general anxiety, depression, phobic anxiety, and phobic avoidance. The author commented on the extreme sensitivity of many patients to anticholinergic side effects, even with low doses. Since Klein reported similar findings in some patients receiving imipramine, this aspect of treatment would repay further study.

## LEUKOTOMY

Although leukotomy is not a drug treatment, it is convenient to discuss it at this point. In the period up to the mid-1960s, a number of agoraphobic patients were treated in this way, and although there is no reason to think that this is any longer an appropriate treatment, some of the changes observed in these patients are relevant to issues that we shall be concerned with in later chapters.

There is no adequately controlled randomized trial of leukotomy for any disorder. For agoraphobia, there is one report of a case-controlled retrospective study of the effects of modified leukotomy in 22 patients with severe agoraphobia by Marks, Birley, and Gelder (1966). These authors studied patients referred for leukotomy by other psychiatrists and treated by neurosurgeons, at two units (referred to as Series A and Series B in Figure 4.1). All of these patients had severe agoraphobia of many years' duration, together with pronounced general anxiety. Those who received leukotomy were matched individually from case note information with patients chosen from a group of 400 agoraphobics treated at one of the hospitals with a variety of drugs and psychological treatments. Ratings of progress were made from extracts of case notes by assessors who were "blind" to the nature of the treatment. The leukotomy patients changed

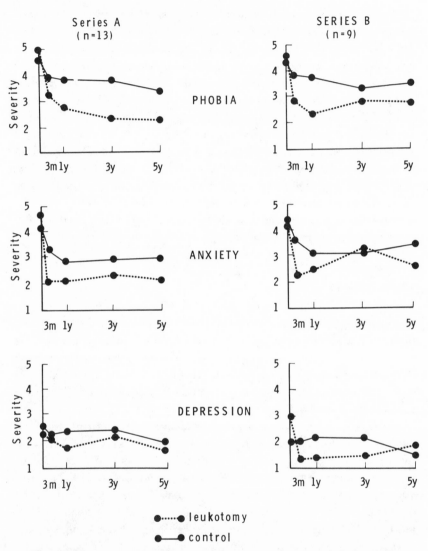

FIGURE 4.1. Mean ratings of the two series of cases immediately before leukotomy, three months after the operation, and at one-, three-, and five-year follow-up.
From I. M. Marks, J. L. T. Birley, and M. G. Gelder, *British Journal of Psychiatry*,
1966, *12*, 761. Reprinted by permission.

significantly more than controls on ratings of both general anxiety and phobias, and this effect was achieved without any marked changes in personality. There were two striking and important features of these results. First, although the maximum improvement in anxiety took place within the first three months after the operation, the phobias continued to improve for a year (Figure 4.1). Second, the patients with an outgoing previous personality showed more improvement in phobias than did those who were shy, although there was no difference in the amount by which anxiety was reduced in the two types of personality immediately after the operation. These results suggest that the immediate effect of the operation is to reduce anxiety, and this supposition is consistent with the results of Kelly, Walter, and Sargant (1966), who studied anxious patients and found reductions in ratings of both anxiety and forearm blood flow six weeks after the operation. However, in agoraphobic patients, there appears to be a second, more gradual process that accounts for the improvement in the phobias. The course of several cases suggested that this process may be concerned with facing the feared situations again.

One patient had received intensive behavior therapy before leukotomy without benefit. Several weeks after leukotomy, she had a further course and this time made rapid progress. A second patient lost much of her anxiety immediately after the operation, but the phobias did not begin to improve until many months later. Up to that time, she had made little effort to go out, but an accident then occurred that caused her to run outside the house for the first time. She did not feel anxious, and from that time, she went out regularly and the phobias improved. This view is consistent with the finding that patients who were depressed did less well than the others, as did those with introverted personalities. It is possible that these factors were important because they were associated with less determined efforts to practice going out again.

The findings do not at first appear to accord with those of Mitchell-Heggs, Kelly, and Richardson (1976), who found that ratings of phobias and general anxiety had both changed maximally two months after limbic leukotomy. However, these authors relied on the Middlesex Hospital Questionnaire for the ratings of phobia, and the findings are from a diverse group of patients and not restricted to agoraphobia. They do not therefore contradict our results.

Before we leave this topic, it is important to make clear that we have presented these data for the light that they may throw on the mechanisms by which phobic symptoms are maintained. We do *not* advocate leukotomy as a treatment for even the most severe cases of agoraphobia, despite the opinion of Bridges and Bartlett (1977) that subcaudate and cingulate operations are indicated in chronic phobic anxiety states.


## CONCLUSION

Although there are many gaps in our knowledge about the effects of drugs on agoraphobia, we can conclude that neither anxiolytics nor antidepressant drugs lead to more than temporary relief of symptoms when given without other measures. Moreover, the simplest explanation of the effects of antidepressant drugs, whether monoamine oxidase inhibitors, or tricyclics, is that they, too, are acting as anxiolytic—rather than as antidepressant—agents, albeit with effects that take longer to appear and to disappear than those of the benzodiazepines. If we can make a link between the effects of leukotomy and those of these drugs, we might conclude that anxiety reduction, however long sustained, affects the phobic symptoms only when it is combined with regular exposure to phobic situations. The evidence is weak, for it comes mainly from the informal observations made in the leukotomy study; none of the studies of monoamine oxidase inhibitors or tricyclic antidepressants have been designed in a way that can give a definite answer to the question. However, this idea would explain the high relapse rate after treatment with monoamine oxidase inhibitors or tricyclics as the consequence of failure to institute regular practice. It is certainly a hypothesis that could profitably be tested systematically in future investigations of these treatments.

These observations also point toward a speculative model of the pathological processes in which a component of generalized anxiety takes on an important role, as do the occasional short-term increases in this anxiety that are manifested in panic attacks. Whether the generalized anxiety is primary or is the aftermath of frequent episodes of phobic anxiety is uncertain, but we cannot conclude, as Klein would have us do, that the anxiety is necessarily primary. In any case, there may be a circular mechanism in established cases in which high levels of general anxiety make it more difficult for phobias to be resolved (hence the effect of leukotomy), while phobic exacerbations maintain the general anxiety—hence the comprehensive improvements observed after successful behavior therapy that are described in Chapter 10. This view is consistent with the model set out in Chapter 3, and it has the additional advantage that it relates the effects of drugs and leukotomy rather clearly to the effects of behavioral treatments.

# 5. Psychotherapy

THIS CHAPTER is concerned with a variety of different forms of psychological treatment that developed separately from the behavior therapies. Most can be broadly grouped as "talking treatments," that is, treatments that attempt to change behavior by some form of discussion with the patient. However, the chapter ends with a brief account of certain techniques of relaxation and meditation that form a bridge between the psychotherapies and the behavioral treatments that are the subject of the rest of this book.

## PSYCHOANALYTIC TREATMENT

Since most psychotherapy is founded on psychoanalysis, it is appropriate to begin by considering this method. We shall see that since Freud, psychoanalysts have made an interesting exception to their general rules when they have treated agoraphobic patients. However, before considering this exception, it may be appropriate to remind the reader about the general rules.

The central idea in the psychoanalytic view of phobias is that the symptoms are the result of two processes: the repression of an emotionally charged idea and the displacement of this internal conflict to an object or situation in the outside world. In the words of Ivey (1959), these psychological processes allow the patient to "transform an inner threat, of which he is unaware, to an outside danger which he can perceive and against which he can protect himself" (p. 39). Such an arrangement may work for a time, but it fails to relieve the true source of the anxiety and at the same time limits the patient's life. The repressed impulses presumably vary from patient to patient, but sexual and aggressive impulses are thought to be those most commonly involved. Psychoanalysis offers an explanation of why the patient's symptom takes the form of agoraphobia rather than any other phobias. Again, more than one cause has been suggested, including sexual desires concerning prostitution, exhibitionism, or adultery or repressed aggressive feelings toward parental figures (Ivey, 1959).

The first requirement of analytic treatment is to uncover the repressed mental contents that account for the agoraphobia. The second is to enable the patient to deal with these directly so that the defenses of repression and displacement can be given up. As in other analytic treatment, the necessary changes are sought through free association and the analysis of dreams. These are subjected to interpretation, with a timing and a speed that depend on the analyst's judgment of his/her patient's readiness to accept and make use of these interpretations. To quote Ivey again:

> By the time treatment is completed, [the patient] should have a good understanding of his previous symptoms and of his own strength in his life situation upon which he can build to gain real satisfaction. In those instances in which the phobias are complicated by other neurotic defenses, indicating a considerable weakness of the patient's ego, interpretation must be rendered carefully, if at all. In such instances, the task of strengthening the ego should receive primary attention in treatment. (p. 47)

We are now ready to return to the exception that analysts agree should be made when phobic patients are treated. This was expressed particularly clearly by Freud (1919/1924b) as follows:

> Our technique grew up in the treatment of hysteria and is still directed principally to the cure of this affliction. But the phobias have already made it necessary for us to go beyond our former limits. One can hardly master a phobia if one waits till the patient lets the analysis influence him to give it up. . . . Take the example of agoraphobia; there are two classes, the one slight and the other severe. Patients belonging to the first indeed suffer from anxiety when they go out alone, but they have not yet given up going out alone on that account; the others protect themselves from anxiety by altogether giving up going out alone. With the last one it succeeds only when one can induce them through the influence of the analysis to behave like the first class, that is to go out alone and to struggle with their anxiety while they are making the attempt. One first achieves, therefore, a considerable moderation of the phobia and it is only when this has been attained by the physician's recommendation that the associations and memories come into the patient's mind, enabling the phobia to be solved. (pp. 399–400)

Since Freud's day, other analysts have confirmed this original observation. Thus Fenichel (1945) recommended that active intervention is required with phobic patients as soon as the analysis has begun to have some effect on the neurosis. And Friedman and Goldstein (1974), in a useful review of psychoanalytic treatment of phobic disorders, also stated that active intervention is needed to encourage patients to face feared situations. Likewise, Ey, Bernard, and Brisset (1974) emphasized the need to encourage patients at an appropriate state in the analysis to face the situations they fear.

The results of psychoanalysis for agoraphobia cannot be assessed. Ey *et al.* (1974) regard it as the treatment of choice, but they give no figures to support this opinion. Nor does it seem that they could, because the literature contains only the reports of individual cases that have been treated successfully. Nowadays most agoraphobic patients who seek psychotherapy are more likely to be treated by one of the briefer methods than to receive psychoanalysis. It is to these methods that we shall now turn our attention.

## ANALYTICALLY ORIENTED PSYCHOTHERAPY

The literature on psychoanalytically oriented psychotherapy is rather less sparse than that on psychoanalysis and contains some reports of series of cases as well as reports on the treatment of individuals. As in the psychoanalytic writings, it is striking how many authors refer to the need to adopt special techniques when agoraphobic patients are treated. Thus Terhune (1949) remarked that "a process of psychological ventilation, in which the patient discusses his mental conflicts, is seldom itself curative. . . . It has been said that discovering and removing emotional conflicts will cure phobias. This is seldom true" (p. 169). And he went on to recommend that patients be encouraged to place themselves in the situations they fear. They should, for example, go for walks and train trips and carry these out in a graduated sequence. At the same time, Terhune drew attention to the need to help patients become less dependent in their personal relationships. He recommended two months of this "psychological reeducation," followed by several months of supervision to ensure that patients will not give up any progress they have made.

Tucker (1956) also advised an active approach. He suggested that the origin of symptoms should be explained to the patient, who should also be reassured strongly that she/he will not become insane. Tucker also drew attention to the need to secure the cooperation and understanding of the spouse and advocated a graduated program of activities intended to rebuild self-confidence. These initial steps can be expected to bring about improvement in the phobias, and it is at this point that Tucker believes that the "real work" begins, the chances of further progress depending on the attitude and the personal resources of the patient. The importance of a dependent relationship between the female patient and her mother was also emphasized by this author, who indicated that this dependence must be modified if progress is to be made. His summary of his views is interesting: "Treatment needs to be strongly supportive and directive in patients of this type and I believe that a non-directive analytic approach is ineffective" (p. 829). Very similar views were expressed by Laughlin (1956).

Andrews (1966) has reviewed the literature on psychotherapy for phobias and has reached two interesting conclusions: first, it is necessary to establish a relationship with the patients that is at once supportive, directive, and not unduly permissive; and second, this relationship should be used to persuade the patient to confront situations that arouse fear. Andrews made the assertion that the personalities of phobic patients are as important as their symptoms. He regards the salient features of the personality of the phobic patient as being undue dependence and the habit of avoiding difficulties. Among the latter, he draws attention to situations in which the patient might have to be assertive or to face challenges. Andrews believes that it is as important to deal with these general attributes of the patient as it is to treat the phobias. To do this, the therapist has to adopt a directive role, but he/she must use it to enable the patient to become more self-assertive. Andrews further suggested that phobic people respond to others in ways that force the other person into action, instead of leaving the patient to master his/her own problems. In this way, the personality features are perpetuated and even enhanced. These ideas of Andrews come close to those of Haley (1963), who viewed symptoms as tactics in a game of human relationships, and psychotherapy as a means of blocking or changing these tactics. In Andrews's words, the patient is, in effect, saying to the therapist, "Please guide and help me because I am unable to deal with difficult and frightening situations on my own," and the crucial point in treatment is the way that the therapist responds to this unspoken message.


## PARADOXICAL INTENTION

One special technique of psychotherapy deserves our attention. This is a procedure that derives from a method of psychotherapy known as *logotherapy* (Frankl, 1970). Logotherapy is rather complicated, but we need concern ourselves with only one aspect of it, the simpler technique of paradoxical intention. Essentially this technique is concerned with anticipatory anxiety, and in broad outline, it takes the following form: the patient is first required to describe something that he/she fears may happen to him/her and then he/she has to attempt to bring about the consequences that he/she fears most. Thus, an agoraphobic patient who fears that he/she may faint when in the street would be asked to make him/herself faint. Naturally, he/she soon discovers that he/she cannot do this to order. According to Frankl, this discovery is followed by a lessening of the fear and a change in the patient's attitude toward it, which he calls an "existential re-orientation." Gertz (1970) has given examples of the ways in which this method can be used with phobic patients. They are required to list the symptoms that disturb them most and then to attempt to produce these deliberately. Since the majority of symptoms that the patients list are autonomic (e.g., blushing or trembling), they are not under direct voluntary control and the patient cannot reproduce them by directly willing them to happen—though the patient might, of course, find indirect ways, such as imagining other frightening events. Patients are also told that when symptoms appear in the course of everyday life, they should not try to diminish them but instead actually attempt to make them worse. Gertz went on to assert that whenever patients relapse after improving with treatment by paradoxical intention, it is because they have slipped back into the old habits of striving to get better. Gertz (1967) has reported his experience with the use of paradoxical intention in 51 phobic and obsessive-compulsive patients in a second paper. However, although he claimed that 90% of these patients improved, the report is descriptive and without quantitative data.

The technique is interesting, and if it were proved effective, this would be of some theoretical interest as well as practical value. It is unfortunate that none of the reports contain evidence that allows an assessment of the method. The question is important, and better research is needed.


## RELAXATION, AUTOGENIC TRAINING, AND HYPNOSIS

Training in relaxation is an important component of many kinds of behavior therapy, but it has also been used on its own. This section is concerned with this independent use of relaxation methods; information derived from behavior therapy studies is considered in Chapter 6.

The most comprehensive account of relaxation training has been given by Jacobson (1938, 1964). His case examples contain few references to phobic disorders, and the table of results (Jacobson, 1938, p. 419) contains only 5 phobic disorders in a total of 231 cases. All 5 are counted among those much improved, but there is no indication whether these were agoraphobics. This account of the method, therefore, supports the clinical impression that relaxation procedures used without any other measures have little place in the treatment of agoraphobia.

Autogenic training is a more elaborate technique described by Luthe and Schultz (1969), in which relaxation is one part of a procedure where great emphasis is given to special training in mental imagery. The treatment is based on the supposition that the autonomic control of organs of the body can be modified by appropriate mental imagery; for example, imagining feelings of warmth in the hand or the forehead is believed to alter the blood flow to the corresponding parts. Autogenic training seems more relevant to psychosomatic disorders than to the neuroses, but Luthe and Schultz stated that phobic reactions respond well. However, they qualified this statement by saying (Vol. 3, p. 78) that many phobias are associated with a psychodynamic disorder and that when such a disorder is present, autogenic training gives less reliable results. Since of all the phobic disorders, agoraphobia is the one that is most often viewed as having complicated psychodynamics, it can be presumed that this comment applies to it.

There are scattered references in the literature over the last 100 years to the use of hypnosis for phobic disorders. Moll (1891) viewed agoraphobia as being due to autosuggestion and he listed it (p. 316) among conditions that he regarded as "particularly suitable" for treatment by hypnosis. The subsequent use of hypnosis has taken two separate forms. The first uses hypnotic suggestion to overcome symptoms directly; the second employs hypnosis as an adjunct to analytic psychotherapy.

An example of the first method is provided by a controlled comparison of hypnosis and desensitization for phobic patients carried out by Marks, Gelder, and Edwards (1968). For our present purposes, it is unfortunate that of the 28 patients who took part, only 12 were agoraphobic. The patients were allocated first to either desensitization or hypnosis, both of which could last for up to three months. However, after six weeks, any patients who had not improved by a predetermined amount were given the other treatment. As a result of this plan, 14 patients received desensitization as the first treatment, and a further 9 received it as a second, while 14 patients received hypnosis as the first treatment and 4 as the second. Hypnosis began with suggestions of relaxation, went on to suggestions about eye closure and arm levitation to deepen the trance, and ended with forcible suggestions that the patient would feel more relaxed when going out and that the phobias would disappear gradually. No imagery was presented and no suggestions were made that the patient should enter any particular situation. All patients were also asked to relax at home between treatments. No graduated tasks were given to the hypnosis group, but patients who received desensitization were asked to practice going into situations once they could imagine these without anxiety. Nearly half the desensitization patients and about 40% of those receiving hypnosis took drugs at some stage of treatment: during the 23 courses of desensitization, 11 patients had a benzodiazepine and 2 an antidepressant; during the 18 courses of hypnosis, 6 had a benzodiazepine and 2 an antidepressant. Multiple ratings were made, and these showed a trend in favor of desensitization. However, since the patients who received this treatment received rather more anxiolytic drugs, the results are difficult to interpret. It is unfortunate also that the small numbers of agoraphobic patients in this investigation make it impossible to draw any firm conclusions about the value of hypnosis for this phobic disorder. Before leaving this type of hypnotic treatment, we can note that Schilder (1956) recommended light hypnosis only for mild cases of phobia, preferring psychoanalysis for the rest.

The second use of hypnosis is to use a deeper trance to facilitate age regression as a means of exploring the dynamic origins of phobic symptoms (e.g., Gill & Brenman, 1943). This technique is recommended by Wolberg (1977), but it does not appear to have been evaluated in a controlled trial.

## CONCLUSION

There is some consistency in the rather scattered literature on the psychological treatment of phobic disorders. Treatments in which the patient takes a passive role do not appear to be helpful; relaxation training used alone, hypnosis, and unmodified techniques of psychoanalysis or analytic psychotherapy all produce limited results. There is a surprising amount of agreement among authors using different methods that it is essential, at some stage of treatment, for the patient to practice returning to the situations that she/he has avoided. Whether psychological exploration is necessary as well has never been demonstrated in a satisfactory way; the literature contains only a series of assertions based on clinical experience. Of the many opinions that have been offered about the central task of the psychotherapist, that of Andrews (1966) is perhaps the most interesting. He suggested that the therapist has to establish a special kind of relationship in which he/she asserts authority over the patient but does so in a way that enables the patient to become more self-reliant. We shall see later that this idea has an interesting parallel with our own conclusions about the task of the therapist who is using behavioral techniques.

# 6. The Behavioral Treatment of Agoraphobia

AGORAPHOBIA has been treated by behavioral methods for a little over 20 years. During this time, three comparatively distinct phases in research and clinical practice can be distinguished. At first, treatment consisted of simple, straightforward methods in which the patient was encouraged to enter the feared situation in a graded manner. This approach, graded retraining, was replaced by imaginal techniques, of which systematic desensitization is the prime example, in which the patient was not exposed to the actual frightening situations but asked to imagine them. The final phase again emphasized experience in the actual feared situation—in this new form, usually called *in vivo* exposure.

## GRADED RETRAINING

It may seem unnecessary to describe the early studies in graded retraining since the research methodology was crude, the therapeutic results were considered disappointing at the time, and the technique was quickly superceded, or, at least, given less emphasis. However, the revival of interest in *in vivo* methods of exposure gives these early studies a topical importance that they lacked a few years ago.

Meyer and Gelder (1963) described the use of graded retraining with five agoraphobic inpatients. They were first taught to relax, and then they were exposed gradually to increasingly fearful situations, while they attempted to remain as relaxed as possible. Then the authors described how

> Case One was taken out daily over gradually increasing distances. Progress was very slow, with much fluctuation from day to day, but steady improvement from one week to the next. . . . Progress was so slow that it took four months to train her to walk a quarter of a mile to meet the therapist. (p. 21)

71

Because progress was so slow, this patient was trained to walk over a route that enabled her to get to work, and her husband was involved in the training, under supervision. The limited improvement that took place was maintained during a 12-month follow-up period. It is notable that the treatment required *140* hours of the therapist's time.

The remaining patients were treated with similar methods for rather shorter periods of time, but never for less than 60 hours. One patient, Case 4, showed a good response that generalized to phobic situations that had not been treated, and this result was maintained at the 18-month follow-up. Case 3 improved well at first but quickly relapsed, while two other very complex cases made little progress: Case 2 had temporal lobe epilepsy and severe obsessions in addition to agoraphobia, and Case 5 was a turbulent adolescent with hysterical fits and dissociated states.

These detailed case reports were supplemented by retrospective studies based on the case notes of patients treated by behavioral methods in the psychology and psychiatry departments of the Maudsley Hospital (Cooper, 1963; Cooper, Gelder, & Marks, 1965; Marks & Gelder, 1965). In the study by Marks and Gelder, the case notes of 32 phobic patients, 21 of whom were agoraphobic inpatients, were rated according to the severity of their phobic symptomatology on a 5-point scale by a "blind" psychiatric assessor. A case control sample of an equal number of agoraphobics, who had not received behavior therapy but who had been inpatients in the same hospital, was also rated. Both groups were well matched for the initial severity of symptoms, and both improved, albeit modestly, while of the two the behavior therapy group showed significantly greater change. The rating scales first introduced in this study continued substantially unchanged for a number of years, so that the results of this early study—illustrated in Figure 6.1—can be compared with later inquiries. It is noteworthy that aspects of functioning not directly related to the phobia changed little with either method of treatment. Because patients who received graded retraining had 66 sessions of treatment, behavioral and other, while the controls had only 27 sessions, the authors concluded that the slight advantage of graded retraining was probably due to this greater amount of treatment —and that "the results did not justify the expenditure of such effort to retrain inpatient agoraphobics" (p. 570).

This pessimistic conclusion did not go unchallenged. Eysenck (1965) criticized the study on a variety of grounds, including the inexperience of the therapists and, most interestingly, the inappropriateness of considering graded retraining as representative of behavior therapy as it was then practiced. He wrote:

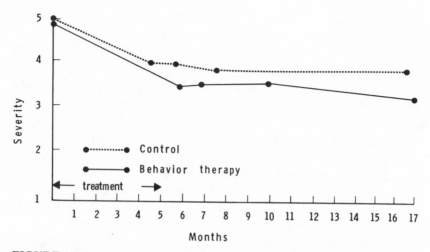

FIGURE 6.1. Assessors' ratings of phobic severity. Modified from I. M. Marks and M. G. Gelder, *British Journal of Psychiatry*, 1965, *111*, 564. Reprinted by permission.

> The retraining method was used on a purely experimental basis and has now been given up because of its poor showing in favour of Wolpe type desensitisation. The review [that of Marks and Gelder] does not deal with an actually practised method, therefore, but with a discarded one which has failed to establish itself. (p. 1008)

This conclusion is strikingly at variance with current thinking, but it does appear to represent a view that was widespread at the time. It led to the rejection or downgrading of the role of practice in entering feared situations and promoted an emphasis on the use of less direct imaginal methods.

## IMAGINAL METHODS

In 1958, Wolpe, in his book *Psychotherapy by Reciprocal Inhibition*, described his method of systematic desensitization and made striking claims for its efficacy. As is widely known, this treatment consists of three basic components. The patient is trained in some response thought to be incompatible with anxiety, usually muscular relaxation. Then a hierarchy of carefully graded fear-provoking situations is constructed, ranging from near neutral to terrifying scenes, and last the patient imagines scenes along this hierarchy, countering any anxiety that arises by using the putative anxiety antagonist. Wolpe anticipated that fear reduction experienced in these imagined scenes would generalize to the experience in the actual situations that they represented. In practice, the treatment was implemented in a rather similar way to traditional psychotherapy. The patient was treated on a regular basis with hour-long sessions in the therapist's office, sometimes for as many as several hundred sessions. Wolpe did not make particular claims for the use of this method with agoraphobia; indeed, his only detailed discussion of this disorder in his 1958 book concerns the use of rather different treatment methods. However, it was clearly an attractive method to use in attempting to reduce agoraphobic fear and avoidance, and it has been vigorously applied and studied by others.

Gelder and Marks (1966) reported what was essentially a prospective version of the retrospective study described already. Twenty agoraphobic inpatients were allocated either to systematic desensitization and graded retraining or to conventional hospital treatment, which included short-term individual psychotherapy. The patients were seen three times per week for three-quarters of an hour. Patients, therapists, and an independent (but not "blind") assessor rated the severity of the phobic symptomatology on 5-point rating scales. Treatment lasted for approximately 20 weeks, that is, 60 or more sessions. The results were disappointing. Figure 6.2 shows that both methods of treatment were associated with modest but equal reductions in phobic severity. There was a slight return of the phobia over the 12-month follow-up period, and this partial relapse

FIGURE 6.2. Combined assessors' and patients' ratings of main phobic symptoms during treatment and follow-up. From M. G. Gelder and I. M. Marks, *British Journal of Psychiatry*, 1966, *112*, 315. Reprinted by permission.

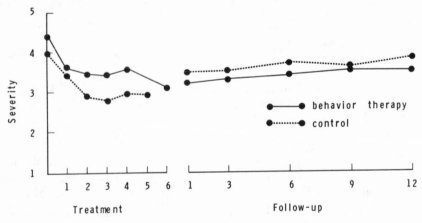

may have been more marked in the control group. Of the 10 patients in behavior therapy, 5 were noted to have made "useful though limited gains in ability to make one particular journey, usually to work" (p. 311). Two patients in the control group made such gains.

The next study in this series considered for the first time the treatment of agoraphobia on an outpatient basis. Gelder, Marks, and Wolff (1967) randomly allocated patients with agoraphobia, social phobias, or simple phobias to 9 months of systematic desensitization, 12 months of individual psychotherapy, or 18 months of group psychotherapy. The numbers in each treatment condition were, respectively, 16, 10, and 16, and all patients were seen weekly for one hour. Graded retraining was not included in any treatment; that is, the therapist did not organize practice from the hospital, although the patients receiving desensitization were set informal homework assignments. The outcome was assessed as before. Figure 6.3 shows that there was a strong effect associated with treatment in this mixed group of phobics. Systematic desensitization was consistently better than either form of psychotherapy, and group psychotherapy had consistently the worst outcome of the three. The difference between systematic desensitization and individual psychotherapy was statistically significant only at the six-month assessment point, but systematic desensitization was nevertheless clearly the most effective of the three treatments studied, and its effects persisted during follow-up. The ratings of patients' phobias, general anxiety, and depression in all three groups are shown in Figure 6.3. It can be seen that there was some improvement in ratings other than those of the main phobia, and while this improvement was most marked in the patients receiving desensitization, it also occurred in those receiving individual psychotherapy. It is unfortunate for our present purpose that only half the patients in this study were agoraphobic, the remainder having specific or social phobias, so that we cannot generalize to the treatment of agoraphobia with complete confidence. However, in studies using such small samples of patients, it is unlikely that statistically reliable effects could be obtained if the differences between the conditions were confined to specific and social phobics. Moreover, seven patients who had received group psychotherapy with little benefit were subsequently treated, after waiting six months, with systematic desensitization. This group showed a striking improvement, which contrasted with their previous response to group therapy; see Figure 6.4 (Gelder & Marks, 1968). This group of seven contained five agoraphobics, so that this very positive response must have been displayed by the agoraphobics. The findings were essentially replicated by

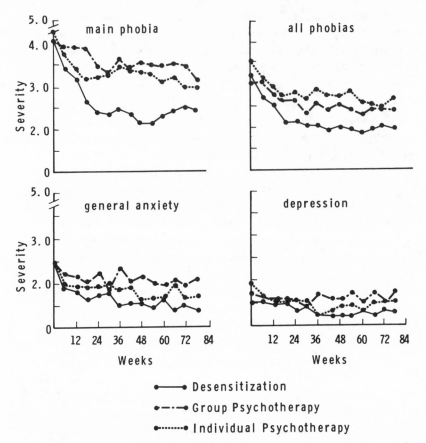

FIGURE 6.3. Mean psychiatric ratings for four symptoms in patients receiving desensitization, individual psychotherapy, and group psychotherapy. Modified from M. G. Gelder, I. M. Marks, and H. H. Wolff, *British Journal of Psychiatry*, 1967, *113*, 59. Reprinted by permission.

Gillan and Rachman (1974), who confirmed that systematic desensitization was superior to individual psychotherapy in a mixed group of phobics. A further study using a similar mixed group of phobics compared systematic desensitization and hypnosis. Systematic desensitization was consistently better, but few differences were statistically significant (Marks, Gelder, & Edwards, 1968).

These studies suggest that systematic desensitization, carried out in imagination with instructions to practice exposure in reality between sessions, is more effective than a variety of other psychotherapeutic procedures with outpatient agoraphobics. The studies also indicate that very similar methods have little specific effect on the behavior of agoraphobic inpatients. It is not clear why the results of systematic desensitization should be so disappointing with inpatients. There appear to be two possibilities; either patients admitted to the hospital are different in some important way from outpatients, or hospitilization reduces the effectiveness of desensitization. Surprisingly, there was little difference in the ratings of agoraphobia, mood, or social adjustment between the in- and outpatient samples in these investigations. However, there could be factors—not reflected in the ratings, such as degree of social support—that determine both the decision to admit and the poor response to treatment. Alternatively, hospitalization may reduce the effectiveness of desensitization by removing the patients from the problem situations, that is, those occurring in their daily life and centered on their local environment. This would not matter if desensitization in imagination automatically transferred to real life, but the poor results with hospitilized patients may indicate that this is not so and that active practice in the problem situations is essential. We shall see that future research makes this seem a most attractive explanation of these findings.

FIGURE 6.4. Ratings of main phobia during group therapy and subsequent desensitization (changes in original desensitization shown for comparison). From M. G. Gelder and I. M. Marks, *British Journal of Psychiatry*, 1968, *114*, 324. Reprinted by permission.

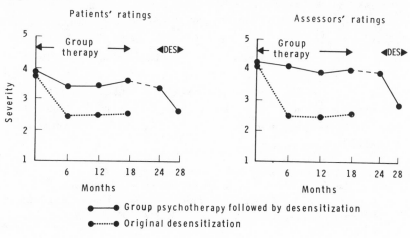

A cardinal feature of the method that we have been describing is that anxiety was avoided whenever possible. Exposure, either to real situations or in imagination, was graded, and as a consequence, the treatment was a slow and rather laborious process. Gelder *et al.* (1967) reported that systematic desensitization took nine months of weekly attendance, and the earlier studies took even more time. A treatment that requires so extensive a professional commitment is unlikely to find widespread acceptance. At approximately the same time, Stampfl and Levis (1967) described a procedure in which patients imagined extremely frightening phobic situations. The imagery also included "dynamic material" that the authors believed related to the genesis of that fear. Stampfl and Levis called their procedure *implosion;* used without the dynamic overlay, it was termed *flooding.* It appeared briefly to be a strong contender as the treatment of choice for agoraphobia.

Marks, Boulougouris, and Marset (1971) described a typical flooding session very clearly. The therapist described several themes for a total of 50 minutes. In these themes:

> an agoraphobic might hear the therapist describe that he went out into the street, became anxious, felt like fainting, was bathed in sweat, screamed in despair and shame, tried to run back home but fainted and was taken by ambulance to a mental hospital. Each theme lasted five or ten minutes . . . those which did not illicit anxiety would be discarded . . . degree of anxiety was judged by clues from the patient such as grimaces, crying, clenching of fists and from an overall rating by the patient at the end of the session on the maximum amount of anxiety experienced. (p. 355)

This method, so spectacularly different from the painful caution of systematic desensitization, was examined by Marks, Boulougouris, and Marset (1971) in a crossover study of a group of 16 phobic patients, of whom 9 were agoraphobics and 5 were inpatients. Treatment consisted of six sessions of systematic desensitization or six sessions of flooding over a period of three weeks. Sessions consisted of 50 minutes of imaginal treatment with, in addition, 70 minutes of exposure to actual situations on the final two treatment sessions in each condition. During flooding in real situations:

> patients were asked to enter the most frightening situation related to the fear that had been dealt with during the fantasy session. . . . While patients were in a phobic situation the therapist intermittently recited the flooding themes and the patients were asked to rehearse these themselves as well, silently or aloud. (p. 355)

Patients being treated by exposure after systematic desensitization were exposed gradually to feared situations with the therapist present to reassure and to attempt to minimize anxiety.

These two very different treatments were compared in a crossover design. All patients received both treatments, half the patients starting with systematic desensitization followed by flooding and the rest receiving the same treatments in the reverse order. The assessment was essentially the same as that used in the studies already described, with the addition of a psychophysiological assessment (described in more detail in Chapter 2). In this study, it consisted of measuring heart rate and skin conductance while the patient was at rest, and then while being confronted with neutral and phobic material.

Flooding was superior to systematic desensitization on most measures, significantly so on independent ratings of phobic behavior and on some physiological measures. Moreover, flooding appeared to be particularly effective with agoraphobics. The mean change in agoraphobics over six sessions was only .22 on the 5-point scale with systematic desensitization, in contrast to 1.29 with flooding. For specific phobias, however, the two treatments were equally effective, the corresponding changes being .74 and .65. This finding is striking. It appeared that a few sessions of imaginal flooding were approximately as effective as the numerous sessions of imaginal desensitization used in previous studies, and very much more effective than the desensitization given in the same study.

If agoraphobics could be helped so successfully and so quickly, then the whole outlook for their treatment would be changed. It was therefore vital that Marks *et al.*'s preliminary observation should be verified. Verification was attempted in a rather complex large-scale study reported by Gelder, Bancroft, Gath, Johnston, Mathews, and Shaw (1973) and by Mathews, Johnston, Shaw, and Gelder (1974). Before describing this study, however, it is necessary to step aside and consider the developments that had taken place in the methodology and design of controlled investigations of psychological treatment.

The studies we have been describing largely relied on simple ratings of the extent to which the patients' phobic symptoms interfered with their life. At the same time as these studies were being carried out, there had developed a large literature of experimental studies on the reduction of minor nonclinical fears, so-called analogue studies. In many ways, the most important impact of this literature has been in deepening our understanding of the issues involved in the evaluation of fear-reduction tech-

niques. In this regard, the work of Lang on the measurement of different
aspects of anxiety (see Chapter 2) and that of Paul on experimental control
are particularly important. Lang proposed in various papers, conveniently
summarized in Lang (1971), that fear and anxiety are composed of three
components, which he characterized as behavioral, cognitive–affective,
and psychophysiological. These components are not considered perfectly
correlated and could therefore vary independently and respond independently to treatment. If this view is accepted, it is necessary to
measure all three aspects of the patient's fear to get a complete understanding of the effects of a treatment. The study by Paul (1966) on the reduction
of public-speaking fears set the standard for adequate outcome investigations for the next decade. Among his most important innovations was a
psychological placebo condition that contained the nonspecific aspects of
the therapy of interest, but not the specific ones. By *nonspecific aspects*, we
mean such features as a persuasive rationale, therapist attention, and
plausible technique, which are present in many therapies. It has recently
been realized that the development of such a nonspecific treatment is very
much more difficult than was originally thought (Lick & Bootzin, 1975)
and, strictly speaking, may be impossible; but in as far as it can be achieved, it offers considerable advantages over the alternative method of studying a comparison treatment. If, for example, systematic desensitization is
compared with individual psychotherapy and desensitization proves to be
more effective, then it can be argued that none of what are considered the
specific aspects of desensitization, such as relaxation and ascending a
hierarchy in imagination, are the effective components. Desensitization
and individual psychotherapy differ in so many ways that it might be some
apparently inert feature that is present in systematic desensitization and
not in psychotherapy that does, in fact, carry all the therapeutic power. It
is therefore a more powerful research method to construct a nonspecific
treatment that contains all the ingredients of desensitization other than the
ones considered critical for their specific effect. In this way, clear conclusions about the importance of the central features of desensitization could
be drawn.

These technical developments greatly influenced the studies by Gelder *et
al.* (1973) and Mathews *et al.* (1974). We wished to examine the relative effectiveness of flooding and systematic desensitization and to discover if
either of these behavior therapies was more effective than a nonspecific
control treatment. Equal numbers of agoraphobics and patients with other
phobias were assigned to systematic desensitization, flooding, or a non-

specific control treatment, 12 patients receiving each treatment. All treatments had the same basic structure and were carried out by the same three therapists, each of whom treated equal numbers of patients in each condition. The treatments all lasted for 15 weekly sessions of approximately 1-1½ hours. The first 3 sessions were assigned to history taking and preparation for the treatments that followed. In the 8 subsequent sessions, the treatment was applied in imagination, while the final 4 sessions were spent practicing the technique.

Flooding and systematic desensitization were carried out along the lines we have already described. The nonspecific control treatment was described thus:

> The therapist presented phobic images as a starting point for free association by the patient, who was asked to describe thoughts and feelings aroused by each image, and to report any new images that occurred to her. The therapist did not attempt to control the content of subsequent imagery, but simply showed interest and concern in anything reported by the patient without attempting to induce relaxation or to focus on anxiety-evoking material. In this way imagery could diverge from specific phobic content towards other areas such as interpersonal relationships. An explanation was given to the patients that exploration of their feelings in this way will lead to a better self-understanding, and thus help to overcome phobic anxiety. (Gelder *et al.*, 1973, p. 448)

This treatment therefore controlled for therapeutic rationale, imagery, goal setting, and attention from the therapist, but not for the specific aspects of treatment, such as relaxation, systematic phobic imagery, and the generation of anxiety. The practice sessions all required the patient to deal with actual feared situations. The main difference between the conditions was the difficulty of the situation to be faced and the level of anxiety to be tolerated. Anxiety was kept at a minimum during systematic desensitization, largely ignored during flooding (during which the emphasis was on maximizing exposure), and allowed to adopt an intermediate level during the control treatment.

The outcome of these procedures was most comprehensively assessed by the use of multiple measures of all the subsystems of anxiety discussed in Chapter 2. The ratings used previously were therefore supplemented with a psychophysiological assessment, very similar to that used by Marks, Boulougouris, and Marset (1971); a cognitive and affective assessment using standardized questionnaires measuring mood (McNair & Lorr, 1964), phobic severity and extensiveness (Wolpe & Lang, 1964), and various semantic differential scales; and, finally, phobic behavior measured direct-

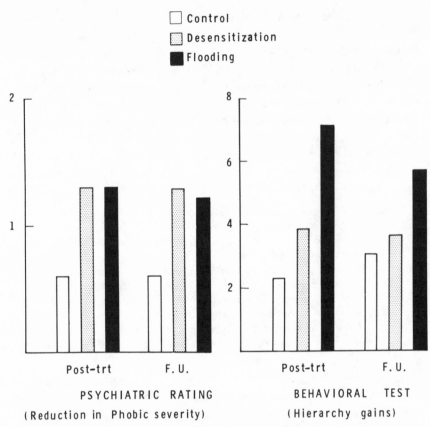

FIGURE 6.5. Change from before treatment in two measures of phobic severity. From M. G. Gelder, J. H. J. Bancroft, D. H. Gath, D. W. Johnston, A. M. Mathews, and P. M. Shaw, *British Journal of Psychiatry*, 1973, *123*, 452. Reprinted by permission.

ly on a behavioral test. This type of testing has been described in Chapter 2. All assessments were carried out by a team of "blind" independent assessors measuring the different aspects of the patients' behavior.

Figure 6.5 shows the results on a number of different outcome measures in the mixed group of phobic patients. The results on these and other measures were consistent, though not always statistically significant. The behavior therapies were superior to the control procedure and did not differ from each other. Improvements during treatment persisted at six-month follow-up. No convincing differences were found between the treatments on physiological responsiveness, although basal heart rate was lower after behavior therapy than after the control procedure. When the groups were subdivided and the agoraphobics were examined separately, flooding and systematic desensitization were found to be equally effective in the treatment of agoraphobia; Marks, Boulougouris, and Marset's (1971) finding that flooding was superior was not replicated. Rather surprisingly, the differences between the behavior therapies and the control condition were rather greater in agoraphobics than in the other phobic patients, as can be seen in Table 6.1. These results, therefore, suggest that systematic desensitization and flooding have specific and worthwhile effects in the treatment of agoraphobia and that these effects are not produced by the nonspecific elements contained in them.

In this study, the main measures were taken before and after a complete course of treatment, but some simple measures were taken by the therapist during every session. Two of these proved interesting. On each visit, patients rated on a 0-10 scale how anxious they felt when imagining the most terrifying item on their personal hierarchy, and how anxious they believed they would feel if actually in that situation. These measures were sensitive to the effects of treatment, and they behaved rather differently. Results are are shown in Figures 6.6 and 6.7. It is clear that on both measures the control treatment was less effective than the behavior therapies. As one might expect, the anxiety that the subjects felt when imagining the situations was affected by the imaginal treatments. However, the anxiety that they anticipated that they would experience when in that situation was affected only by the *in vivo* treatment. This finding suggests that while imaginal treatment modifies some aspects of anxiety and may potentiate later *in vivo* treatment, the *in vivo* treatment may be more effective in producing changes in patients' estimates of what they will actually experience if required to enter the real situation. Exploring this possibility brings us to the final phase of the research that we are describing.

TABLE 6.1. Change in assessors' ratings of phobia from pre- to posttreatment[a]

|  | Agoraphobics | Nonagoraphobics |
| --- | --- | --- |
| Nonspecific control | .3 | .8 |
| Desensitization | 1.7 | 1.0 |
| Flooding | 1.4 | 1.3 |

[a]From Gelder, Bancroft, Gath, Johnston, Mathews, and Shaw (1973).

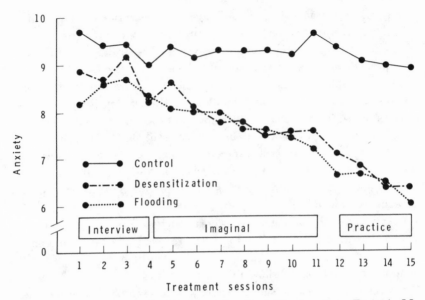

FIGURE 6.6. Anxiety when "thinking about" phobic situations. From A. M. Mathews, D. W. Johnston, P. M. Shaw, and M. G. Gelder, *British Journal of Psychiatry*, 1974, *125*, 262. Reprinted by permission.

FIGURE 6.7. Anxiety estimates for actual phobic situations. From A. M. Mathews, D. W. Johnston, P. M. Shaw, and M. G. Gelder, *British Journal of Psychiatry*, 1974, *125*, 262. Reprinted by permission.

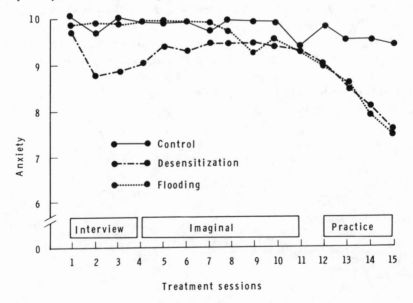

## IN VIVO EXPOSURE

In addition to the suggestive evidence described above, other lines of inquiry suggest that *in vivo* exposure may be a critical aspect of the treatment of fear. Bandura, Blanchard, and Ritter (1969), following Ritter's earlier work on contact desensitization, showed that methods involving direct exposure were more effective than those using imaginal or symbolic modeling in reducing the fear of snakes in moderately severe snake phobics. Sherman (1972) studied fear of swimming in people unable to swim and demonstrated that imaginal desensitization had no effect on this fear, although *in vivo* exposure was highly effective. Good results with *in vivo* methods were reported in preliminary studies of specific phobias (Watson, Gaind, & Marks, 1971) and in a mixed group of phobias, including agoraphobia (Crowe, Marks, Agras, & Leitenberg, 1972), and in agoraphobics treated in groups (Watson, Mullett, & Pillay, 1973). Independently two groups of research workers, using virtually identical experimental designs, chose to investigate the relative power of *in vivo* and imaginal methods in agoraphobic patients.

Mathews, Johnston, Lancashire, Munby, Shaw, and Gelder (1976) and Johnston, Lancashire, Mathews, Munby, Shaw, and Gelder (1976) sought to determine whether *in vivo* exposure was more effective than imaginal flooding, and whether imaginal flooding potentiated later *in vivo* exposure. Thirty-six female agoraphobic patients were assigned at random to one of three treatments. These were 16 weekly sessions of exposure to actual phobic situations; 8 weekly sessions of flooding in imagination followed by 8 sessions of exposure to actual phobic situations; and 16 sessions in each of which flooding and *in vivo* exposure were given during each session. Assessments followed closely the methods used in earlier studies. They were carried out before treatment, after 8 weeks, at the end of the treatment period, and six months later. In addition, a variety of assessments were carried out before, during, and after each treatment session. Figure 6.8 shows the main outcome results at the assessment points. Figure 6.9 shows the week-by-week reductions in estimates of phobic anxiety given by the patient prior to each treatment session. These were obtained by summing patients' estimates on a 0–10 scale of their anxiety in the 15 situations used in the behavioral test hierarchy. No difference was found among any of the treatments on any of the outcome measures at any time. All treatments produced steady—indeed, linear—decreases in fear over the 16 weeks. Imaginal flooding was apparently as effective as *in vivo* practice and did not facilitate later *in vivo* practice, irrespective of whether the latter was car-

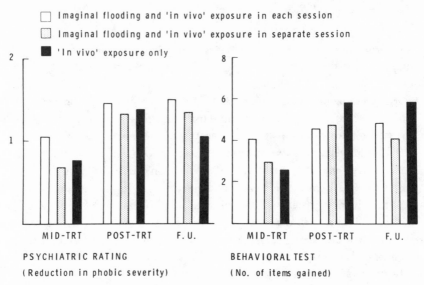

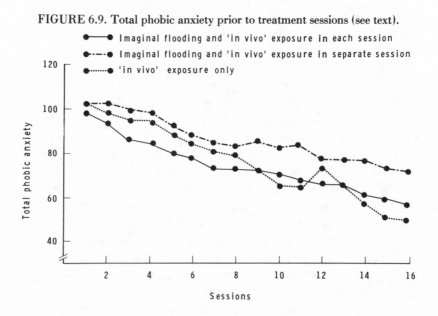

FIGURE 6.8. Change from before treatment on two measures of phobic severity.

FIGURE 6.9. Total phobic anxiety prior to treatment sessions (see text).

ried out immediately after flooding or after a number of flooding sessions had been given. These findings were totally at variance with the authors' expectations, since it had been expected that *in vivo* exposure would be more effective than imaginal flooding.

Patients also completed semantic differential scales immediately before, halfway through, and at the end of each treatment session. On these scales, they rated their attitude toward the phobic situation that was being treated during the corresponding session, on evaluative, safety, and calmness scales. Table 6.2 shows the difference produced on these various scores by flooding and *in vivo* exposure in the three treatment groups. Imaginal flooding produced virtually no change on these measures, whereas *in vivo* exposure produced large reliable and positive changes, so that the agoraphobic patients rated the treatment situations as generally better, safer, and calmer after *in vivo* exposure. There is therefore a clear conflict between the short-term and long-term effects of imaginal and *in vivo* treatments. In addition, there is a conflict between this study on agoraphobics and earlier, rather similar studies of people with minor fears. Finally, and most seriously, this study conflicts markedly with the results of another very similar study carried out on agoraphobic patients.

Emmelkamp and Wessels (1975) studied 22 agoraphobic volunteers from a phobia society and compared four sessions of imaginal flooding with four sessions of *in vivo* exposure and four sessions of a combination of the two. All clients then received a common treatment for the remaining eight sessions. The assessments used in this study were broadly similar to those adopted in our own investigations. The main points of difference were that the rating scales of Emmelkamp and Wessels separated out fear and avoidance and used a 9-point rather than a 5-point scale (the implications

TABLE 6.2. Mean change in semantic differential ratings during treatment sessions[a, b]

| Semantic differential | Flooding and practice on each session | | Flooding and practice on different sessions | | All practice | |
| | Flooding | Practice | Flooding (sessions 1–8) | Practice (sessions 9–16) | Practice (sessions 1–8) | Practice (sessions 1–16) |
| --- | --- | --- | --- | --- | --- | --- |
| Evaluative | .62 | 4.07 | .76 | 3.21 | 2.95 | 3.20 |
| Safety | .11 | 2.54 | −.56 | 2.88 | 2.84 | 2.52 |
| Calmness | .99 | 4.25 | .55 | 4.87 | 3.78 | 4.08 |

[a]Positive scores indicate improvement.
[b]Modified from Johnston, Lancashire, Mathews, Munby, Shaw, and Gelder (1976).

of variations in measurement procedures such as this were discussed in Chapter 2). Emmelkamp and Wessels used the form of behavioral test, also described in Chapter 2, in which the subject was asked to remain outside his/her home for as long as possible without experiencing anxiety, and the time spent out of the house was taken as an outcome measure. No psychophysiological assessment was used. The results of this behavioral test and of a composite of the fear and avoidance rating scales are shown in Table 6.3. The authors' analyses confirm the impression from this table that *in vivo* exposure was markedly more effective than imaginal flooding on both these measures, while the composite treatment occupied an intermediate position.

The explanation that we proposed for this conflict of evidence had a profound effect on our conception of how treatment should be conducted, and it has heavily influenced the treatment methods we describe in Chapter 8. It is therefore necessary to go into the problem in some depth. The two studies used very similar treatment methods and adopted experimental designs that were formally almost identical. The main differences lay in the location, duration, and frequency of treatment; there were some dif-

TABLE 6.3. Effects of treatment on behavioral test and phobic ratings[a]

| | Pretreatment | Posttreatment |
|---|---|---|
| *In vivo* exposure only | | |
| Behavioral test (min) | 11.1 | 49.9 |
| Combined fear and avoidance rating (0–8) | 5.5 | 3.0 |
| Imaginal flooding only | | |
| Behavioral test (min) | 14.6 | 17.9 |
| Combined fear and avoidance rating (0–8) | 6.0 | 5.4 |
| Imaginal flooding and *in vivo* exposure in each session | | |
| Behavioral test (min) | 12.3 | 26.1 |
| Combined fear and avoidance rating (0–8) | 6.4 | 3.5 |

[a]Modified from Emmelkamp and Wessels (1975).

ferences in the method of assessment as well. We treated patients in a hospital outpatient department, and when they were required to go out, it was from there. Our patients were seen weekly for 16 weeks and were strongly encouraged to practice returning between treatment sessions to actual situations that they feared. Finally, our behavioral assessment was carried out in the environs of the patient's home, that is, in situations quite independent from those used in treatment.

By contrast, Emmelkamp and Wessels treated their patients at their homes; they carried out four sessions of treatment over a period of about 10 days; and the behavioral assessment was carried out in situations virtually identical to those used for treatment. Moreover, they did not encourage their patients to practice between sessions, and Emmelkamp has stated that it was unlikely that the patients had much opportunity to do so because the treatment was so intensive (Emmelkamp, 1979). Consider, then, the situation that presented Emmelkamp and Wessels's patient and therapist when they had to judge the patient's progress shortly after these four treatment sessions. The main evidence available to patient and therapist at that time was what had happened during the therapy sessions and the results of a behavioral test that was virtually identical to one type of therapy. For this reason, it seems very likely that Emmelkamp and Wessels's study was maximally sensitive to changes in the therapeutic sessions. It therefore provides very good evidence that *in vivo* exposure is more effective than imaginal flooding in reducing fear of specific situations in agoraphobia. This is an important finding and it has greatly influenced the later treatment of agoraphobics, but it has to be considered in conjunction with our failure to find a difference between the two methods. If it can be argued that Emmelkamp and Wessels maximized the effects of the treatment sessions on outcome measures in their study, it can also be argued that our study went in the opposite direction and maximized the possible role of effects that took place between sessions. Thus our treatment was spaced over many weeks; moreover, and this is particularly important, the patients were strongly encouraged to practice facing the feared situation. Under these circumstances, the nature of the therapy practiced during the sessions at the hospital had no effect on outcome in the long run, although it did affect ratings taken immediately after treatment. Hence the semantic differential showed changes within each treatment session that were quite compatible with the findings of Emmelkamp and Wessels. Therefore it does not appear that our treatment was necessarily different from that used by Emmelkamp and Wessels.

The hypothesis we proposed to explain the discrepant findings was that sessions of both the imaginal and the *in vivo* forms of exposure are sufficient to enable a patient, in the interval between treatment sessions, to practice entering the actual situations that they fear. We further hypothesized that when this practice between sessions is allowed to develop, it becomes the main determinant of outcome. The predicted importance of the instruction to practice between sessions has recently been confirmed by McDonald, Sartory, Grey, Cobb, Stern, and Marks (1979), who showed that the instruction to practice and the planning of practice with the therapist had an effect on agoraphobia that was not present if such instructions were not given. On the other hand, the effect of instructions to practice was not great, and it is clear that instructions used alone are not a sufficient treatment for agoraphobia. Various other findings fit into place if the distinction is made between the relatively pure effect of the treatment session and the more long-term effects of the interaction between these treatment sessions and the opportunities and likelihood of practice in the patient's home environment. The analogue studies—such as the study of snake phobics described by Bandura *et al.* (1969), which showed that *in vivo* exposure was markedly more effective than imaginal flooding—can now be seen as particularly sensitive to the effects of the treatment sessions, since few snake phobics are likely to be able to practice with snakes between treatment sessions. It also offers an explanation for the discrepancy between the various studies of flooding. The treatment approach adopted by Gelder *et al.* (1973) allowed practice between sessions, while Marks, Boulougouris, and Marset (1971) used a much more intensive form of treatment, so that when assessments were carried out it is likely that they were strongly influenced by what had gone on in the treatment sessions. In particular, one might expect that patients receiving flooding would experience very vigorous *in vivo* exposure in the final treatment sessions and that this exposure would powerfully affect the ratings.

While this hypothesis did make possible an integration of findings that previously had seemed discrepant, this integration was much less important than its implication for the way on which treatment should be carried out. In all the treatments we have described, the main emphasis in treatment had been on events during the treatment session. The new hypothesis suggested that we should be more concerned with what happens *between* treatment sessions, and that the main aim of treatment should be to encourage patients to practice exposure between sessions in an effective and efficient way. What had previously been seen as a comparatively minor aspect of treatment now became its main concern. The effect of this hypothesis on the treatment of agoraphobia is described in Chapter 8.

At this point, it may be helpful to the reader to review the main findings of almost 20 years' outcome research on the behavioral treatment of agoraphobia. It is clear that systematic desensitization, flooding, and *in vivo* practice are effective in reducing the fear and the avoidance of agoraphobic patients, and it is likely that these treatments all operate through a specific factor, probably involving exposure to the phobic object. Treatments that do not involve exposure to the feared situation are less effective, whether they be active treatments, such as group or individual psychotherapy, or control treatments designed to mimic the nonspecific elements in behavioral treatment. How exposure is carried out does not seem particularly to affect long-term outcome, although the immediate effect of *in vivo* exposure is much greater than that of imaginal exposure.

One striking feature in the development of the treatment for agoraphobia has been the reemergence of *in vivo* methods, which inevitably raises the question of why graded retraining, an *in vivo* method, was so ineffective when first tried. The most striking difference between the graded retraining carrried out in the early 1960s and the exposure treatment carried out in the most recent studies is in the vigor with which the patient is exposed to the feared situation, and the location in which therapy is carried out. As we have written above, graded retraining was based on the assumption that fear and anxiety had to be avoided at all times during *in vivo* exposure, and therefore both patient and therapist anticipated that progress would be slow. This expectation led to long periods of exposure to situations that were not very threatening, such as walking a few hundred yards from the hospital. As we shall see in the next section, this is probably not the most effective form of exposure. In addition, it seems quite likely that exposure in the home environment is more effective than exposure from the hospital.

## FACTORS THAT INFLUENCE THE EFFECTIVENESS OF EXPOSURE

### EXPOSURE TO WHAT?

As we have written above, there is now a general consensus that exposure to feared situations is an important, possibly a critical, feature of the effective treatment of phobias. Before going on to consider the factors that influence the effectiveness of exposure, it is necessary to acknowledge one discrepant finding. In a group of people with a variety of phobias, Watson and Marks (1971) compared conventional imaginal flooding with imaginal flooding to themes that were irrelevant and often beyond the subjects' possible experience, for example, being eaten by a tiger. A reasonably comprehensive outcome assessment failed to demonstrate any difference between the two types of fearful stimuli, and the effects of each form of exposure were convincingly similar. If this result is of wide generality, then it could suggest, among other things, that the therapeutic mechanism in exposure is not some form of extinction to certain classes of situations but is rather the extinction of the fear of fear itself, which we have seen to be an important component of phobic disorders. In some ways, this is an attractive notion, but it should be recalled that this was an isolated study that examined techniques that produced only modest reductions in phobic behavior. Until this study is replicated and extended, it is parsimonious to maintain the view that exposure to the feared situation is an essential part of the mechanism of fear reduction. We are now ready to examine some of the factors that influence the results of such exposure.

DURATION AND SPACING OF EXPOSURE

Stern and Marks (1973) reported a study in which agoraphobic patients received *in vivo* exposure for two hours, either continuously or in four 30-minute periods separated by 30-minute periods spent in an environment that did not raise the patient's anxiety. The effects of these two procedures were assessed just before the next treatment session began, and it was found that continuous exposure for two hours was more effective than exposure for 30-minute periods. It is not clear quite how to interpret this finding. Anxiety levels in the two conditions were very similar, so that it does not seem likely that longer continuous exposure led to a more effective extinction of fear. Moreover, it is not clear from the report that the patients were exposed to identical situations in the two conditions. Clearly, more ambitious goals could have been set when two continuous hours were available for treatment, and equally clearly, constraints might have been placed on the therapist when an item had to be successfully achieved within 30 minutes. It is possible, therefore, that continuous exposure was also exposure to more difficult and more threatening phobic situations. It should be noted, however, that there is now reasonably convincing evidence from the study of volunteers with mild specific fears that very brief periods of exposure are less effective and may even be harmful (Marshall *et al.*, 1979).

It is our strong clinical impression that extensive periods of exposure to actual situations are more effective in reducing fear in agoraphobia.

ANXIETY DURING EXPOSURE

Much research effort has been directed at clarifying the role of anxiety during therapeutic exposure. Should it be minimized as in desensitization, maximized as in flooding, or firmly ignored as Mathews *et al.*'s (1976) *in vivo* practice? The question is difficult to answer because anxiety and exposure cannot be completely untangled. The most effective way of making sure that anxiety is not experienced is the method used by the patients themselves, that is, avoidance. When exposure is used as a therapeutic method, is inevitable that the patient will experience some anxiety and that attempts to minimize that anxiety will nearly always reduce exposure at the same time. The most common way out of this impasse is to use drugs to alter anxiety during exposure, although behavioral methods (in addition to relaxation) have also been attempted, albeit rather unsuccessfully (Hafner & Marks, 1976; Solyom, McClure, Heseltine, Ledwidge, & Solyom, 1972). We shall confine our discussion in the following section to the use of drugs to facilitate the immediate effects of behavioral treatment. The reader is referred to Chapter 4 for a discussion of studies that have combined behavior therapy and the long-term use of drugs.

Friedman (1966) used intravenous methohexital sodium (Brevital) to relax patients as an alternative to muscular relaxation during imaginal desensitization. He claimed impressive results when this technique was used with patients presenting a variety of phobias. Friedman and Silverstone (1967) and Mawson (1970) carried out small controlled studies of phobics and claimed that Brevital-assisted desensitization was superior to standard desensitization. However, the results obtained with this technique have not been consistent. Yorkston, Sergeant, and Rachman (1968) reported a careful study of the method with agoraphobic inpatients. Their report is illuminating in various ways. Patients were treated for five days with daily one-hour sessions of Brevital-aided desensitization or various control conditions. Assessment was carried out immediately before and after the five sessions, and patients were told *not* to practice between sessions. Psychiatric ratings and behavioral tests were used as outcome measures. There was no advantage of Brevital; indeed, none of the treatments produced a statistically significant improvement. We can note in passing that this appears to be the only study in the literature on behavior therapy with agoraphobics in which no change was produced. It also appears to be the only study in which purely imaginal treatments were used with no opportunities for *in vivo* exposure. It is therefore powerful, if indirect, evidence that exposure to the feared situation in reality is vital in the treatment of agoraphobia. Hussain (1971) treated socially phobic and agoraphobic outpatients with either Brevital-assisted desensitization or with saline-placebo-assisted desensitization. Brevital did not confer any advantage. However, he also compared imaginal flooding carried out either with Brevital or with saline, and in this case, Brevital was helpful.

These studies therefore suggest that reducing anxiety with drugs has little value during imaginal desensitization. This does not necessarily mean that anxiety is unimportant, since the alternative treatment, standard desensitization, goes to considerable lengths to reduce anxiety, and it may simply mean that drugs are no more effective than muscular relaxation in reducing anxiety. This could not have been the case, however, in Hussain's study of imaginal flooding, in which patients received either Brevital or saline, because no other anxiety-reducing agent was used. Therefore his results suggest that anxiety level during imaginal exposure may be important and that lower levels of anxiety are beneficial. Chambless, Foa, Groves, and Goldstein (1979) have recently compared Brevital-assisted flooding, standard flooding, and supportive psychotherapy in the treatment of agoraphobics. They predicted that Brevital would reduce the effectiveness of flooding because they felt that the "fear of fear" has to be extinguished in effective therapy, and for this to happen, the fear of fear has first to be evoked. In marked contrast to Hussain, they found that Brevital led to slightly less improvement than did standard flooding, and this result was particularly evident in patient's self-ratings. Both forms of flooding were superior to supportive psychotherapy, supporting the conclusions reached on the basis of earlier studies. There is no obvious reason for the discrepancy between the two studies (nor did Chambless *et al.* provide one), and so the role of Brevital in flooding remains obscure.

Brevital has many disadvantages as an adjunct to behavior therapy (Sergeant & Yorkston, 1968), not the least being the intravenous route of administration, which precludes its use during *in vivo* exposure of agoraphobics. Many of these disadvantages can be avoided by the use of diazepam, taken by mouth. Marks, Viswanathan, Lipsedge, and Gardner (1972) showed that diazepam increases the effectiveness of *in vivo* exposure used for specific phobias. This finding was followed up in a small study by Johnston and Gath (1973) of four agoraphobic inpatients, in which imaginal flooding and *in vivo* exposure were used with or without diazepam. The patients received all four possible combinations of imaginal plus *in vivo* exposure with diazepam or placebo given under two conditions of instruction (see below). Assessments were made on the days before and after each three-day block of treatment, when the effects of the drug would no longer be present. In two of the treatment blocks, diazepam syrup was given, and in the other two, the patients were given an indistinguishable placebo syrup. They were told that they would receive a calming drug in half the sessions but were given no reason to believe that the syrup was to be the vehicle for this drug. Instead, the syrup was said to be an aid to psychophysiological measurement. The patients were also given a large capsule, which was, in fact, always inert but which they were led to assume contained the calming drug. This design made possible the investigation of the effects of the drug separately and in combination with the effects of the patients' belief that they had ingested a calming agent. The conditions were active syrup plus capsule; inactive syrup plus capsule; active syrup without capsule; and inactive syrup without capsule. The results were not what we had expected. The patients did best when they had received diazepam during treatment and when they knew this. They performed at an intermediate level either when they thought they had received an active drug but had not or when they had received diazepam but did not know it. The worst performance was obtained in the condition in which patients received no drug and knew it. The results therefore suggest that the therapeutic effects of exposure are increased by diazepam, as Marks *et al.* (1972) had shown in specific phobics, and that knowledge about the drug increases the effects further. Although the latter result might be due to the effect of placebo on reducing anxiety, it is not necessarily the case that reduction of anxiety is the only important factor. During the *in vivo* phase of treatment in particular, the main determinant of treatment is what patients will tolerate, and they are much more likely to enter very threatening situations if their confidence has been increased by the knowledge that they have ingested a drug. However, the effect of diazepam taken without the patient's knowledge presumably indicates that anxiety reduction has an effect as well, but it does not make clear whether this effect is direct or secondary to the more vigorous exposure that it makes possible.

This interpretive difficulty may have been avoided in a study by Hafner and Marks (1976) in which diazepam and placebo were compared in 41 agoraphobic patients treated in groups by *in vivo* exposure. Since all the patients in any one group were inevitably exposed to very similar phobic

situations, and each group contained patients on placebo and on diazepam, any differences observed in fear reduction are likely to have been due
to the different anxiety levels experienced. While within-session measurements appeared to show that some of the predicted differences in anxiety
level were found, no differences in outcome were apparent. This result implies that if exposure is kept constant, anxiety is of little significance and,
by implication, that the effects of diazepam in the other studies that we
have discussed were related to the greater exposure made possible by the
drug.

Two studies have examined the effects of reducing somatic symptoms of
anxiety with beta-blockers. Hafner and Milton (1977) compared propranolol with placebo using the group exposure technique already described.
They expected that propranolol would reduce some of the somatic manifes-
tations of anxiety during exposure to feared situations and would thereby
facilitate exposure. Propranolol, far from aiding treatment, appeared to
hinder it, and in the month after treatment, patients who had received propranolol actually traveled alone significantly less than patients who had
received placebo. Presumably the patients in the two conditions had been
exposed to the same situations, since they were in the same group for their
behavioral treatment, and so it would appear that it was the nature of their
experience during exposure that affected outcome. Hafner and Milton included in their study intensive measurement of their patients' state during
exposure. Those receiving placebo showed a steady reduction in anxiety,
panic attacks, and heart rate over the exposure sessions. Those receiving
propranolol showed a rather different pattern. Anxiety did not decline, nor
did panic attacks; indeed, these tended to increase, while heart rate showed
little sign of slowing. Hafner and Milton interpreted these findings as suggesting that as the effects of propranolol wore off, the patients began to
have difficulty in coping with the reappearance of somatic symptoms, so
that exposure, instead of becoming less threatening, became more so as the
treatment session progressed. This finding implies that the absolute level of
anxiety during exposure may be of less importance than the direction of
change in anxiety.

Unfortunately, methodological weaknesses vitiate this interesting study.
Hafner and Milton relied exclusively on questionnaires and diary measures
of patients' actual behavior, all of which were completed after treatment;
that is, no pretreatment measures were used. In studies as small as this,
with 12-15 patients per treatment group, it is not sound practice to allow
chance to determine the matching of groups without including some check

on the adequacy of that matching. Without this information, it cannot be concluded that the differences obtained after treatment were necessarily due to the effect of treatment rather than to the characteristics of the patients' behavior before treatment began.

Ullrich, Ullrich de Muynck, Crombach, and Peikert (1975) also examined the effects of a beta-blocker (alprenolol) on *in vivo* exposure. They compared three conditions: exposure with alprenolol or placebo and exposure alone. Exposure was carried out individually and so could vary in response to the drug. In contrast to Hafner and Milton, who used the drug only immediately before exposure, Ullrich *et al.* gave the drug four times a day for the 15 days of the course of treatment. These latter authors showed that alprenolol conferred little advantage apart from a reduction in what they termed "autonomous anxiety."

The information on the effects of anxiety-reducing agents during exposure is therefore somewhat contradictory, and no truly convincing conclusion can be drawn. A working generalization that has guided our research is that if exposure is held constant, anxiety-reducing agents have weak and contradictory effects, but if such agents are used to bring about exposure to situations that would otherwise be avoided, then the effect may well be beneficial. This benefit is particularly likely if the drug is used only shortly before or during the period of exposure, rather than being taken for prolonged periods. We would like to emphasize that the levels of anxiety studied to date have all been fairly low. It would be unsafe to generalize those findings to very high anxiety levels and panic. It seems very unlikely that exposure to a frightening situation that induces panic without the opportunity to remain in that situation until panic decreased would be an effective treatment.

## SUMMARY

In the 20 years in which the behavioral treatment of agoraphobics has been studied experimentally, there have been some surprising twists and turns in our understanding of the best method of treating these patients. However, a number of conclusions can be proposed, admittedly with varying degrees of confidence. It seems clear that a variety of behavioral treatments, all of which involve exposure to the feared situation, lead to a reduction of fear and avoidance in agoraphobic patients, and that this reduction is greater than that achieved by a variety of psychotherapeutic techniques or by a nonspecific therapy. It is more difficult to be certain about the best behavioral technique to use with agoraphobic patients. In this matter, a distinction has to be drawn between studies that have examined the comparatively pure effects of the patient's immediate experience of treatment and those that have studied the more complicated effects of the interaction of therapy with other aspects of the patient's life—especially the opportunities for practice between sessions.

If we consider first those studies that allow the comparatively pure effects of treatment to be examined, it seems clear that exposure to the actual feared situations is superior to "imaginal" exposure. However, it is not clear whether the form of that exposure to real situations is important, although there is some indirect evidence that prolonged exposure to difficult situations is the most effective procedure. Anxiety level during that exposure does not seem to be crucial. It is possible that diazepam increases the effectiveness of exposure, but it may do this by enabling the patient to tolerate more difficult situations.

If we turn to studies that allow an examination of the interaction of exposure and other aspects of the patient's life, it appears that it makes little difference what form of exposure is used in therapy. It can be imaginal or *in vivo*, gradual or vigorous. However, this is not a reason for ignoring the other evidence and doing whatever is most convenient or pleasing, but rather an indication that it is important to examine ways of making better use of what the patient does between the sessions of treatment, so that exposure to feared situations in the local environment is made as effective as possible. We shall return to this topic in Chapter 8.

# 7. Social Influences on Exposure to Phobic Situations

T HE TREATMENT METHODS described in the previous chapter depend to a large extent on the direction by the therapists of the patients' behavior. Therapists usually plan the course of exposure to phobic situations, decide whether it shall be in imagination or in real situations, select targets for practice, praise patients for counterphobic behavior, and so on. It is appropriate to ask whether the social influence of the therapist contributes in any important way to the effectiveness of exposure treatment.

Analogue studies of specific fears have not provided any convincing evidence that the provision of systematic social reinforcement (e.g., praise for progress up a hierarchy) increases the effectiveness of systematic desensitization (Oliveau, Agras, Leitenberg, Moore, & Wright, 1969). However, it can be argued that feedback of information about behavioral progress has a powerful reinforcing effect of its own, and as this effect is present in in desensitization, the addition of praise might have little further influence (Mathews, 1978).

Single-case investigations of three agoraphobic patients in Agras, Leitenberg, and Barlow (1968) provide some evidence about the effect of social reinforcement in the form of praise from the therapist. In these patients, it was only when progress was followed by praise that distance or time out increased steadily from session to session (see Figure 7.1). Because these results are based on only three cases, it remains uncertain how far they can be generalized. In a subsequent series of single-case studies, Leitenberg, Agras, Allen, Butz, and Edwards (1975) obtained results suggesting that praise alone may not be effective with all patients, and that by contrast, when the therapist provided feedback of information about progress there were more general effects. For example, one agoraphobic patient was first praised for progress during practice but was not given

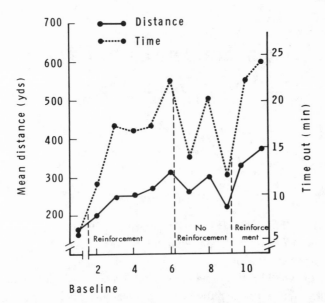

FIGURE 7.1. The effect of social reinforcement (praise) on the performance of an agoraphobic patient during practice. From W. S Agras, H. Leitenberg, and D. H. Barlow, *Archives of General Psychiatry*, 1968, *19*, 426. Copyright 1968 by the American Medical Association. Reprinted by permission.

specific feedback; then feedback was added; and finally feedback was withdrawn. As can be seen from Figure 7.2, praise was without effect until feedback was added.

An alternative way of providing feedback of results is to ask patients to monitor their progress. In a treatment condition described by Emmelkamp as "self-observation," agoraphobics were asked to practice going out while keeping careful records of their progress. This treatment was compared in a crossover design with a procedure, called "successive approximation," which involved similar practice of exposure, but with the addition of contingent verbal praise from the therapist. The two treatments were found to have similar effects (Emmelkamp & Ultee, 1974), possibly because self-monitoring and contingent verbal praise have equivalent reinforcing effects on practice. However, in the absence of a control group of patients who received neither praise nor feedback, it is possible to argue that both are unnecessary and that the instructions to practice are a sufficient explanation for the improvement observed in both groups. Never-

theless, such a conclusion is inconsistent with the findings of the single-
case studies discussed previously, and it runs contrary to the impression of
most clinicians, including ourselves.

In one study (Mathews *et al.*, 1976), patients were asked, after treatment, to rank a number of possible reasons for their progress. Some of
these reasons related to the technique of exposure, while others were included as nonspecific items. Unexpectedly, it was one of the latter—encouragement given to patients for their own efforts—that was judged the
most important reason for progress by the majority of patients. Obviously, this choice could merely reflect the demand characteristics of the test
situation and might have little bearing on the real mechanisms of treatment. However, for other reasons (discussed in Chapter 6), one of the conclusions from this study was that outcome may largely depend on practice
at self-exposure carried out by patients between treatment sessions, and
this conclusion is entirely consistent with the opinions recorded by the patients.

In view of the suggestion that some agoraphobics are overdependent, it
is of interest to know whether the importance attached by patients to encouragement from the therapist is related to this characteristic. Thus patients who become dependent on support from their therapists might re-

FIGURE 7.2. The effect of praise alone, and feedback plus praise, on time spent by
an agoraphobic patient in practice. From H. Leitenberg, W. S. Agras, R. Allen, R.
Butz, and J. Edwards, *Journal of Consulting and Clinical Psychology*, 1975, *43*,
399. Copyright 1975 by the American Psychological Association. Reprinted by
permission.

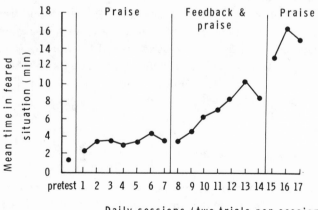

spond well during treatment but be unable to make further progress when this support is withdrawn.

At the end of time-limited treatment, many patients are left with mild to moderate residual handicaps (Mathews, 1977). In our experience, both therapist and patient expect that these will diminish with the continuing application of the simple principles that the patient has learned in treatment. However, if the influence of the therapist is a crucial motivating factor in exposure to real phobic situations, removal of this influence would be expected to bring further progress to a halt. In fact, most studies that have included a follow-up period show little or no change in group scores of phobic anxiety or avoidance after the end of treatment (see Chapter 10). Such an average result must, of course, conceal the fact that some patients continue to improve while others relapse, but it remains true that the majority do not change. The belief that removal of social support or influence is important in this failure to change is supported by anecdotal reports from patients who, at the end of treatment, were optimistic about further progress. Some of our patients described how they were able to succeed in overcoming anticipatory anxiety and in dealing with occasional setbacks as long as they were encouraged by their therapist but found it impossible to continue in the face of a complete lack of interest on the part of their families. Even very supportive families and friends may not understand why, after a period of treatment, a patient cannot live a normal life, and they become impatient with the need for continuing practice. In the next chapter, we shall consider how the family of the agoraphobic might be organized to provide an effective alternative to long-term support by a professional therapist.

An alternative is for the patient to obtain help and support from fellow phobics. Many agoraphobics have formed their own associations, while others have been asked to join groups created by a therapist. Both approaches offer the possibility of beneficial modeling influences and long-term social support—and they save the time of the therapist. To what extent have these possibilities been realized?

## PHOBIC ASSOCIATIONS

The proliferation of patients' associations as a way of arranging mutual support and gaining social recognition has been documented in a number of surveys (e.g., Robinson & Henry, 1977). Several societies for phobics have come into being in the United Kingdom and elsewhere (e.g., the Open Door, the Phobic Trust, the Phobic Society, Out and About), and membership is overwhelmingly of agoraphobics, though a minority have other phobias (McGennis, Nolan, & Hartman, 1977). Informal surveys of those who have joined suggest, not surprisingly, that they think membership helpful, and that many are highly critical of the lack of effective treatment available elsewhere. Nevertheless, there is little or no evidence to date that either the symptoms or the disabilities of agoraphobics improve as a result of joining such groups, and no attempts seem to have been made to use behavioral methods within them.

Most associations issue newsletters that reach members who cannot attend group meetings. Their contents usually include a mixture of constructive advice about ways of obtaining treatment and about the use of self-help methods, together with letters describing symptoms and personal problems written in a way that seem unlikely to be helpful to the readers.

In one survey (Marks & Herst, 1970), 33% of the Open Door members reported that they had never seen a psychiatrist, and 5% had never consulted their family doctor about their problem. As might be expected, those who had not seen a psychiatrist appeared to be less severely handicapped than the rest, but, unexpectedly, this was not true of those few who had never consulted any doctor about the problem. This minority were characterized by a lack of social confidence that may have explained their reluctance to seek help except through contact with fellow sufferers. It seems likely that this function of providing comfort and reassurance to people who are unable to seek out effective treatment is one of the major benefits of these organizations.

It is clear that associations of this kind offer a potentially valuable service to large numbers of agoraphobics, but in the absence of evaluative research, it is difficult to know whether any of this potential is being realized. Our experience with groups suggests that although the social influence exerted by fellow patients can be very powerful, without appropriate direction it is not always beneficial. Thus some patients assume that the purpose of group meetings is to discuss anxiety symptoms, and as a result, meetings may degenerate into a "symptom competition," with each patient claiming to be worse than the others. Subsequent attempts to shift toward active self-help may then be blocked by objections such as "You couldn't possibly understand how bad I feel." As Hand *et al.* (1974) have pointed out, relatively successful groups, such as Weight Watchers or Alcoholics Anonymous, have behavior change as their criterion of membership, and not just common problems. Perhaps phobic groups could profit from this example by having willingness to engage in self-help determine membership rather than the phobia alone.

## INTENSIVE GROUP EXPOSURE

Although group methods of exposure have sometimes been used clinically for reasons of economy, the possibility that they might have superior long-term effects was first suggested in a study reported by Hand *et al.* (1974). Two conditions of group exposure were compared: one called *structured*, the other *unstructured*. In the structured condition, patients met for half an hour before going out together and discussed situations they found difficult. They were also encouraged to help each other during exposure. In the unstructured condition, although the patients went out at the same time, all contact and discussion among them was discouraged.

In all other ways, the treatment programs were similar. The patients were given standard instructions to enter phobic situations and then to allow anxiety to decline without avoidance. They were also instructed to use the therapists as "trainers" and not to rely passively on them as "doctors." Although exposure was to proceed at the pace of the slowest patient, in practice the strong group pressure to go forward resulted in surprisingly rapid progress. For example, a patient in a structured group who complained of becoming "paralyzed" with fear was ignored until she actively tried to cope. Moreover, during exposure, the patients used first names, held hands, or even put their arms around each other.

Progress was more rapid in the structured groups. These patients had usually entered the most feared situations (e.g., crowded city streets) by the end of the first session, while those in the unstructured groups reached an equivalent point only in the course of the second session. Treatment was intensive, with three exposure sessions of four to five hours each in the space of one week. After this, the structured groups met for discussion and mutual encouragement four times over a six-month follow-up period, while the unstructured groups met their therapists individually for equivalent periods.

The most striking result of this study was that while both types of group treatments led to rapid and significant improvement in phobic anxiety and avoidance, only the structured groups continued to improve after the end of treatment and up to the three-month follow-up (see Figure 7.3). This

SELF-RATING

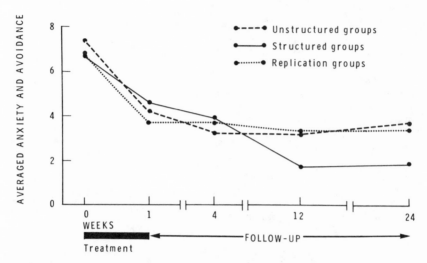

FIGURE 7.3. Self-ratings, averaged for anxiety and avoidance, showing the effects of exposure carried out in structured and unstructured groups. From J. D. Teasdale, P. A. Walsh, M. Lancashire, and A. M. Mathews, *British Journal of Psychiatry*, 1977, *130*, 188. Reprinted by permission.

latter finding is of considerable interest in view of the earlier discussion of restricted long-term benefit, and it is worthy of further consideration. If the significant difference reported on follow-up is to be attributed to social influence, it is necessary to show that the groups differed in relevant ways. Hand *et al.* offered in support of this idea ratings made by their patients of mutual help and liking for each other, all of which were greater in the structured groups (see Table 7.1).

Before any definite conclusions can be drawn, however, two reservations must be introduced. The first concerns the small number of patients on whom the final follow-up ratings were made: because of lost data, the supposed superiority of the structured condition is based on information from only seven patients from only two of the three groups. Second, Teasdale *et al.* (1977) attempted to replicate the structured group conditions and, while achieving similar immediate effects, failed to show any change during the period of follow-up. The results of this latter inquiry are also shown in Figure 7.3, while the corresponding social cohesion ratings are in the accompanying table. Since the social cohesion ratings in this replica-

TABLE 7.1. Mean social cohesion ratings[a]

| Study | Help from whole group | Help from individual patients | Help to individual patients | Liking from other patients | Liking of other patients |
|---|---|---|---|---|---|
| Hand et al. (1974), unstructured | 4.0 | .6 | 0 | 1.9 | 3.9 |
| Hand et al. (1974), structured | 6.2 | 3.0 | 1.0 | 3.4 | 5.2 |
| Teasdale et al. (1977), structured | 5.7 | 1.3 | .9 | 2.8 | 4.6 |

[a]From Teasdale, Walsh, Lancashire, and Mathews (1977).

tion study are between those for the structured and unstructured groups in the study of Hand *et al.*, it could be argued that a critical level of cohesion necessary for long-term benefit had not been achieved in the replication. Even if this was so, the failure to replicate indicates that this critical level of cohesion may not necessarily be achieved despite the most careful attention to the procedures described by Hand *et al.*, and this lack of replicability reduces the clinical usefulness of the method. However, it is difficult to sustain the argument that there is a critical level, since it seems likely that the more exposure is socially reinforced, the better results should be. In any case, neither a social reinforcement explanation nor alternatives, such as observational learning of new coping methods from other patients, can explain why the effect of social cohesion did not appear until follow-up. From our own experience of running these groups, we believe that it is more likely to be the continuing motivational influence arising from patient contacts *after* treatment that are responsible for this continued progress. In the meetings of structured groups during the follow-up period, suggestions were often made by patients about exposure practice for themselves and others, and the outcome of these efforts was discussed at the following meeting. Additionally, some patients entered into informal agreements to telephone and meet each other between group sessions. Since these contacts were not arranged by the therapist nor measured systematically, it is impossible to be certain of their role, but uncontrolled variations in these factors could well account for the different results reported in the two studies.

Only a few studies have compared group and individual exposure directly, and these have found no outcome differences. Hafner and Marks (1976) used a complex design involving various drug conditions within groups as well as a high- versus low-anxiety condition with patients treated individually. The groups were said to be "moderately cohesive" (although no cohesion ratings were reported), discussion took place before exposure, and the patients were described as spontaneously helping one another. Among the patients who did not receive an active drug, a comparison of those treated individually with those treated in groups shows no significant differences in phobic avoidance at any time. Furthermore both patients treated in groups and those treated individually changed rapidly during the treatment phase (12 hours of exposure during a two-week period) but showed a complete lack of change during the six-month follow-up.

In another comparison of group and individual exposure ("self-observation"), Emmelkamp and Emmelkamp-Benner (1975) also reported no advantage from group treatment either at the end of the four 90-minute sessions or at one-month follow-up. No ratings of social cohesion were made, and the only details given of group sessions were that the first half-hour of each session was used to acquaint patients with each other.

Although these results do not suggest that groups are an effective way of harnessing social forces in treatment, two arguments can be used for group treatment in clinical practice. First, Hafner and Marks reported that patients treated in groups improved more on measures of general and leisure adjustment, suggesting that the experience of group exposure produced some additional social benefits. Second, group treatment requires less time from a professional than does individual exposure, because one therapist can manage up to seven patients in each exposure session.

## PROBLEMS ARISING FROM EXPOSURE TREATMENT

The place of group treatment in clinical practice is evaluated more fully after an alternative approach has been presented in the following chapter. Before turning to this chapter, however, an attempt will be made to summarize the problems that are thrown up by the consideration of the outcome studies described in this and the preceding chapters:

1. Little attention has been paid to factors that help patients practice self-exposure to phobic situations, although these may be crucial to long-term success.

2. Treatments that require therapists to arrange each exposure session require much professional time.

3. Patients often attribute progress to the help that they receive from the therapist, and thus they feel dependent on continuing contact with him/her.

4. Possibly as a result, progress does not usually continue after treatment has ended even though most patients still have some residual symptoms and disability.

5. Patients who later experience a recurrence of acute anxiety may be unable to cope successfully without the help of the therapist, and so they relapse.

For these reasons, treatment should emphasize the practice that patients carry out by themselves; it should either involve nonprofessional helpers or better still encourage complete self-reliance; and it should plan for long-term improvement and teach methods of coping with panic. Our attempts to achieve these ends are the subject of the next chapter.

# 8.  A Home-Based Treatment Method: Programmed Practice

F OLLOWING THE LINE of argument presented in the previous chapter, a new behavioral program was developed in an attempt to overcome the deficiencies that we saw in other exposure methods. Although some aspects of the program are based on clinical experience and may need to be modified in the light of further research, the program as a whole has been shown to be both effective and efficient. In distinction to those in the rest of the book, the present chapter describes this one treatment program in enough detail to enable clinicians to carry it out in a relatively standardized way. Thus the description that follows is intended to serve as a manual for therapists, to be used in conjunction with the manuals for client and partner that appear as appendixes at the end of this book. Summaries appear at intervals in the chapter, and these are collected together in Appendix 3, which can serve as an *aide-mémoire* for the therapist.

The term *client* will be used in this chapter in preference to *patient*, since the present program may be used for people who have not presented at a clinic or hospital (though it is important that it be used under the direction of a qualified professional). Similarly, the generic term *partner* has been adopted because although in practice it is usually the client's spouse who joins in treatment, other family members or friends may be involved if more appropriate.

Therapists who plan to use the program must be thoroughly familiar with the manuals that have been prepared for the client and the partner. Indeed, a first reading of these manuals (Appendixes 1 and 2) is recommended before proceeding further with the present chapter, since many points from them are assumed in what follows. The development of these detailed manuals was thought to be the best way of providing all the information that would be needed to enable the client and the partner to understand the nature of the problem and to be able to carry out the treatment procedures themselves.

In this new program, practice in self-exposure is not considered incidental to some other procedure; it forms the core of the treatment, thus following the conclusions of Mathews *et al.* (1976). This transfer of responsibility for the detailed management of the program to the client and the partner serves the double purpose of reducing the professional time that would otherwise be needed to supervise exposure and of diminishing the client's dependence on continuing contact with the therapist. The involvement of a partner is also seen as a method of increasing social reinforcement for regular practice. In the absence of any clear evidence of differences attributable to alternative types of exposure, graded practice has been adopted as the most acceptable and practical from the client's point of view. However, unlike earlier forms of graded practice, in which anxiety was minimized, a vigorous approach is used in which clients are told to expect and learn to cope with moderate levels of anxiety. The regular use of tranquilizers is discouraged, but clients who are already taking anxiolytic medications are advised that it may be helpful to use them occasionally just before attempting new or difficult items (cf. Johnston & Gath, 1973). However, much more emphasis is placed on helping clients to find other methods of coping with anxiety. These are based on calming self-instructions, and the recommended self-instructions are expressed for convenience in the form of 10 rules. These include reminders that anxiety symptoms are not harmful, that they will dissipate in time, and that they can be reduced more rapidly by the avoidance of "frightening thoughts." In this way, the client's attention is directed toward the need to overcome the major maintaining factor for avoidance, namely, the fear of provoking a panic attack.

Before we go further, the main points of programmed practice can be summarized as follows:

1. From the start it is made clear that the client, rather than the therapist, will be responsible for running the treatment program.

2. Whenever possible, a suitable person is recruited to help in the day-to-day running of the program (this is usually the client's spouse but need not be).

3. The client (and the partner) are provided with detailed but simple manuals that outline the nature of agoraphobia, the principles of

graded exposure, and methods of coping with anxiety and of encouraging regular practice.

4. The therapists present themselves as advisers or educators and do not take any active role in exposure practice.

5. Meeting with the therapist is usually in the client's home and takes the form of discussions among the therapist, the client, and the partner about the practice program and any problems that have arisen.

6. The time spent with the therapist is limited to about five visits over a month, after which the meetings with the therapist are phased out while the client and the partner continue the program (see Appendix 3).

## SELECTION AND ASSESSMENT

Programmed practice is designed for agoraphobics who have a relatively consistent pattern of avoidance, for example, of everyday situations such as crowded public places and of travel from home alone. The method is not likely to be appropriate in the unusual cases where there is phobic anxiety but no avoidance, nor where avoidance concerns situations that are encountered rarely. One important aim of the selection interview is therefore to assess the extent of phobic avoidance. A second aim is to describe any factors that increase or decrease phobic anxiety, for example, the presence of other people, the ease of potential escape, the distance from home, and the appearance of particular bodily feelings or frightening thoughts. A description of the form, frequency, and intensity of anxiety reactions also helps to ensure that the account given in the patients' manual will be appropriate for the client who is being assessed. Frequent panic attacks with no obvious external cue—for example, when relaxing at home—may suggest the need for some additional or alternative treatment method, such as anxiety management training.

Because this is a self-help method, it is important to ask about reactions to any previous treatment, and to assess the attitude of both client and family toward a program that may involve a great deal of effort on their part. If there is an extremely difficult marital relationship, marital counseling or group exposure methods may seem preferable; the latter is also appropriate for clients who are socially isolated. As will be seen later, however, it is very unusual to find a degree of marital disturbance that makes programmed practice unworkable; a marriage must be very severely disturbed before this happens, since relationships usually improve as the partners work together on the agoraphobic problem.

We have not found the concomitant use of medication to be a problem. If clients are already taking tranquilizing drugs, it is appropriate to discuss how their use can be integrated with the behavioral program. Although the prolonged use of minor tranquilizers such as the benzodiazepines is counterproductive, their occasional use to enable a difficult item to be accomplished for the first time can be recommended, although the aim should be to discontinue medication completely.

A baseline assessment should always be carried out before treatment with programmed practice begins. For reasons that were discussed in Chapter 2, two self-report measures are appropriate in most cases; these are a standard fear questionnaire (Marks & Mathews, 1979) and a diary of all the time spent out of the house. Copies of both are included in Appendix 4. Self-monitoring with the behavioral diary for at least one week is a particularly useful way of providing information about the general level of functioning before treatment and about particular phobic difficulties.

## TREATMENT VISITS: GENERAL CONSIDERATIONS

Every treatment visit involves both client and partner, although occasionally one person may be seen alone for a short time. For example, during practice (normally the second visit), the therapist may take advantage of being alone with the partner to discuss the ways in which success should be reinforced or panic dealt with. In general, the therapist should lay great stress on the client's independence, and the partner should be instructed to be kind but firm in encouraging the client to do as much as possible for him/herself. If the client is socially isolated, it may be impossible to recruit a suitable partner. In this event, although the program will obviously need some modification, the essentials remain the same. The clients' manual is still used, and the importance of self-reliance and self-reinforcement is emphasized even more strongly.

As a rule, all visits are to the client's home, but if, after the first session or two, the therapist has gained a reasonably clear idea of the domestic situation and the immediate environment, other suitable meeting places may be chosen.

## FIRST TREATMENT VISIT

As a rule, the first visit is the longest, and an hour or more may need to be set aside for it. Time will be saved if the therapist makes sure that both client and partner have understood the general nature of the program and have carefully read both manuals before the first visit. In the rare event of the manuals not having been read in time, the therapist should emphasize the client's responsibility and suggest in a friendly way that further discussion would be better postponed until the manual has been read.

Otherwise, a typical visit begins with an explanation by the therapist of the likely length and content of the session. After clarifying the answers to any questions that were not covered in the assessment interview, the therapist should normally proceed immediately to set an agenda for the visit. This should include a discussion of the clients' and the partners' manuals, negotiation of and agreement on a treatment contract, the collection of diary records, and the selection of initial practice targets.

Discussion of the manuals can usefully begin with the answers given to the check questions on each page, for these should reveal any gross difficulties in understanding. Clients or partners who have reading difficulties may be embarrassed to admit these, and therapists must be able to handle this problem tactfully and suggest another way in which the material could be presented, that is, by tape recorder. If no major misunderstandings are apparent, comments or questions should be invited about each part of the manual. Possible difficulties include a persisting belief in physical causes and the need for medication, or the idea that the approach is too superficial. These problems can usually be overcome if the therapist suggests that the client give the suggested method a fair trial before rejecting it, pointing out the evidence that supports the program's effectiveness. It is important, however, that a realistic picture of outcome be given, with particular attention to the persistent effort that will be required.

At this stage in the visit, it may be useful to review the whole treatment approach with the client and the partner, emphasizing the following points by discussion and reference to the appropriate parts of the clients' manual:

1. Since the method depends on self-help, the therapist will be acting as adviser and guide. It is the client and the partner who will be responsible for carrying out the program. Visits by the therapist will therefore be for the purpose of reviewing progress and discussing problems that have arisen. The number of visits is limited, so that dis-

cussion should concentrate on issues directly relevant to the practice program. Improvement can be confidently expected, but it will require persistent effort that must continue after the therapist's regular visits have ceased.

2. Regular practice in facing increasingly more difficult situations is the key to success. Therefore it is what the client and the partner do between the visits of the therapist that is the real treatment. Daily practice is strongly recommended, and any obstacles (e.g., long working hours, the care of young children) should be discussed with the therapist. Solutions to these problems will depend on the targets selected for practice and may involve practice in the evenings and on weekends, or a rearrangement of working hours.

3. Graded practice involves the learning of new ways of coping with fear, to take the place of avoidance. Clients will need reassurance that if they remain in the phobic situation, fear will always decline and that it will do so more rapidly if it is not maintained unnecessarily by the client's own thoughts or behavior. Specific fears about the outcome of panics should be dealt with by a review of the explanation that agoraphobia is a learned emotional reaction, unconnected with any serious physical or mental disease. The 10 rules for coping with panic should be used to provide a framework for developing an alternative, more positive plan directed toward overcoming "fear of fear."

4. Some clients may be taking anxiolytic drugs regularly. They should be told that although the eventual aim is to stop all medication, minor tranquilizers can be put to good use when new and difficult items are practiced. Their use should be occasional, not regular, and should be timed to exert the maximum effect when maximum difficulty is expected.

After any further questions arising from the clients' manual have been discussed, the way in which the client and partner work together should be reviewed, with emphasis on the following points:

1. The partner must agree to being present at all the meetings with the therapist and to take an active part in the program. The partner's role is not to do things for the client, but to firmly encourage independence.

2. Signs of excessive concern over panic are to be avoided, since they will focus the client's attention on anxiety symptoms. However, the partner needs to understand and be sensitive to the client's experience of anxiety, while reinforcing any efforts to practice despite the presence of anxiety.

3. Support and encouragement of regular practice are essential. It is most important to discuss each day what has been achieved, to show sincere appreciation of the client's efforts, and to praise these. It is also desirable that specific reinforcement should be agreed on for particular targets to be achieved.

4. The partner is to be involved in the selection of targets for practice and in planning practice attempts. Some targets will also require the partner to be actively involved in practice, either by going out with the client or by arranging meetings when the client is out.

THERAPY CONTRACT

Although not essential, a written contract sometimes helps to prevent misunderstandings and may increase the sense of commitment. If used, such a contract should specify (for example) the number and the approximate timing of the therapist's visits; should state clearly the respective responsibilities of client and partner (in running the program) and therapist (in being available as adviser); and should contain agreement about the frequency of practice attempts and the keeping of diary records and target sheets.

SELECTION OF TARGETS FOR PRACTICE

It is useful to look at the diary record immediately before a discussion of targets. This examination will reveal any problems that have arisen in keeping the diary and helps to clarify the extent of avoidance. The therapist then asks the client and the partner to suggest practice targets, guiding them toward appropriate items when this is necessary.

The first target should be something that is usually avoided at the time but is nevertheless thought possible to achieve with effort and is judged important by both client and partner. If the only targets that can be agreed on seem unduly difficult, further guidance may be needed to define intermediate practice items. When a clearly defined behavioral target of appropriate difficulty has been jointly agreed on, this item should be recorded on a target list, preferably by the partner. Some discussion may be necessary about anticipated obstacles and the need to avoid inflexible advance decisions about how far to go in any one practice session. Instead, clients should be asked to regard early attempts at practice as experiments that are carried out to explore their present limits. It is usually better to postpone further detailed discussion until the therapist has observed a practice session on the second visit. This should be arranged to take place within a day or so of the first.

1. Explain the purpose of the visit and set an agenda.
2. Make sure that the manuals have been read and are understood.
3. Review the treatment approach: (a) the self-help nature of the method; (b) practice as the real treatment; (c) panic management methods; (d) the importance of firm encouragement from others.
4. Negotiate a treatment contract.
5. Help the couple to select targets.
6. Discuss the importance of daily records (diary and target sheet).
7. Arrange a meeting place and a target for the next session.

## SECOND TREATMENT VISIT

The second meeting is usually devoted to observing a practice session in which both client and partner take part. It may be necessary to provide some guidance at first, to make sure that the aims of the session have been understood clearly. The client and the partner should arrive at an agreed-on plan, which may involve going out together toward the target, going out separately but remaining in sight of each other, or the client's going alone on a complete outing that is discussed with the partner before and afterwards. The therapist should offer advice when this is appropriate but should avoid taking complete control of the session since this may prevent misunderstandings from coming to light. If possible, the therapist should simply observe all interactions between the client and the partner, see that the agreed-on practice has been carried out, and when it is over, discuss possible improvements. However, if difficulties arise that threaten the success of the treatment, the therapist should intervene with advice or modeling during the practice. If this happens, a further practice session should be watched to make sure that the difficulty has been overcome.

The partners should be strongly encouraged to prompt and reinforce with praise all attempts at coping by the client, whether or not the practice target has been completed as planned. After the session, the discussion should include the client's assessment of the support received from the partner, any suggestions about improvements in the arrangements for practice that could be incorporated in subsequent sessions, and the extent of the anxiety experienced during the practice.

Although the extent of the anxiety during practice should be noted, lengthy discussions should usually be discouraged, since they focus unnecessary attention on symptoms. Nevertheless, it is important that the partner appreciate the extent of anxiety experienced by the client in order to know how much help to give and when a new target should be suggested. If the partner has found it difficult to decide how to react to the client's anxiety during practice, appropriate behavior should be discussed and modeled. Whenever possible, the client should be helped to remain in the phobic situation until anxiety begins to subside. The partner should not communicate excessive concern about anxiety and should encourage attempts at coping through self-instruction, should ignore self-critical or defeatist comments, and should redirect the client's attention to whatever has been achieved, no matter how little.

This is a convenient time in the visit to discuss the client's confidence in dealing with anxiety, and specifically to check on the use of the 10 rules for panic management that appear in the clients' manual (see Appendix 1). Some clients find it helpful to carry this list with them and use it to remind themselves of what they should try to do when feeling anxious. They can be encouraged to add to the list if they find any other helpful methods. If anxiety is interpreted by the client as evidence of failure, it can be pointed out that the primary purpose of practice is to learn how to cope with anxiety by keeping it within manageable bounds, so that practice completed in the presence of anxiety should be seen as a success. The session ends with a discussion of any problems that are anticipated in future practice sessions. The next visit should be arranged to take place in about a week's time.

SUMMARY OF SECOND VISIT (practice session: allow ¾ hour)

1. Accompany the client and the partner during exposure: (a) encourage them to take responsibility for practice; (b) praise their achievements and coping behavior.

2. Observe the behavior of both client and partner: (a) model appropriate behavior if a panic occurs; (b) prompt the partner to reinforce the client's achievements; (c) suggest further practice.

3. See that diaries are being used correctly and arrange the next visit.

## SUBSEQUENT VISITS

The remaining visits are likely to be rather similar in form, and 30 minutes is usually sufficient. After agreeing on an agenda, the therapist should ask to see the diary and target sheets and should then ask about progress since the last visit. We have found it useful to direct the first questions to the partner, both to ensure that he/she is in touch with current progress and to prompt praise for any significant achievements by the client. For example, the therapist may use questions such as "What do you feel has been achieved since we last met?" After eliciting the partner's opinion, and prompting praise if this is appropriate, the therapist can direct a similar question to the client. In addition, the client may be asked to comment on the quality of support he/she has received since the last visit, in order to provide effective feedback for the partner. Any misunderstanding between client and partner is likely to become apparent in the course of this exchange, and this allows the therapist to prompt or model more appropriate supportive behavior.

A common difficulty with clients who have been treated before is that they expect to form a doctor–patient relationship with the therapist and tend to exclude the partner. This can be prevented by repeatedly referring the client's comments or questions to the partner and asking an opinion. Excessive complaints directed to the therapist should be dealt with by a reminder that too much concentration on anxiety symptoms may strengthen them, or by referral to the relevant part of the manual. In general, it is most important that the therapist always encourage the client and the partner to attempt to solve the problem themselves before any alternative solution is offered.

Reference to the diary should make it clear whether regular practice has been carried out along the agreed-on lines. Clients should be praised for regular practice and for completing the diary. If practice is not being carried out regularly, the possible reasons must be explored and the client's responsibility for keeping to the contract emphasized. It may be necessary to make clear the distinction between practice and target completion; clients (and partners) have the responsibility to practice, but not to complete specific targets by a particular time. At times, the level of difficulty of targets or intermediate items may need to be adjusted, but this adjustment does not reduce the need for regular practice.

If there is difficulty in making progress with targets, it may be necessary to discuss specific techniques to overcome obstacles. Examples, listed at the end of the partners' manual, include having another person close by but out of view, arranging in advance an easy "emergency exit" from situations, and making sure that any other people who are involved know about the problem. Although it is usually necessary to work persistently on one target at a time, it may occasionally be useful to bypass an item that is giving unexpected difficulty and come back to it later after success with a different item.

Discussion of the technicalities of practice sometimes results in a client's losing sight of the main target of treatment, namely, an increase in the ability to control or tolerate phobic anxiety. It may be necessary to give frequent reminders that the best method of practice is to find a level of difficulty that provokes a manageable amount of anxiety, and to extend this level when anxiety has declined noticeably.

Clients should also be reminded that they must expect variations in their ability to achieve targets, and that a little done under difficult conditions can be more valuable than much done without anxiety. Regular inquiries should be made about the appropriate use of self-instructions to manage panic feelings, and praise should be given for increases in coping ability.

PHASING OUT THE MEETINGS WITH THE THERAPIST

Once regular practice has been established and any immediate difficulties have been resolved, the therapist should begin to introduce some discussion of the need to establish future targets and of possible problems in maintaining progress when the visits have ended. If possible, a list of increasingly difficult targets should be agreed on, while it is made clear that these may need to be modified appropriately in the light of subsequent experience. Encouragement should be given for plans to find a job, to join clubs or classes, or to visit friends more.

If it has not been discussed previously, this may be an appropriate moment to talk to the client and the partner about a reward system to mark the achievement of particular targets. The suggestion that family members should buy presents as rewards for progress is often interpreted as bribery. If this attitude is held strongly, it may be better not to persist with the suggestion, but it could be pointed out that the client may find that continuing regular practice over a period of months is rather difficult to sustain, particularly if progress seems to be slow. The anticipation of something pleasant can help to counteract anxiety and make practice less of a chore. Rewards are sometimes more acceptable and seem less artificial if they take the form of preferred activities that follow naturally from the target that has been achieved, for example, buying a small gift in a large store when the patient can go there regularly. However, attention and praise are more important to most clients than material rewards and may be a more natural expression of the partner's pleasure at what has been achieved.

Finally it is important to discuss setbacks. In their more severe form, these usually result from unexpected panic attacks, although minor setbacks may be no more than natural fluctuations in the condition. Clients should be advised that at least one setback is to be expected, and that they should not be discouraged when it occurs. Instead, they should try to look on setbacks as occasions for learning from their mistakes. They should also realize that although it may be necessary to go back a stage in practice, this lost ground is usually recovered quickly. Before leaving, the therapist should indicate that if any difficulties arise in the program, the patient and the partner should first look through the manuals and try to solve the problem themselves; however, if this fails to solve the difficulty, they should know under what circumstances emergency contact can be made with the therapist.

SUMMARY OF SUBSEQUENT VISITS (each about ½ hour)

1. Set an agenda for the visit.
2. Check diaries and target sheet.
3. Discuss the importance of regular practice, prompting reinforcement and feedback.
4. Discuss any specific difficulties encountered by the couple during practice, and encourage efforts at problem solving.
5. Discuss long-term plans: (a) continuing practice; (b) setting new targets; (c) increasing social activities; (d) anticipating setbacks; (e) rereading the manuals to help solve problems.
6. Arrange further appointments.

## FOLLOW-UP VISITS

These are appropriately arranged at increasing intervals after the end of regular contact, for example, after two weeks, one month, three months, and six months. The main purpose of these follow-up visits is to make sure that the practice program is continuing as planned; if there are no difficulties, the visits can be very brief, and when specific difficulties have arisen, possible solutions should be discussed. However, we have found that the most common problem is a gradual reduction in the time devoted to practice as the more immediate targets are achieved. Therapists who are used to using other forms of exposure treatment may sometimes find it difficult to accept the priority that clients place on different targets. Because this is a self-help program, clients select targets that have special importance to themselves and may ignore areas of avoidance that they see as irrelevant (e.g., public transport if a car is available). Although the advantages of a complete elimination of avoidance should be mentioned, it is probably not productive to insist on targets that clients see as unimportant.

Active family cooperation is also likely to fall away over time, particularly where other relationship problems are present. For this reason, both clients and partners should be encouraged to continue working together on any targets that have not yet been achieved.

SUMMARY OF FOLLOW-UP VISITS (about ½ hour)

1. Discuss any problems that have arisen during practice.
2. Give support and encouragement for achievements so far.
3. Encourage the client and the partner to set targets that are outside the client's daily routine (e.g., shopping in large towns, long-distance trips, vacations).
4. Emphasize the need for continuing practice and the involvement of the family.
5. Make the next appointment, and discuss the procedure for making any extra appointments in case of difficulty.

# 9. Results of Programmed Practice

PROGRAMMED PRACTICE was developed within the context of the research that has been described in earlier chapters. In the first stage, patients who had been treated unsuccessfully within previous trials, or who relapsed, were offered a second course of treatment. In this second course, an attempt was made to combine our various findings and conclusions. This approach eventually led to the home treatment method using programmed practice. The results were encouraging in that some of these previously unresponsive patients succeeded better with the new program than they had with the earlier exposure treatments. They also seemed less likely to relapse.

Once the home treatment program had been developed to a relatively standard format, it was evaluated with 12 agoraphobics referred as new patients (Mathews *et al.*, 1977). All these new patients were married women, but apart from this restriction, they were selected on the criteria adopted in the earlier series. They did not differ from earlier samples in either severity or chronicity; for example, the mean rating of phobic severity before treatment corresponded to definite disablement in several aspects of everyday life (4 on the 1–5 scale), and the mean duration of the problem was nine years.

An independent psychiatric assessor rated these patients for phobic severity, generalized anxiety, depression, and marital and sexual adjustment and estimated the willingness of the spouse to help. In fact, all the husbands agreed to help with the program when they were asked to do so. After this interview, a second independent assessor visited each patient at home and administered a behavioral test that employed a hierarchy of 15 items selected for each individual. The couples were then asked to read both manuals before the first therapy visit.

Three therapists, all with previous experience in using conventional exposure treatments, began by treating pilot cases and meeting to standard-

122

ize the way they followed the procedure described in Chapter 8. Four new patients were then assigned randomly to each of the three therapists. Eight home visits were arranged in the course of one month: three times in the first week, twice in the second and third weeks, and once in the fourth. Both partners were asked to be present at each meeting, and full collaboration between them was encouraged—although the therapists were not permitted to attempt marital counseling. At the end of this month, brief follow-up visits were arranged two weeks, six weeks, and three months later. The average time required to treat a patient was 17 hours. However, more than half of this time was spent in traveling, and the average time spent in actually treating the patients was only 7 hours, with a further 2½ hours for the follow-up visits.

Behavioral diaries showed that the patients spent 15 hours per week outside the home before treatment began, and that the amount of time rose to 22 hours afterwards. The diary records also showed that in some cases, a large part of the time outside the home was spent in the homes of other people or at work. Therefore, to obtain a more accurate estimate of the amount of time spent in phobic situations, this other part was excluded. The residual part of the mean time spent outside the home was 4.6 hours per week before treatment and increased to 10 hours at the end of the first four weeks, remaining at this level when it was estimated again six months later (see Figure 9.1). Similarly, the results of behavioral testing showed that all but one patient could perform additional items after four weeks, and nine patients improved further during follow-up (Table 9.1). Independent psychiatric ratings showed similar changes, with reductions in phobic anxiety, general anxiety, and depression in the majority of patients. Ratings obtained from the spouses showed a similar outcome.

Although there was no randomized control group in this study, the results can be placed in perspective by a comparison with those obtained during hospital-based exposure treatment in the immediately preceding study (Mathews *et al.*, 1976), for as we have noted already, the patients were initially similar on all measures. Table 9.2 shows that, on the four main measures of phobic avoidance and anxiety, the home treatment program was at least as effective despite a reduction in treatment time from over 20 hours to about 7. However, the more interesting finding is the striking difference in the proportion of the overall change that occurred during the follow-up period. Whereas exposure treatment carried out from the hospital produced all its benefit during the period of treatment and none during follow-up, in the home-based program about half as much change took place after the treatment as during its course.

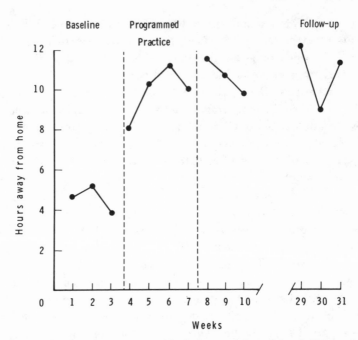

FIGURE 9.1. Average time spent outside the home each week (excluding work and visits) before, during, and after programmed practice. From A. Mathews, J. Teasdale, M. Munby, D. Johnston, and P. Shaw, *Behavior Therapy*, 1977, *8*, 919. Reprinted by permission.

There were no difficulties in obtaining the cooperation of the spouses, although there was some suggestion of a low-level positive correlation between ratings indicating poor marital relationship and smaller changes in phobic severity ($r = +.43$, NS). Using the same program with 18 agoraphobics, Cole (1978) reported that severe marital conflict was associated with poorer cooperation by the spouse. In Cole's study, cooperation was assessed from compliance with suggestions that spouses should monitor their partners' progress in a number of ways. The derived measure was predicted only by intelligence level ($r = +.56$) and ratings of marital relationship ($r = +.58$). These findings suggest that the quality of the marital relationship should be assessed before treatment. If severe conflict is found, the therapist should consider whether it is appropriate to involve the spouse in the treatment. In such a case, there is no compelling reason that additional helpers, such as close friends or other family members, should not be sought.

TABLE 9.1. Most difficult item performed on behavioral test by each patient, with approximate total time required and initial rank of items (1–15)[a]

| Patient | Baseline | | | After four weeks | | | Follow-up | | |
|---|---|---|---|---|---|---|---|---|---|
| | Description | Time (min) | Rank | Description | Time (min) | Rank | Description | Time (min) | Rank |
| A | Walk to end of road | 5 | 2 | Car to nearest town[b] | 90 | 9 | Car to farther town[b] | 270 | 13 |
| B | Walk to local store | 10 | 5 | Shopping in nearest town | 30 | 7 | Shopping in nearest town | 30 | 7 |
| C | Walk to bus stop | 2 | 3 | Bus to nearest town | 30 | 11 | Bus to farther town | 240 | 13 |
| D | Walk to local store | 20 | 4 | Shopping in nearest town | 90 | 10 | Shopping in farther town | 60 | 13 |
| E | Walk to nearest store | 20 | 3 | Bus to nearest town | 15 | 8 | Walk to nearest school | 20 | 5 |
| F | Walk to nearest store | 10 | 3 | Short bus trip | 10 | 4 | Walk to shopping center | 10 | 6 |
| G | Walk to next street | 15 | 3 | Bus to shopping center | 60 | 8 | Bus to nearest town | 120 | 11 |
| H | Bicycle to nearest store | 5 | 2 | Walk to shopping center[b] | 30 | 7 | Bus to nearest town | 60 | 13 |
| I | Walk to next street | 10 | 5 | Shopping in nearest town | 60 | 12 | Visit social club | 180 | 14 |
| J | Bicycle to shopping center | 20 | 4 | Bus to nearest town | 25 | 10 | Shopping in nearest town | 45 | 11 |
| K | Walk to friend's house | 5 | 2 | Walk to farther store | 25 | 6 | Bus to nearest town | 180 | 14 |
| L | Walk to local store | 20 | 5 | Walk to local store | 20 | 5 | Walk to nearest store | 10 | 2 |

[a]From A. Mathews, J. Teasdale, M. Munby, D. Johnston, and P. Shaw, Behavior Therapy, 1977, 8, 920. Reprinted by permission.
[b]Items not carried out alone.

TABLE 9.2. Comparison of programmed practice with hospital-based exposure on four main measures of phobic avoidance and anxiety

| | Pretreatment | Posttreatment | Follow-up | Improvement | |
| --- | --- | --- | --- | --- | --- |
| | | | | Pre–post | Post–follow-up |
| *Programmed practice* (Mathews et al., 1977) | | | | | |
| Behavioral test (1–14) | 3.3 | 7.4 | 8.8 | 4.1 | 1.4 |
| Total phobic anxiety (0–150) | 108 | 75 | 54 | 33 | 21[a] |
| Assessors' rating (1–5) | 6.0 | 4.0 | 2.8 | 2.0 | 1.2[a] |
| Self-rating (1–5) | 5.4 | 3.6 | 2.6 | 1.8 | 1.0[a] |
| *Exposure from hospital* (Mathews et al., 1976) | | | | | |
| Behavioral test (1–14) | 3.0 | 8.0 | 7.9 | 5.0 | .1 |
| Total phobic anxiety (0–150) | 99 | 65 | 69 | 34 | –.4 |
| Assessors' rating (1–5) | 6.8 | 4.0 | 4.6 | 2.8 | –.6 |
| Self-rating (1–5) | 5.8 | 3.6 | 3.8 | 2.2 | –.2 |

[a]Significant change post-follow-up.

The results obtained in this uncontrolled series of patients suggest that programmed practice may be the treatment of choice for the majority of agoraphobics. There were surprisingly few problems of administration, and the therapists found the program easy to manage. In general, the couples welcomed the opportunity to collaborate in a clearly structured program, and many commented that this was the first time that they had ever been offered an explanation of the problem and clear guidance on how to manage it. Perhaps as a result, there was little evidence of the type of uncooperative behavior that others have described in the families of agoraphobics. Similarly, comments from both partners indicated that they attributed their success more to their own efforts than to those of the therapist and therefore felt less dependent.

It is obviously difficult to interpret these results because the comparison was with the results of earlier hospital-based treatment. An appropriate evaluation of the program clearly requires comparison in a design that allows random allocation to a control treatment. It is also obviously important to replicate the promising results in a further sample of patients. These were the aims of a subsequent controlled study (Jannoun, Munby, Catalan, & Gelder, 1980). The first step was to develop an alternative procedure that was also a "self-help" treatment and was matched with programmed practice in terms of treatment time, the use of home visits, the involvement of the spouse, and the use of manuals, but that differed in the type of treatment instructions given to the patients. To match the manuals that give the details of programmed practice, a manual was written to describe this control procedure. The instructions that this manual contained dealt with any problems of everyday life that were experienced as stressful. It went on to describe ways of resolving these problems that the patient and spouse could use together. The rationale given for this approach was that agoraphobia persists as a result of a generalized anxiety, which, although interpreted by the patient as a fear of going out, can best be overcome by reducing the stress in her life. Instead of being given strong instructions to practice going out, patients in this alternative program were merely told that they should go out as and when they felt able to do so; no further specific advice was offered about the way in which they should do this.

Twenty-eight agoraphobic women, each with a husband or a close friend willing to act as a helper, were allocated randomly to programmed practice or the problem-solving comparison treatment. The patients were selected according to the criteria used in earlier investigations. In the sample as a whole, the mean rating of severity was 6 on a scale of 0-8 points (this corresponds to 4 on the 1-5 scale used previously), and the average duration of the phobia was six years. In each treatment condition, equal numbers of patients were allocated to one of two experienced female therapists, who saw both partners together and advised them on the use of the self-help method to which they had been allocated. Programmed practice was conducted as before, with the single exception that the therapists visited only five times over the first four weeks: twice in the first week and once in each of the three following weeks (see Appendix 3). This schedule halved the time spent in contact with the patients, which was the same for the two conditions. Thus the two conditions were matched as far as possible for nonspecific factors, but differed in their specific content of treatment.

Psychiatric ratings were made as in the previous investigation (i.e., before treatment, after four weeks, and again at six months), but in this case, the assessor was "blind" to the treatment condition. Self-ratings were also made as in the earlier study, except that behavioral testing was replaced by a complete record of outings from home using a behavioral diary (the reasons for this approach were given in Chapter 2). Overall, the results showed that programmed practice reduced phobic severity on all the main measures of anxiety and avoidance. Most of the change occurred in the first four weeks of treatment, although a modest improvement continued on at least some of the measures in the three months after treatment (see Figure 9.2). The change appeared to be at least as great as that observed in the previous series, which was a convincing replication since the actual treatment had been reduced to 3½ hours over the four-week period (see Appendix 3). Even after allowing for the additional time required for traveling and for follow-up contact, this treatment compared very favorably with the other treatments for agoraphobia, including exposure in cohesive groups.

A comparison of the major studies that we have carried out shows a striking increase in the efficiency of treatment over the last decade. Thus Table 9.3 shows the changes achieved on comparable phobic scales in very similar groups of patients with different forms of exposure treatment. If we can assume that such a comparison is not distorted too much by the differences that may exist in the population of patients and variations in the methods of rating, programmed practice stands out as a very economical treatment. However, the absolute magnitude of change has improved on-

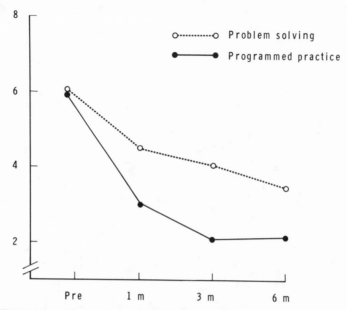

FIGURE 9.2. Independent ratings of phobic severity following programmed practice and a control problem-solving treatment. Redrawn from Jannoun, Munby, Catalan, and Gelder (1980).

ly slightly, suggesting that there are some factors that limit the extent of improvement.

In the comparison of programmed practice with the problem-solving treatment, most outcome measures revealed significant main effects in favor of programmed practice. However, these must be interpreted with caution, since a significant interaction was found between the type of treatment and the identity of the therapist. While the two therapists who took part obtained identical results with programmed practice instructions, their results with the comparison treatment were different. One achieved equivalent results with the problem-solving treatment and programmed practice, while the other did not. In view of this unexpected result and its implications, it becomes necessary to consider the results in more detail.

After four weeks of programmed practice, the patients of both therapists had clearly increased the number of hours spent away from home, and this result did not occur with the problem-solving treatment. However, in the

TABLE 9.3. Independent ratings of phobic severity with treatment time required[a]

| Source | Treatment | Pre | Post | Follow-up | Change | Treatment time |
|---|---|---|---|---|---|---|
| Gelder et al. (1973) | Nonspecific | 6.4[b] | 5.6 | 5.6 | .8 | 18 hr |
| | Desensitization | 7.6 | 4.4 | 4.6 | 3.0 | |
| | Flooding | 6.0 | 3.2 | 3.0 | 3.0 | |
| Mathews et al. (1976) | Flooding + exposure | 6.6 | 3.8 | 3.8 | 2.8 | 32 hr |
| | Flooding/exposure | 7.0 | 4.0 | 4.0 | 3.0 | |
| | Exposure alone | 6.8 | 4.0 | 4.6 | 2.2 | |
| Treasdale et al. (1977) | Group exposure | 5.2 | 3.6 | 3.2 | 2.0 | 15 hr (5 hr/patient) |
| Mathews et al. (1977) | Programmed practice | 6.0 | 4.0 | 2.8 | 3.2 | 7 hr (+ travel) |
| Jannoun et al. (1980) | Programmed practice | 6.1 | 3.1 | 2.2 | 3.9 | 3½ hr (+ travel) |
| | Problem solving | 6.1 | 4.5 | 3.7 | 2.4 | |

[a]All figures based on 0–8 scales, converted from 1–5 scales where necessary.
[b]Includes only the agoraphobic patients in this study.

case of one therapist only, the patients in both treatment groups had improved by an equivalent amount in this respect by the final follow-up. It would seem, therefore, that some of the patients given the problem-solving treatment were also enabled to go out more during the follow-up period even though they had received no specific instructions about self-exposure. The nature of this change and its implications for understanding both etiology and treatment mechanisms will be discussed at greater length in Chapter 11. At present, it is sufficient to note that despite this complication, we can conclude that programmed practice is a reliable and effective treatment for agoraphobia and that it has produced similar good results in the hands of four different therapists in two separate investigations.

The finding that programmed practice exerts such a powerful effect with so few hours of treatment raises the question of whether it is necessary for the patient to see the therapist at all. Weekes (1973) reported an uncontrolled series of 500 agoraphobic patients who were sent, by mail, instructions on her methods. Satisfactory results were claimed in about 60%, but this figure is apparently based on the results of a mailed questionnaire. Without further details of the study and in the absence of clear objective criteria for change or an appropriate control group, it is difficult to evaluate this claim. However, despite the lack of convincing evidence of its efficacy, a number of features make the approach an appealing one. Thus patients who are unable or unwilling to attend a clinic might be helped by instructions sent by mail; indeed, this method might maximize self-help and minimize dependence on clinicians. Even if the results were less good than those of conventional treatment, any improvement would be worthwhile if it could be obtained with clients who would otherwise be inaccessible. Moreover, very little professional time would be required.

For these reasons, we attempted to evaluate the instruction manuals developed for use in programmed practice, using them without any direct contact between the agoraphobic person and the therapist (Mathews & Munby, in prep.). Applications were invited from the members of a phobic society, and about 50 volunteers who met our criteria and who returned the questionnaire and diary measures were randomly assigned to one of three groups. The 14 clients in the first group were sent two instruction booklets, one for themselves and one for a partner, whom they were asked to recruit from their family. In the second group of 15, only the clients' booklet was sent, while in the third—a wait group—the 15 clients were told that there would be a delay before any instructions could be sent. After one month, all the groups were reassessed, and the clients in the wait group were sent booklets. All groups were finally reassessed six months later. There are obvious limitations on the kind of measures that can be obtained by mail, but comparisons using the Middlesex Hospital Questionnaire, the fear questionnaire, and diary records suggested that at the beginning these volunteers were as severely handicapped as—or more handicapped than—the agoraphobics attending outpatient clinics. For example, 39 clients of the 44 who completed the study were taking psychotropic medication, and 26 had received hospital treatment in the past. The mean duration of the problem was 7½ years, and the mean self-rated severity (0–8 scale) was 5.6, compared with 5.5 in the study of Jannoun *et al.* (1980).

On the agoraphobia scale of the fear questionnaire (Marks & Mathews, 1979), the mean initial score for these phobic volunteers was 28, compared with 25 for the group of agoraphobics treated in the previous study. The change on this scale was also similar to that observed in the other treatments. As can be seen from Figure 9.3, both the group with a partner and the group without one changed more than the wait group, and the apparent initial superiority of the group with a partner did not reach significance. On other self-report and diary measures, the pattern of results was similar, although in general the extent of change was less than that usually achieved with a therapist. Self-rated phobic severity, for example, was reduced by 1.8 points, compared with 2.4 in the equivalent condition

FIGURE 9.3. Agoraphobia scores on the fear questionnaire before and after programmed practice or a wait period, without direct therapist contact. From Mathews and Munby (in prep.).

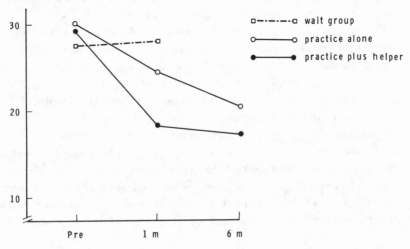

reported by Jannoun *et al.* (1980). Although this outcome suggests clear limits to the effectiveness of this self-help program, the results show that instructions without any personal contact with a therapist can have a useful effect that continues for at least six months. The lack of any significant differences due to the involvement of a partner suggests that having a partner is not important when neither client nor partner sees a therapist, although more research is needed before a firm conclusion can be drawn. Moreover, there has been no direct comparison of a self-help program carried out with a therapist and one carried out by mail.

Although knowledge is incomplete, the clinician has to make decisions about treatment on the basis of the incomplete information available. Our own experience to date supports the use of programmed practice carried out from the client's house, although some of the meetings with the therapist may sometimes be arranged more conveniently at a health center or clinic. On balance, we also favor the involvement of family members in the program, and we believe that whenever possible, therapists should meet patients and family members. Our evidence indicates that the professional time required to do this need not exceed about four hours on the average.

# 10. Persistence, Generalization, and Prediction

THIS CHAPTER IS concerned with three loosely related topics that draw heavily on the results and arguments presented previously. These topics are the long-term follow-up of the effects of behavior therapy; the extent to which behavior therapy affects areas of functioning other than the phobic symptoms, whether this effect is beneficial or not; and finally, the prediction of the effects of behavioral treatment in the individual patient.

## THE LONG-TERM FOLLOW-UP OF BEHAVIOR THERAPY

As we have noted in Chapter 6, the effects of behavioral treatment generally persist unchanged for the six-month follow-up period that is usually reported. There are only two significant exceptions. The first is the study of group *in vivo* exposure by Hand *et al.* (1974), in which an improvement during follow-up was seen although this effect could not be replicated by Teasdale *et al.* (1977). The second is the study of programmed practice (Mathews *et al.*, 1977) that has been described in Chapter 9. In this program, an improvement was observed during follow-up but was less marked in the replication (Jannoun *et al.*, 1980). It seems safe to conclude that the behavioral methods used to date, with the possible exception of programmed practice, lead to effects that persist more-or-less unchanged for at least six months.

The clinician, of course, hopes for more lasting effects. There are, however, formidable problems in establishing whether such effects do indeed exist. Inevitably patients who fail to respond to treatment or who relapse seek additional or alternative treatment, so that no firm conclusions can be drawn about the effects of the original treatment. Nevertheless, such

134

studies do at least make it possible to arrive at some estimate of the long-term effects of behavioral treatment.

Four studies are now available of the long-term effects of behavioral treatment for agoraphobics. All agree about the remarkable persistence of the beneficial effects of treatment. Marks (1971) followed the patients from the trials carried out by Gelder *et al.* (1967) and Marks *et al.* (1968). A psychiatric social worker—or, in a few cases, a psychiatrist—interviewed more than 90% of the patients about four years after the end of their treatment, rating them on the scales used at the time of the original investigation. Thirty-six of the patients seen at follow-up were agoraphobic. Over this four-year period, the patients' symptoms had not changed in intensity except in those cases that had received additional behavioral treatment, in which case some further improvement was observed. No further change was observed when treatment stopped again. Emmelkamp and Kuipers (1979) reported on 70 of the 81 patients treated about five years before in Emmelkamp's previous studies of *in vivo* methods of exposure (see Chapters 6 and 7). These authors found that agoraphobics did not worsen in the five years after treament; indeed, on some measures, there was evidence of further significant improvement. However, the latter findings should be interpreted cautiously because the patients were not interviewed; instead, they completed questionnaires sent by mail. For this reason, there is a greater possibility of falsification than there was in the study reported by Marks. Moreover, seven patients did not return their questionnaires, and they could not be traced in other ways. Their omission could have led to systematic bias in the assessment of outcome.

McPherson, Brougham, and McLaren (1980) have also reported the results of a study using questionnaires sent by mail to follow-up agoraphobics. This study is unusual in that the patients were treated not in clinical trials but in the everyday practice of a hospital within the British National Health Service. Moreover, only patients who had responded to treatment were followed up. The authors identified 81 agoraphobics who had been treated by behavioral methods, and 56 were successfully reexamined after an average interval of 4.3 years. As a group, the patients had received on average 11.3 treatment sessions of *in vivo* exposure (61%), imaginal desensitization (14%), or other unspecified behavioral methods. As in the previous studies, the effects of treatment persisted unchanged for four years. On the 0–4 rating scale used by McPherson *et al.*, these patients' self-ratings of agoraphobia before treatment were on average 3.10; after treatment, this rating had reached .56, and at follow-up .63. During the follow-up period, five patients had received further treatment for agoraphobia, all behavioral. While some caution must be accorded to findings based on a follow-up rate of 69%, the study remains an impressive demonstration of the durability of the effects of behavioral treatment for agoraphobia. It is particularly impressive because all of these patients had responded very well to treatment (as the means show), so that there was much more room for deterioration than improvement during follow-up.

We have recently completed a comprehensive follow-up study of agoraphobics treated by behavioral methods in our own previous investigations (Munby & Johnston, 1980). We followed the patients treated in the clinical trials reported by Gelder *et al.* (1973) and Mathews *et al.* (1976, 1977), all of which have been described in previous chapters. The time between these treatments and the occasion of follow-up was 8.6, 6.8, and 5.3 years, respectively. Of the 66 agoraphobics so treated, 65 were found; 63 were interviewed, and incomplete information was obtained on the remaining 2. The study therefore has a more complete data base than the studies of Emmelkamp and Kuipers or McPherson *et al.* Our patients were reassessed with the same outcome measures that had been used in the original trials. The assessors' and the patients' ratings of phobic severity are shown in Figure 10.1. For patients from all three trials, the effects of treatment lasted almost unaltered for up to nine years. Moreover, when a subsample of patients who had responded particularly well was analyzed separately, it showed equally lasting improvement, a finding that repeats that of McPherson *et al.*

It is difficult to draw causal conclusions from follow-up studies such as these. However, in the study by Munby and Johnston (1980) a correlational analysis of the relationship between measures taken at the time of the original treatment and those taken at follow-up suggests that treatment was indeed the main identifiable determinant of outcome. Table 10.1 shows the correlations between the main measures of agoraphobia made before treatment, six months after treatment, and six years later. The data are from the patients reported by Mathews *et al.* (1976), since this is the largest single sample of agoraphobics in our studies. Ratings of behavior six months after treatment were a much better predictor of outcome six years later than were ratings of the same behavior immediately before treatment. If treatment had not been a significant determinant of long-term outcome, these two correlations could be expected to be approximately the same. That they are not strongly suggests that treatment led to the changes in the patients' behavior and that these changes persisted.

Another interesting feature of the results of this investigation was a sug-

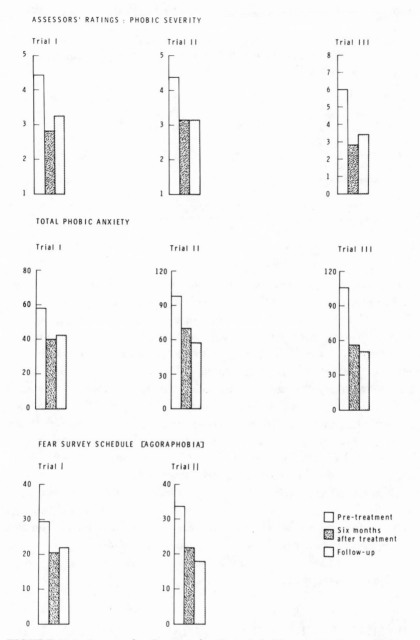

ASSESSORS' RATINGS : PHOBIC SEVERITY

TOTAL PHOBIC ANXIETY

FEAR SURVEY SCHEDULE [AGORAPHOBIA]

☐ Pre-treatment
▨ Six months after treatment
☐ Follow-up

FIGURE 10.1. Assessors' and patients' ratings of phobic severity of agoraphobics followed up 5–9 years after behavioral treatment. From M. Munby and D. W. Johnston, *British Journal of Psychiatry*, 1980, *137*, 421. Reprinted by permission. Trial I, Gelder *et al.* (1973); Trial II, Mathews *et al.* (1976); Trial III, Mathews *et al.* (1977).

TABLE 10.1. Correlations between values of assessors' ratings of phobic severity and two self-report measures at follow-up and values prior to treatment and six months after treatment ended[a]

| Variable | n | Pretreatment with follow-up | Six months after treatment with follow-up |
|---|---|---|---|
| Phobic severity | 34 | .18 | .58[b] |
| Total phobic anxiety | 34 | −.02 | .65[b] |
| Fear Survey Schedule (agoraphobia) | 35 | .17 | .51[b] |

[a]From Munby and Johnston (1980).
[b]$p < .05$.

gestion that the programmed practice described in Chapter 8 had succeeded in making patients and their spouses more self-reliant. As can be seen in Figure 10.1, the reductions in ratings of agoraphobia brought about by programmed practice lasted for over five years. Moreover, only 1 of these 12 patients had had further contact with the psychiatric services during the follow-up period, and she was also the only one to claim that her phobia had worsened at *any time* during the follow-up period. Most of the patients in the two earlier clinical trials had made further contact with the psychiatric services, and almost half reported severe but short-lived exacerbations of the phobia during the years of follow-up. Several explanations could be put forward for the difference between these results and those of programmed practice, but the data are certainly consistent with our expectation that programmed practice should teach patients and their spouses to deal with the problem of agoraphobia with a minimum of professional help.

These four studies, which involved the behavioral treatment of over 200 agoraphobic patients and follow-up periods between four and nine years, all point to the same conclusion: behavioral treatments for agoraphobia produce substantial and enduring effects.

## EFFECTS OF BEHAVIOR THERAPY ON AREAS OF FUNCTIONING OTHER THAN THE PHOBIAS

Unlike the more traditional psychotherapies, behavior therapies are directed at the patient's main overt problem (agoraphobia), and it is not usual to treat other areas of disordered functioning unless the disorder is particularly severe. Nonetheless, the evidence generally suggests that after behavior therapy, there are small improvements in a number of psychological and behavioral domains that have not been treated directly. For example, in the study by Gelder *et al.* (1967), ratings of general anxiety, depression, and relationships with others all improved significantly during treatment and did so at least as much in systematic desensitization as they did in psychotherapy. In the more recent comparison of flooding, systematic desensitization, and a control treatment (Gelder *et al.*, 1973), improvement was noted on several mood scales and on self-ratings of depression; this improvement was significantly greater after behavior therapy than after the control treatment. Similarly, Mathews *et al.* (1976) found a significant improvement on tension–anxiety and depression ratings after imaginal flooding or *in vivo* exposure.

Emmelkamp's group has also examined mood changes during and after behavior therapy using ratings of anxiety and a Dutch version of the Zung Depression Inventory. They consistently found small improvements in anxiety and depression with their *in vivo* treatment methods. However, they also found a significant worsening of anxious mood in patients receiving imaginal flooding in a study that compared this treatment with *in vivo* exposure (Emmelkamp & Wessels, 1975). We did not find this increase of anxiety in our comparable study (Mathews *et al.*, 1976), although a few individual patients did find the flooding process distressing.

The persistence of these effects on mood was examined in our recent follow-up study (Munby & Johnston, 1980). The assessor rated the patient on anxiety and depression scales, and the patients completed anxiety and depression measures from the McNair and Lorr (1964) Mood Scale. The relevant means are shown in Figure 10.2, in which the modest reductions, over the treatment period, in anxiety and depression already referred to can be seen. It is also clear that in the judgment of the assessor, these gains had not persisted and the patients had returned to levels near those before treatment. However, the patients' own ratings suggest that the effects were more enduring than this. This persistence of the reduction in patients' self-ratings of depression was also reported by Emmelkamp and Kuipers (1979) and McPherson *et al.* (1980) in their follow-up studies.

All the findings we have reported so far show that some (possibly unstable) improvement in mood is the result of the behavioral treatment of agoraphobia. Nonetheless, many believe, on the basis of psychoanalytic theory, that direct behavioral treatments that successfully remove the patient's symptomatology have a hidden cost. It is argued that since the hypothesized underlying cause has not been dealt with, the removed symp-

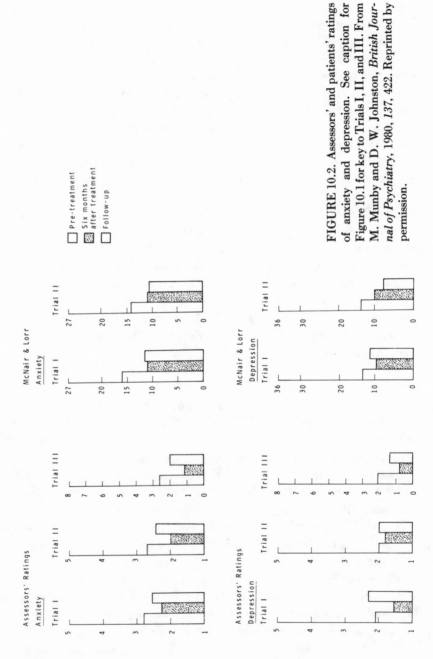

FIGURE 10.2. Assessors' and patients' ratings of anxiety and depression. See caption for Figure 10.1 for key to Trials I, II, and III. From M. Munby and D. W. Johnston, *British Journal of Psychiatry*, 1980, *137*, 422. Reprinted by permission.

140

tom will be replaced by another and that if the patient's life is viewed as a whole, no real gain will have been made. Considerable confusion exists about the idea of symptom substitution, and it is as well to keep two points in mind: (1) psychoanalytic theory predicts that symptom substitution will appear in those patients who have had their symptoms successfully removed by behavioral treatment (i.e., the most successful patients are the ones most likely to show the appearance of other symptoms), and (2) if other symptoms are found to occur after behavior therapy, they cannot be assumed to be the result of that therapy or peculiar to that therapy unless it has been compared with a psychoanalytic therapy that has dealt with the underlying cause. In addition, all therapy has hazards: an unsuccessfully treated patient may be depressed and demoralized; a successfully treated patient will have to learn to cope with new patterns of behavior, and these may be disturbing to the patient or the patient's relatives. This hazard is not peculiar to behavior therapy and should not be counted as symptom substitution. Clinicians should, of course, be aware of this danger and attempt to deal with it.

In general, it has been found that few new symptoms appear during treatment or in the period immediately following it, and that such symptoms are no more likely to occur after behavior therapy than after other therapies. We cannot improve on the statement made by Gelder *et al.* in their 1967 paper on the comparison of psychotherapy and behavior therapy, in which it will be recalled systematic desensitization was more effective than psychotherapy in the reduction of phobic behavior. They wrote:

> It has often been suggested that symptom substitution will follow behaviour therapy. We therefore searched carefully for evidence that improvement in phobias with desensitisation was associated either with the appearance of new symptoms, which were sustained, or more restriction in the patient's social adjustment. Several sources were considered; patients' and therapists' ratings, case notes and the P.S.W.'s [psychiatric social worker's] interview notes. Some examples were found of transient increases in depression lasting for a week or two but these occurred as often in the two groups receiving psychotherapy. No patient whose main phobias improved markedly with desensitization developed any new and sustained symptoms and no patient whose phobia was rated improved had achieved this at the expense of more limited social adjustment. Indeed, there was much evidence to the contrary; patients whose main phobias improved markedly also showed improvement of other symptoms of social adjustment. (p. 64)

Zitrin *et al.* (1978) also made the same comment about their comparison of psychotherapy and behavior therapy: "Symptom substitution did not occur in any of the patients. Whenever clinical regression occurred it consisted of a recurrence of the original symptoms" (p. 315). These two direct comparisons of behavior therapy and psychotherapy therefore suggest that symptom substitution, if it occurs at all, is very rare and is not more likely after behavior therapy than after psychotherapy.

The results of the four follow-up studies have been equally positive. Marks (1971), Emmelkamp and Kuipers (1979), and McPherson *et al.* (1980) all commented on their failure to find any negative effects of behavior therapy in agoraphobics. In our follow-up study, we paid particular attention to the possible negative effects in patients who had responded very well to treatment. In common with previous writers, we found no evidence of new symptomatology in these patients, and indeed, they were *less* depressed and *less* anxious than the patients who had responded poorly. In this study, in our earlier studies, and in our clinical practice, we find no convincing evidence of symptom substitution or particular negative effects that are peculiar to behavior therapy.

Hafner (1976) came to much less sanguine conclusions about the possible risks of behavior therapy and, in particular, *in vivo* exposure in groups. He presented an analysis of one year's follow-up of 39 agoraphobics treated by *in vivo* exposure in groups (Hafner & Marks, 1976) and stated, "It is inescapable that a proportion of patients who receive a standard symptomatic treatment will be worse one year later. There is strong evidence that this worsening derived from treatment itself" (Hafner, 1976, p. 382). We do not understand how Hafner came to this conclusion. He presented no convincing evidence that any patients showed a significant deterioration on any of his measures. Even if he had such evidence, this study would not allow him to attribute this outcome to behavior therapy as distinct from any other therapy or indeed from the passage of time. We are not convinced by this study.

Behavioral treatment of agoraphobia has now been studied extensively and intensively, and all the evidence points to a conclusion that symptom substitution has never been demonstrated and that there are no consistent negative effects of any of the treatments we have described, certainly no more negative effects than one would anticipate with any therapy, including psychoanalysis, for the same problem.

## PREDICTION OF OUTCOME

Agoraphobic patients do not respond uniformly when given the same behavioral treatments: most improve; some improve a great deal; and a few are unchanged. It would clearly be of some practical and theoretical value to be able to predict who would benefit most from a particular method. In clinical practice, patients are rarely given a standard treatment package; rather, treatment is, to a greater or lesser extent, tailored to suit the individual. This tailoring can take the form of the therapist's choosing one type of treatment rather than another or treating additional problems other than the agoraphobia (e.g., marital disharmony) that he/she believes may be maintaining the phobia or interfering with treatment. The study of predictive factors offers the hope of putting these judgments on an empirical rather than an intuitive basis. Unfortunately, to date, few useful predictors have been found.

Nearly all published reports of behavioral treatment have included a section on prognostic factors that describes efforts to improve patient selection. The results have been almost uniformly disappointing. In 1966, Gelder and Marks contrasted agoraphobics who had improved considerably and those who had not, following either a behavior therapy or a control treatment. Because the two had very similar effects, the two methods of treatment were combined in the analysis. Among the measures taken were pretreatment ratings of the patient's phobia, other phobias, anxiety, depression, obsessions, age, symptom duration, IQ, social adjustment, work adjustment, and the E and N scores of the Eysenck Personality Inventory. Only two measures related to outcome. Patients who did well had fewer symptoms on the Cornell Medical Index and a better work adjustment record prior to treatment. Ten years later, the picture had not changed. Hafner and Marks (1976) studied 57 agoraphobics who were treated with *in vivo* exposure. All they felt it necessary to write was "Many variables at the start of treatment and during treatment were correlated with outcome. No consistent pattern of predictors of response emerged" (p. 85). Stern and Marks (1973) reported the study of 16 agoraphobic patients treated with imaginal and *in vivo* exposure. They correlated 26 variables measured before treatment and 5 variables measured during treatment with 23 outcome variables. The only results that they reported were a few scattered correlations between psychophysiological responsiveness prior to treatment and psychophysiological responses after treatment.

Stern and Marks also included in their study three measures of the patient's expectations about treatment. Unfortunately, they gave no details of these measures except to report that they did not predict outcome. Emmelkamp and Wessels (1975), using the same measures, found that they did predict outcome after four sessions of treatment but not after a further eight. Expectancy was also found to be a significant predictor of outcome in the study of 36 agoraphobics reported by Mathews *et al.* (1976). In this study, to avoid the problems produced by multiple very specific outcome measures, one composite outcome score was used. This was obtained by selecting those outcome variables that intercorrelated satisfactorily, adjusting them for pretreatment level, converting each to a standard score, and then summing these. This composite score reflected patient, therapist, and independent assessor's ratings of phobic behavior. Expectancy was assessed by requiring the patients to estimate, before treatment, how likely they thought they were to achieve each of 15 phobic situations in the behavioral hierarchy. The patients who were more confident about improvement were more likely to improve. Another simpler rating of patients' expectations of benefit from treatment did not predict outcome, but we have evidence that such simple expectancy ratings are unrealistic. Thus we found (Mathews et al., 1974) that ratings of expectation of benefit from treatment, made weekly before each treatment session, did not change, even in patients who were manifestly not benefiting from treatment. This finding illustrates one of the many complexities of measuring expectancy (see Lick & Bootzin, 1975).

It is increasingly apparent that much behavior is situation-specific and that more powerful prediction is likely if this is recognized. In part, this specificity is confirmed by the predictive power of measures of patients' expectancies, since such measures are more specific to the treatment than are, for example, general personality measures. It is also likely that a patient's initial response to treatment will be a guide to the eventual outcome. We explored this likelihood in the 36 agoraphobics treated with *in vivo* or imaginal flooding (Johnston *et al.*, 1976). Patients estimated on a 0–10 scale how anxious they would be in 15 phobic situations. The sum of these estimates, termed the *total phobic anxiety* (TPA), was completed before each treatment session, as well as at the main assessment points. To measure the effect of treatment, we calculated the change from before the first treatment session to before each of the 15 successive treatment sessions. The resulting 15 scores were correlated with the composite outcome score described above. The change in TPA over the complete course of therapy (i.e., between Weeks 1 and 16) was also correlated with the change prior to each treatment session. The resulting correlations are shown in Figure 10.3. Weekly change in TPA correlated with total change in TPA, became significant after three weeks of treatment, and reached a high level (.8) halfway through treatment. The correlations with the composite score were naturally smaller, but they became significant after six weeks of treatment and approached an asymptote by nine weeks, with a correlation of almost

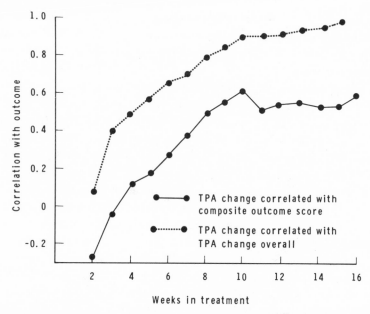

FIGURE 10.3. Change in total phobic anxiety between Week 1 of treatment and each successive week, correlated with two measures of outcome (see text).

.6. This latter correlation, while low, is approximately the level at which the total change in TPA correlated with the composite outcome score and is therefore unlikely to be exceeded by a score derived from this measure. Both these forms of correlational analysis suggest that patients who were showing little sign of improvement halfway through the course of treatment were not going to do well.

The studies described above were all concerned with prediction of the response to treatment. It would also be useful to be able to predict those patients who are likely to relapse after successful treatment. As we have seen in an earlier section, enduring relapse is not a major problem among successfully treated agoraphobics. A corollary is that it is extremely difficult to predict those few who do relapse, and there are few guidelines that we can offer. We have examined the relationship between ratings of anxiety and depression made before treatment and relapse during a prolonged follow-up and failed to find any relationship. Barlow and Mavissakalian (1981) have recently suggested that relapse is more likely if there is a marked difference between the various aspects of the patient's fear after treatment, for example, if the patient has ceased to avoid most situations but is still highly aroused autonomically when in these situations. This is an appealing view, and it was part of the reason for the interest in psychophysiological measurement in the early 1970s. Unfortunately, there is no convincing evidence to support it to date.

Neither therapist nor theoretician has learned much that is positive from the many analyses of prognostic factors in the treatment of agoraphobics. However, the lack of significant correlations is not in itself a negative thing, because it indicates that there is so far no *a priori* reason that any particular agoraphobic should do badly in treatment. The therapist need not be daunted by patients who are very anxious, are slightly depressed, or have phobias of considerable severity or great duration. This research and our clinical experience suggest that treatment should be undertaken with all agoraphobics who request it; surprising results can be achieved with even the most handicapped or disadvantaged patients. What this research does show is that therapists should seriously reconsider their plan of treatment if an agoraphobic patient is not improving after a few weeks of behavioral treatment, since there is quite a high probability that this patient will not benefit if the treatment is continued. That is not to say that such a patient could not eventually benefit from treatment or that treatment should be discontinued, but only that the therapist should look for obstacles to progress and be prepared to explore new avenues.

# 11. Future Directions in Theory and Research on Agoraphobia

## TOWARD AN UNDERSTANDING OF TREATMENT MECHANISMS

IN THE COURSE of developing programmed practice as a treatment for agoraphobia, questions about mechanisms have been largely ignored. However, if we are to extend and improve the treatment effects that have been described in the previous chapters, we need to understand how they are produced. In the discussion that follows, programmed practice is taken as the procedure whose effects are to be explained because, although simple in principle, it is at least as effective as the other behavioral treatments that we have evaluated. Necessarily, many of the explanations to be offered in this section are speculative, but it is our hope that nonetheless they will be heuristic and testable. For convenience, programmed practice is considered here under three headings: the effects of exposure to phobic situations, the facilitation of self-exposure practice, and methods of modifying patients' experience of anxiety.

## THE EFFECTS OF EXPOSURE

Surprisingly there is still no general agreement about the mechanism by which exposure to feared situations reduces phobic anxiety and avoidance. Perhaps this is less surprising when it is remembered that in the apparently much simpler situation of avoidance conditioning in animals, there is no single accepted theory of how exposure coupled with response prevention produces extinction (Mineka, 1979). The assumption that the crucial element is unreinforced exposure to the conditioned stimuli for avoidance, leading to a decrement in conditioned fear, has recently come under heavy attack. Thus, in response prevention, there is no obvious relationship between indexes of conditioned fear (e.g., autonomic reactivity) and subsequent tendency to avoid. As Mineka put it, while extinction of conditioned fear may be sufficient to eliminate avoidance, it does not seem to be necessary; some other kind of learning can apparently take place and prevent avoidance without the need to extinguish all signs of fear. The evidence from experiments with animals may have a parallel in human phobias, since a number of cases have been reported in which there is a degree of dissociation between avoidance behavior and other indexes of fear. For example, Barlow and Mavissakalian (1981) described a patient who could enter all phobic situations during treatment and considered herself cured despite evidence of a marked acceleration of heart rate during practice. Although this patient subsequently relapsed, it is by no means clear that such dissociation of indexes of phobic anxiety always carries with it a poor prognosis.

Returning to studies of conditioned avoidance, other authors have suggested that during response prevention, animals may learn alternative behaviors that subsequently interfere with avoidance. Hence Baum (1970) argued that animals may acquire relaxation responses (e.g., grooming or social behavior) during response prevention that inhibit response to the fear conditioned stimulus. Although vulnerable to the same criticisms as conventional extinction theory, this idea does account for the facilitating effects of social stimuli, forced exploration, and so on, which may relate to the use of distraction strategies by agoraphobic patients.

A final influential theory is the cognitive model proposed by Seligman and Johnston (1973). In simple form, these authors argued that like humans, animals learn that avoidance will lead to the absence of punishment, and that they must learn new expectancies during exposure and response prevention. In this theory, conditioning plays a role only in the early stages of learning, so that conditioned autonomic responses may not parallel avoidance, which is determined by the expectation of punishment. Cognitive theories of this sort can thus account for autonomic–behavioral dissociation. However, they are extremely difficult to test, since no objective indexes of expectancy exist.

In the case of agoraphobia, it is probable that avoidance is motivated in part by the anticipation of high levels of anxiety and panic attacks. During treatment, patients are increasingly exposed to phobic situations and learn that the anxiety provoked is less than expected, occurs less frequently, or is more easily tolerated. Thus one consequence of exposure may be a cognitive change: a reduction in the expectation that uncontrollable anxiety will occur. However, before this cognitive change can occur, it is necessary that the anticipated panic not take place, that it be less severe than was expected, or that the patient remain long enough in the feared situation to experience the decline of the panic without avoidance.

A complicating feature, the discussion of which will be postponed until later, is the possibility that the patient's own behavior or cognitions sometimes create or maintain, or alternatively dissipate, the panic state. For the moment, however, it is convenient to assume that prolonged exposure, especially to situations of graded intensity, usually leads to moderate but declining anxiety, rather than the panic that the agoraphobic person anticipates. As we have seen in Chapter 6, within limits the level of anxiety experienced during exposure does not appear to affect crucially the long-term outcome of treatment. On the other hand, during the development of the phobia, patients may have experienced extremely severe attacks of anxiety that were terminated only by avoidance behavior—usually by returning home or going to some other place of safety. It is likely that such avoidance in response to feelings of panic produces what Eysenck (1976) has termed *incubation*, that is, an increment in the strength of the conditioned fear—or, in cognitive terms, an increase in the expectancy that panic can be terminated only by avoidance. In experiments with volunteer subjects, extremely brief but intense exposure has indeed been shown to produce incubationlike effects (Marshall, Gauthier, & Gordon, 1979), but the equivalent in agoraphobics must remain conjectural. In contrast, the exposure carried out in the course of a treatment such as programmed practice is arranged to produce a degree of anxiety that usually declines without provoking avoidance.

To the extent that phobic anxiety during exposure is believed to be the result of fear conditioning, this decline in anxiety can be seen as reflecting the process of extinction. As indicated earlier, however, extinction of conditioned fear does not seem to be the only way in which avoidance can be prevented. On the other hand, if exposure can be brought about, conditioned fear will be reduced, provided that the exposure continues for long enough. In the case of agoraphobia, it is possible that high levels of trait anxiety and autonomic reactivity may have amplified any conditioned or unconditioned reactions to environmental stimuli (see Chapter 3). Moreover, having avoided phobic situations for some time, agoraphobics may become sensitized (or dishabituated) to the intense, complex, and demanding social stimuli that characterize these situations. Thus the reduction in fear during practice may be attributable to habituation of these autonomic responses as well as to extinction.

Finally, and perhaps more important in determining future behavior, the patient in usually aware of the declining autonomic anxiety reactions, and this awareness in turn may lead to cognitive changes. Whatever the true explanation for the reduction in autonomic anxiety, the patient's intention to reenter a phobic situation is likely to reflect beliefs about the consequences of that behavior. It is to this area that we now turn our attention.

## FACILITATION OF SELF-EXPOSURE PRACTICE

Self-exposure practice may be usefully seen as the end result of a decision process, in which patients decide to approach rather than to avoid phobic situations, as they have done previously. If this process is assumed to be similar to other behavioral decisions, then theories that have been productive elsewhere may help in an understanding of agoraphobic behavior. Subjective utility theory (Slovic, Fishoff, & Lichtenstein, 1977) suggests that decisions are made by computing the product of probability and value for each outcome, and choosing the action that maximizes this product. Although it is already clear that human behavior often violates this model in a number of ways (see Tversky & Kahneman, 1974), the theory points to an important idea. This is that behavioral intentions are determined (at least, in part) by beliefs about the positive and negative outcomes consequent on that behavior. In the case of phobic behavior, one expected negative outcome is the occurrence of a panic attack and all that this implies. Additional possibilities that could be put forward include the increased demands that might be made following recovery. The expected positive outcomes are less easily identified, but they probably include social incentives (see Chapter 7), perceived progress toward recovery, and the resumption of activities that were previously found rewarding. Persisting practice in self-exposure is made more likely when—as in the home treatment program—family support is encouraged, patients monitor their own progress, and patients select targets that are personally significant. Exposure may therefore be facilitated, on the one hand, by a belief that panic is less probable or less terrible than previously supposed and, on the other, by the belief that it will lead to the approval of friends and relatives, to a feeling of mastery, and to the attainment of rewarding goals.

Agoraphobic behavior can thus be thought to represent the result of an approach–avoidance conflict: an equilibrium reached between the advantages of going out and the fear of doing so. However, as others have argued, in the area of compliance with medical advice (Becker & Maiman, 1975) an outcome balance in favor of an action may be insufficient if there are no prompts or cue stimuli to remind patients of their intentions. After a long period of avoidance, changes in habits and lifestyle may have removed many of the normal cues and prompts to go out, because others have taken over duties such as shopping, or visitors come to the house instead of meeting the patient elsewhere. For this reason, an otherwise effective change in the balance of incentives in favor of going out may be insufficient to change behavior. The thought or idea of going out may simply not arise any longer without external prompting. A number of features in behavioral treatments might help to overcome this, and among these possibilities are the aftereffects of imagined or real-life exposure sessions themselves. Thus, after sessions of treatment, agoraphobics seem more likely to think about going out and in this way may be prompted to practice self-exposure. Within programmed practice, this function is fulfilled by instructions given in the manual, by the self-monitoring of practice, and by discussions with the partner.

One remaining problem that many patients report is that anticipatory anxiety remains high before they attempt any new and more difficult tasks. From a cognitive viewpoint, it would seem that the expectancy changes in such patients are rather specific (concerning particular situations) rather than general (concerning overall ability to overcome obstacles and tolerate anxiety). Programmed practice attempts to induce a more general change in self-confidence by passing a large share of the responsibility of running the program to the patients and their families. Thus they can take credit for what has been achieved and make their own plans to extend self-exposure practice, rather than depending passively on a therapist.

## ANXIETY EXPERIENCED DURING EXPOSURE

It has been emphasized that avoidance is partly maintained by fear of provoking acute anxiety attacks. Such attacks can be extremely aversive in their own right, but they are made more so by ideas that they may lead to physical collapse, illness, insanity, or public humiliation. It therefore seems unlikely that programmed practice could be effective in the long run if these fears and the anxiety experienced during practice were not reduced also. The simple interpretation of anxiety as conditioned fear or autonomic overreactivity is complicated by the fact that agoraphobics appear to have secondary reactions to their own physical symptoms and often interpret these in an alarming way. Indeed, some authors, such as Beck and Rush (1975), have gone so far as to argue that such ideas are the primary cause of phobic anxiety. While not accepting this extreme position, we find it at least plausible that the construction placed on physical signs of anxiety may play a part in increasing or maintaining them. Agoraphobics may attend selectively to minor physical symptoms and then add to them by interpreting the symptoms in a frightening way, thus forming a vicious circle. Apart from cognitive reactions, they may also behave in ways that increase physical symptoms. For example, tensing up to "fight off" panic, rushing to escape, and breathing deeply to the point of hyperventilation may all lead to new symptoms. Such counterproductive responses can be modified in a number of ways.

First, patients can be educated and reassured about the nature of anxiety, so that they are enabled to relabel symptoms as harmless. Second, this approach can be extended to helping the patient to identify particular thoughts or actions that increase anxiety and to develop ways of countering them. For example, the fear of possible loss of control in public might be countered by the idea that it has never happened before, that others would be available to help if required, and so on. Third, patients may be helped to ignore physical symptoms by the use of distracting tasks, such as holding a conversation about unrelated topics, or by paying close attention to their surroundings.

Unfortunately, there is no direct evidence of how effective—if at all—any of these techniques is in controlling anxiety. Our impression is that distraction methods alone are ineffective when anxiety has already reached a high level, as it then becomes difficult to prevent the intrusion of symptoms or frightening thoughts into awareness. For this reason, the first two methods form the basis of the instructions for coping with anxiety that are used in programmed practice. Further research is needed to establish whether the use of these methods gives patients real control over anxiety, including its autonomic component. Even if it does not have a direct effect, some justification for the use of the method in clinical practice is provided by experimental work on the reduction in distress brought about by perceived (rather than actual) control over aversive stimuli (Averill, 1973).

In the hope that it will stimulate future research, we will summarize the main points of the preceding discussion in a strong and, we hope, testable form. The effectiveness of programmed practice is thought to depend on three procedural components. In common with other behavioral approaches, it increases exposure to feared situations in such a way as to allow conditioned (or unconditioned) fear to decline without avoidance. Awareness of this decline reduces expectations of subsequent panic and thereby influences behavioral intentions. In other words, we suggest that cognitive change is secondary to self-observation of changes in behavior, but that subsequently the altered expectations act so as to facilitate further self-exposure practice.

## COGNITIVE CHANGE IN THE TREATMENT OF AGORAPHOBIA

The account that we offer of the changes in programmed practice may be seen as similar to those described by Bandura (1977). In Bandura's view, all behavioral change following the treatment of fear depends on changes in self-efficacy expectations; that is, individuals come to believe that they are capable of performing successfully the previously avoided behavior. In this account, efficacy expectations are distinguished from outcome expectations, which are defined as beliefs about the consequences of the newly acquired behaviors, and which are not accorded a crucial role in the treatment process. The application of this model to agoraphobia is made difficult by the vagueness of these definitions and of the distinction between the two concepts.

We have suggested that both beliefs about panic and the perception of control may change during treatment. It is not entirely clear whether these should be described as changes of self-efficacy or outcome expectations, since this designation depends on exactly what is meant by the belief that one can successfully perform the avoided behavior. In a strictly behavioral sense, agoraphobic patients know that they are able to go out but do not do so because of the risk of panic. Given sufficient incentive, however (e.g., a real threat to survival), patients quickly show themselves capable of going out. Before treatment, panic may be regarded as being beyond the control of the individual, while afterwards it is seen as controllable by anxiety management techniques. In this case, it is possible to argue that patients have actually acquired new behavioral skills in the control of panic and that this is the crucial change. Alternatively, patients may simply become aware that as they practice going out, the fear they experience becomes less. In this case, rather as Borkovec (1978) has argued, any change in expectancy seems more explicable as a consequence of behavior change rather than its cause. As was argued earlier, however, it seems likely that a two-way interaction may come to exist between expectations and self-exposure practice.

The only obvious way of testing whether or not cognitive changes are causal rather than merely secondary to self-observation of behavior would be to develop treatments that alter expectations directly. More specifically, we need to know if exposure to the feared situation is always necessary before phobic anxiety can be eliminated, or whether prior cognitive change can produce equivalent effects. Since there is a trivial sense in which behavioral change cannot be observed in the absence of exposure, the latter term is taken to refer to *systematic* practice in situations previously avoided because of anticipated anxiety. The nearest approach to answering this question would seem to be provided by investigations of the effects of cognitive or other nonexposure treatments on agoraphobia.

In the earlier discussion of the study by Jannoun *et al.* (1980), it was noted that some of the patients who received the problem-solving treatment improved as much as patients given the programmed practice instructions. It is possible that the therapist whose patients responded well to the problem-solving approach may have given encouragement to practice, even though this was not part of the plan of the treatment. This possibility is consistent with the observed tendency for the "blind" assessor to rate these patients as improved in phobic severity after the first four weeks of treatment. However, this rating is a composite of the phobic anxiety anticipated and the actual avoidance behavior reported. Diary records show that despite the rated improvement, none of the patients given the problem-solving treatment spent more time out of the house or made more trips at this stage, when contact with the therapist was greatest. For this reason, we suspect that the assessor was responding—at least, in some cases—to changes in anticipated anxiety rather than to changes in avoidance. And we conclude that it is unlikely that the changes observed in these patients were the result of covert encouragement to practice.

At least two other possibilities exist. One is that in the hands of the more successful therapist, the comparison treatment was particularly successful in achieving its aim of encouraging patients to adopt a problem-solving set, and that this set was later applied to the problem of phobic avoidance. A related possibility is that the successful solution of life problems gave these patients a heightened sense of confidence in dealing with obstacles, and this facilitated practice without any special instructions being needed.

Alternatively, since the stated target of the problem-solving treatment was the reduction of general anxiety, it is possible that one therapist was more successful in this respect. There was a tendency for the patients who subsequently avoided less to show an early decrease in generalized anxiety, although this was not statistically significant. Such a decrease might conceivable lead to a greater willingness to go out, or to lower levels of phobic anxiety when out, or to both. We cannot, of course, be certain which—if any—of these suggestions are correct. However, if there is any truth in the last two possibilities, exposure may not after all be the only route to the reduction of phobic avoidance and anxiety.

An alternative approach to treatment that does not necessarily involve exposure is cognitive restructuring. As used by Emmelkamp *et al.* (1978), cognitive restructuring consists of three cognitive modification procedures. The first is the provision of a rational explanation for the patient's fear; the second is discussion of underlying irrational beliefs; and the third is practice in replacing negative self-statements with more positive ones. In a comparison of five sessions of cognitive restructuring and *in vivo* exposure (each given for one week in a crossover design), exposure was found to be by far the more effective treatment. However, in a subsequent study (Emmelkamp, 1980) of eight sessions of cognitive restructuring, *in vivo* exposure, or both combined, the results were more complex. Immediately after treatment, outcome resembled that of the earlier study; that is, cognitive restructuring apparently had little effect. However, one month after treatment, there was much less difference between the groups because further improvement had taken place in those who had received the cognitive restructuring treatment; this effect was seen particularly in ratings of phobic anxiety (see Figure 11.1). Unfortunately, the treatment that combined exposure with cognitive restructuring was no better than either alone. Thus it is not clear that cognitive restructuring adds to exposure treatment, but again, there are indications that exposure (as we have defined it) may not always be necessary for improvement. It is of interest that the effects of cognitive restructuring were not always immediately obvious; perhaps time is required, either to consolidate the cognitive changes induced, or to allow them to be translated into behavior. This possibility leaves unresolved the question of whether cognitive change may in some way reduce anxiety, as implied by the suggestion that phobics may add to their experience of anxiety by frightening thoughts. Alternatively,

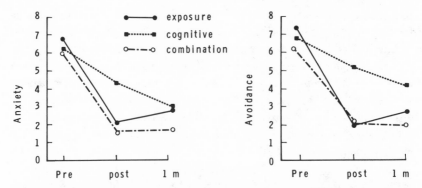

FIGURE 11.1. Changes in phobic anxiety and avoidance following exposure, cognitive restructuring, and a combination of both. From P. M. G. Emmelkamp, in A. Bellack, M. Hersen, and A. Kazdin (Eds.), *International handbook of behavior modification and therapy.* New York: Plenum Press, 1980. Reprinted by permission.

cognitive modification may be effective for a different reason: because it acts as an incentive, motivating patients to test themselves out in phobic situations.

## IMPLICATIONS FOR FUTURE RESEARCH

It appears that while we have an economical treatment that can be offered to agoraphobics with some confidence that it will be beneficial, we have only a very rudimentary understanding of how it works. It is clear that many now believe that cognitive theories will offer more satisfactory explanations of treatment mechanisms than did earlier noncognitive learning theories. Such ideas are attractive—and we have discussed some of them in the previous section—but as yet, they lack compelling empirical support as explanations for current therapies, and they have not led to the development of powerful new treatment techniques. Our understanding of the cognitive processes thought to be crucial to behavior change would be greatly increased by experimental assessments of the effectiveness of the manifestly cognitive aspects of exposure treatment (e.g., anxiety and panic management instructions); by the development of better measures of the cognitive variables that are thought to mediate behavior (e.g., expectancy); and above all by the development of cognitive therapies capable of producing powerful behavioral effects on agoraphobia.

It has to be acknowledged that a minority of patients fail to respond to exposure methods. We suggest that it would be appropriate to direct cognitive treatments at helping such patients. There is an obvious need for improvements in the treatment of these patients, and any gains made would be powerful evidence for cognitive theories and treatment methods. We would also suggest that further efforts be made along more traditional behavioral lines to explore the social situation of these patients, seeking information on factors that might maintain fearful and avoidant behavior. Another issue that may relate to the treatment of this subsample of patients is the use of antidepressant drugs in combination with behavior therapy. From the available evidence, it is not possible to draw firm conclusions on the use of drugs, and further studies are needed both of patients who are not responding to behavioral treatment and of agoraphobics in general. We hope that in future investigations of antidepressants, considerable attention will be paid to the measurement of possible treatment mechanisms such as alterations in mood or reduction in frequency of panic attacks. As well as increasing our understanding of the effects of antidepressants in agoraphobia, this information might also increase our knowledge of cognitive factors in other therapies in which similar mechanisms could be operating.

In writing this monograph, we have been impressed by the vigor with which the treatment of agoraphobia has been investigated, as well as by the comparative lack of studies on the etiology of the condition. In Chapter 3, we presented a model of the development of agoraphobia from which four main research topics readily arise: (1) the role of life events in setting a high level of background anxiety prior to the onset of agoraphobia; (2) the putative similarity between the early stages of agoraphobia and anxiety states; (3) the tendency of agoraphobics to attribute threat to immediate external stimuli; and (4) the tendency of agoraphobics to respond to such threats by dependent and/or avoidant behavior.

There are immense practical difficulties in testing etiological models of this kind. However, the model could at least be disconfirmed by the careful study of existing populations of agoraphobics and anxiety states. We are clearly predicting that agoraphobic patients attribute threatening events to the external environment and respond to these threatening events by dependent or avoidant behavior. If they were not to do so more than patients with generalized anxiety, the model would have to be modified. As we wrote in Chapter 3, studies of dependence in agoraphobia have not been illuminating—we believe partly because of an overwide concept of dependent and avoidant behavior. We see no reason that agoraphobics should be more dependent in a general sense than people with anxiety states; that is, agoraphobics should be as able to mend a fuse or cope with their child's school difficulties as well as those with other anxiety states. We do maintain that they will be more dependent in frightening situations. Therefore investigations should concentrate on their response to fear, either by examining their actual behavior in generally fearful situations or by questionnaire investigations of their beliefs about how they would or do respond in various life situations.

If such studies either confirm the model or lead to its replacement by a powerful alternative, then it might be worth mounting a prospective study, since this is the only way in which etiological questions can be convincingly answered. A prospective study of the kind necessary to test the model would inevitably be a large, difficult, and expensive undertaking. It would clearly be impractical, or at least wasteful, to investigate agoraphobia alone in this way, but agoraphobia could be usefully studied as part of a more wide-ranging study of mental health problems. A large-scale survey of an "at-risk" population—for example, women in their late teens or early 20s—would certainly provide enough subjects who would become agoraphobic over the next 10 years for an adequate investigation of the role of high levels of trait anxiety, external locus of control, and dependent or avoidant behavior. Testing the role of life events and the level of anxiety immediately before the onset of agoraphobia is much more difficult since it demands that patients with agoraphobia and anxiety states be interviewed at the onset of the condition or very shortly afterwards. Unless a prohibitively large sample were interviewed, we doubt whether sufficient patients could be collected for an adequate investigation of these issues. It might be more practical and more useful if a smaller sample were interviewed regularly for many years. This is clearly a daunting undertaking, but if it did succeed, our understanding of the causes, effects, and maintaining conditions of agoraphobia and anxiety states would be markedly increased.


## SOME GENERAL IMPLICATIONS OF OUR FINDINGS

From the beginning, our studies of agoraphobia have had two aims. The first is the obvious need to develop more effective treatment for a common and disabling disorder. The second is more general. We hoped that by studying agoraphobia, we should learn lessons that might apply more widely to the behavioral treatment of other conditions. The first aim has been discussed; before the book ends, we should attend briefly to the second.

The general lessons from this work are clear and can be stated briefly. First, progress in research on behavior therapy is more likely to be made when the aim is to identify the behavior that needs to be changed and the simplest procedures that are effective in bringing about change. The alternative, which is less satisfactory, has always attracted clinicians. It is the idea that if a simple treatment is found to have limited value, patients will benefit more if other procedures are added to it. It is a line of thought that is seen in the progressive elaboration of psychotherapeutic techniques, while in behavior therapy it is reflected in so-called multimodal treatment. Research into the treatment of agoraphobia shows, instead, the value of concentrating effort by eliminating techniques that are ineffective and then examining the precise conditions under which the remaining simple method (in this case, exposure) can be made to work effectively.

The second lesson is that having identified an effective simple method, the research worker has to consider whether patients are likely to be able or willing to carry it out. Poor results with behavior therapy are often due to a failure to carry out treatment, just as powerful drugs will have weak therapeutic effects if they are not taken persistently. We have shown how this failure can be analyzed as a behavioral problem in its own right and can in this way be overcome. It may arise partly because the patient does not understand clearly what he/she is required to do, or because he/she is poorly motivated to do it. The lessons we have learned about the delivery system that is needed for exposure treatment—the partner and the instruction manual—are likely to be just as relevant to problems such as the treatment of anxiety states by relaxation or anxiety management training or, away from psychiatric disorders, to those problems of medical rehabilitation in which patients may have to persist in repetitive and uninteresting exercises.

The final lesson from this work on agoraphobia concerns the value of an interchange between basic and clinical research. That laboratory findings can illuminate clinical problems is no new idea, but we would emphasize the value of a less-well-recognized form of research; that is, experiments carried out with patients, using good experimental methods to study short-term changes in behavior and symptoms. Information from these sources is often a much surer guide to action by the clinician than are the results of experiments with animals or even with so-called analogue populations. The substantial progress that has come from the research in several countries, directed toward the treatment of agoraphobia, suggests that an equally sustained and systematic attack on other behavioral problems would lead to comparable advances in the basic knowledge of psychopathology and in the care of patients.

# Appendix 1.
# Programmed Practice:
# Clients' Manual

## INTRODUCTION

This booklet is designed for people suffering from agoraphobia.[1] It has been written to help them understand their problem and find ways to help themselves in overcoming it.

When you have read this introduction, turn to the section headed "What is Agoraphobia?" where you will see a short text dealing with one aspect of the problem. Read this carefully and thoroughly. If you do not understand it clearly read it again more slowly.

When you understand the text, read the statement at the bottom of the page. Read the four alternative answers to each question and circle *one* that best completes the statement. Then turn over to the next page to see if you have answered correctly.[2] The *most* accurate alternative is always followed by the word *correct*.

If you have chosen an incorrect alternative, read the accompanying explanation. This tells you why we consider it less satisfactory than the one we have chosen as correct. Then turn back and read through the text and questions again. By doing this, you will be able to make sure that you understand each page before you turn to the next. This is very important. You must on no account omit the question at the bottom of each page.

If you have chosen the correct answer, you can turn immediately to the section headed "What Causes Agoraphobia? (I)." Repeat the same procedure with every page until you have mastered the whole booklet.

1. These self-help instructions are intended for use by professionals or under their direct guidance. The authors strongly recommend against their unsupervised applications and assume no responsibility for any effects resulting from such use.
2. This appendix is available as a separate offprint for clients. Because it is not desirable for clients to have the answers on the same page as text and questions, the answers in that version will appear on the next page.

Remember:

* Always circle your answer to each question *before* you turn to the next page to find the correct answer.
* Read the booklet several times to make sure that you understand everything and can remember the contents.
* If you do not remember everything, do not be disheartened; go back to the booklet and read it again.
* If you do not understand one of the points in the booklet, write it down and remember to ask your therapist the next time you meet.

## CONTENTS

WHAT IS AGORAPHOBIA?

An agoraphobic is someone who has a fear of going far from home, a fear of being alone or far from help, and a fear of crowded public places such as streets, stores, and buses.

Most agoraphobic people also fear that they will lose control over their own reactions, and that their fear will get completely out of control and lead to a panic attack or something worse.

Because of this fear, they tend to avoid places that could trigger it, and this avoidance tends to become a habit. Often they feel better with someone they know well, and so they come to depend on having a companion when they go out. Once a person regularly avoids going out alone or avoids many different places for this reason, he/she is said to have agoraphobia.

Agoraphobia is quite a common problem: about 1 in 160 people suffer from it. More than two-thirds of agoraphobics are women.

---

Someone with agoraphobia is likely to be afraid of:
  (a) Open spaces in the country.
  (b) Losing control in crowded public places.
  (c) Staying at home with someone.
  (d) Being with other people.

---

(a) *Open spaces in the country.*
Agoraphobia is often called a fear of open spaces but this is misleading. This fear is sometimes present, but so is a fear of small, enclosed spaces.

(b) *Losing control in a crowded public place.*
*Correct.* This common fear develops in most people with agoraphobia.

(c) *Staying at home with someone.*
Staying at home instead of going out is a common problem. However, agoraphobics are not usually afraid at home unless they are alone.

(d) *Being with other people.*
On the contrary, a companion—especially a familiar person—can prevent the fear, although crowds may be frightening.

## WHAT CAUSES AGORAPHOBIA? (I)

Agoraphobia is *not* connected with serious mental disease (such as schizophrenia), nor is it connected with any known physical illness.

It is caused, in the first place, when the body reacts to everyday situations as if they were dangerous and frightening. In the second place, it is caused by the worry caused by these strange feelings, and in the third place, by the fact that agoraphobics tend to avoid places connected with these feelings.

To understand this, think about the way your body reacts at a time of real danger—say, a near miss in what could have been a fatal accident. Your heart may beat hard and fast, your stomach may churn, you may sweat and tremble, and so on. The exact reaction varies from person to person, but it is usually strong enough to cause a feeling of "shock" after an accident.

In agoraphobia, it is as if this bodily reaction has become *oversensitive*, so that it tends to be triggered automatically, by quite ordinary situations that are not dangerous.

---

Agoraphobic panic is different from ordinary fear or shock because:
  (a) It can't be controlled very easily.
  (b) It causes bodily changes, such as your heart's beating faster.
  (c) It is an automatic bodily reaction.
  (d) It is the same as fear but without any real danger.

---

(a) *It can't be controlled very easily.*
No fear, whether agoraphobic or of other kinds, can be controlled easily.

(b) *It causes bodily changes.*
All kinds of fear, agoraphobic and others, can cause bodily changes, such as your heart beating faster.

(c) *It is an automatic bodily reaction.*
All kinds of fear, agoraphobic and others, involve an automatic bodily reaction.

(d) *It is the same as fear, but without any real danger.*
**Correct.** There are no obvious differences between the *experience* of extreme fear and agoraphobic panic, only between the *situations* that trigger them.

## WHAT CAUSES AGORAPHOBIA? (II)

It is not always possible to say what started the oversensitivity that leads to the first panic reaction. Sometimes it follows a physical illness or pregnancy, when physical resistance is low; sometimes it follows an emotional shock; and in some cases, it happens at a time of prolonged tension that has some other reason.

Whatever the cause, once it has taken place a few times, it starts to happen more frequently in certain places.

The reason for this is a special kind of learning called *conditioning*. To understand this, think of the reaction of a child when it meets a dog for the first time. If by bad luck the dog barks loudly and frightens the child, then the next time the child sees a dog, he/she may feel nervous and even run away.

*Conditioning* is the name given to the way that fearful reactions come to be associated or connected with particular things or places. This association is learned in a completely *automatic* way—it happens whether you want it to or not.

---

*Conditioning* means:
    (a) Association of a reaction with a situation.
    (b) Learning to be afraid.
    (c) An oversensitive state following an illness.
    (d) Learning that two things always go together.

---

(a) *Association of a reaction with a situation.*
**Correct.** *Conditioning* describes the way in which everyone learns to react automatically to particular things or places.

(b) *Learning to be afraid.*
Learning to be afraid of some situations would be an *example* of conditioning, but the question asked for the general meaning of *conditioning*.

(c) *An oversensitive state following an illness.*
No. This state may cause panic feelings, but the word *conditioning* refers to the way the feelings are later attached to particular things or places.

(d) *Learning that two things always go together.*
This is not quite accurate, since it does not indicate that reactions become *automatically* associated with particular things.

## WHAT CAUSES AGORAPHOBIA? (III)

The child's first reaction of fear to a dog is not abnormal since some dogs may be dangerous and it is best to learn caution. In time, provided the child meets friendly dogs and is not bitten, the automatically "conditioned" fear will die away. But if dogs are avoided after the first frightening encounter, the fear may persist. If this happens it can lead to a permanent fear of dogs—a "dog phobia."

In the case of agoraphobia, panic reactions become attached to particular situations (and ideas) by the same process of conditioning. Even after the "oversensitive" state that caused the fear reactions in the first place has died away, the *conditioned* fear keeps on. Since this fear results in the avoidance of places associated with these reactions, there is no reason for the phobia to get better.

---

If a child has been frightened by a large, fierce dog, would it be best to:
(a) Keep him/her away from dogs for a while.
(b) Tell him/her to be braver next time.
(c) Give him/her candy to cheer him/her up.
(d) Introduce him/her to a more gentle dog.

---

(a) *Keep him/her away from dogs for a while.*
If this is done, the conditioned fear is left untouched, and it may even get worse.

(b) *Tell him/her to be braver next time.*
Talking does not usually do anything to reduce conditioned fear. A different kind of experience with a dog is necessary.

(c) *Give him/her candy to cheer him/her up.*
This may cheer the child up, but it will not do anything to reduce the fear—unless perhaps you give the child candy when he/she is getting *nearer* to a dog.

(d) *Introduce him/her to a more gentle dog.*
*Correct.* This will reduce the conditioned fear and stop it from spreading to *all* dogs, without preventing the child from being appropriately cautious with fierce ones.

SUMMARY SO FAR

1. Agoraphobia usually starts with panic reactions coming "out of the blue."
2. They are more likely to happen when one is alone or away from home.
3. These reactions tend to be associated with the particular places where they happened.
4. This conditioning leads to avoidance of these places, which tends to become a habit.

---

Agoraphobia is:
   (a) A mental disease such as schizophrenia.
   (b) Due to physical illness.
   (c) A learned emotional reaction.
   (d) Caused by a lack of willpower.

---

(a) *A mental disease such as schizophrenia.*
No. The two things are quite different. Go back to "What Causes Agoraphobia?" and read it again.

(b) *Due to physical illness.*
The first panic attack may have followed a physical illness, but there is no reason to think that agoraphobics continue to be physically ill in any way. Go back to "What Causes Agoraphobia?" and read it again.

(c) *A learned emotional reaction.*
*Correct.* Although other kinds of *behavioral* learning occur later (like learning to avoid places), the emotional reaction is usually learned first.

(d) *Caused by lack of willpower.*
It makes no more sense to call it a lack of willpower than it does to say that about someone who jumps when there is a loud noise. Go back to "What Causes Agoraphobia?" and read it again.

WHAT KEEPS AGORAPHOBIA GOING? (I)

You might expect that if conditioned fear reactions were ignored and the person kept on going out, the reactions would gradually fade away. Why does this not happen in agoraphobia?

The main reason is that the natural reaction to feelings of panic that cannot be understood is to avoid the places in which they happen. Unfortunately, this seems to have the effect of actually *strengthening* the conditioned fear. The longer the avoidance goes on, the stronger it can become.

People often feel that they can help by getting things for an agoraphobic so that he/she doesn't have to go out. However, this only makes the habit of avoidance stronger.

It is very common to find that people with agoraphobia depend, for going out, on other people who are close to them. This is because a familiar, reassuring person can make frightening situations seem safer. The trouble is that depending on other people tends to become a habit, just as avoiding places does.

---

If you avoid a store where you had a panic attack:
 (a) You will find it more and more difficult to go back.
 (b) In time you will be able to go back without trouble.
 (c) You should wait until you are well before going back.
 (d) You should get someone else to go into the store for you.

---

(a) *You will find it more and more difficult to go back.*
**Correct.** Avoidance tends to strengthen conditioned fear.

(b) *In time you will be able to go back without trouble.*
No. Time is likely to have the opposite effect.

(c) *You should wait until you are well before going back.*
You are probably as ready to begin now as you will be. Waiting too long may make it more difficult.

(d) *You should get someone else to go to the store for you.*
If you do this, you will be helping to establish a habit of avoidance and the fear will grow stronger. You would *not* be helping yourself.

WHAT KEEPS AGORAPHOBIA GOING? (II)

When you are frightened by a real danger, your whole mind is usually occupied with *doing* something about it. In the case of agoraphobia, the same feeling of fear seems to start and keep on, for no reason at all. There seems to be nothing that can be *done* about it. For this reason, there is a tendency to dwell on the feelings themselves. This just makes them worse.

Agoraphobic people may feel dizzy or breathless, get a feeling of weakness in their legs, or experience their heart pounding. Some feel that everything seems unreal, like a dream. Worrying about these feelings tends to get them more firmly fixed, like a habit. It is only too easy to get in to the vicious circle of worrying and being *afraid of the feelings of fear* themselves. Some people think that they might make a fool of themselves in public, that they might faint or be sick, or collapse and perhaps injure themselves. Some even fear permanent loss of control or insanity.

In actual fact, agoraphobics run no more risk of any of these things than anyone else does.

---

Agoraphobic symptoms often include:
   (a) Acting insanely.
   (b) Feeling faint or strange.
   (c) Collapse through physical overstrain.
   (d) No special feelings.

---

(a) *Acting insanely.*
Agoraphobics often fear that they will act insanely but never do.

(b) *Feeling faint or strange.*
**Correct.** These feelings and others of the same sort are very common, and although alarming, they are quite harmless.

(c) *Collapse through physical overstrain.*
Agoraphobics often fear that they may collapse, but they are no more likely to do so than anyone else. Often they get little exercise, so they *feel* exhausted when they practice going out, but this does no harm.

(d) *No special feelings.*
With the exception of those who have given up and never go out, agoraphobics *do* experience feelings that are unusual for most people in ordinary circumstances.

## HOW CAN AGORAPHOBIA BE TREATED? (I)

If you have followed so far, you already have some idea of how agoraphobia should be treated—it is just the opposite of the way it is kept going.

The most important step is to stop avoiding the feared places. It is only by gradual practice *in* these places that the fear will be overcome. And because the fear has been developing for a long time, you will need a long time to get rid of it. This means that you will have to practice facing the feared situations over and over again until your confidence returns. In other words, a person with agoraphobia must get into the *daily* habit of leaving home to practice walking, going into stores, traveling on buses, or facing the feared things, whatever they are. Of course, you cannot expect all these things to be done at once; each situation has to be practiced in stages, one step at a time. You build up confidence by doing the easier things first before gradually doing more and more difficult ones.

---

If you succeed in going to a particular place that you have avoided for some time:
- (a) It won't give you any more trouble.
- (b) It will be even more difficult the next time.
- (c) It won't have made any difference one way or the other.
- (d) It will probably be slightly easier the next time.

---

(a) *It won't give you any more trouble.*
Fears that have got worse over a period of years won't go away as quickly as that.

(b) *It will be even more difficult the next time.*
No. It is usually only the experience of panic attacks or the avoidance of a place that makes it more difficult to go there. Go back to "What Keeps Agoraphobia Going?" and read it again.

(c) *It won't have made any difference one way or the other.*
It may not make any obvious immediate difference in every case, but on average it is likely to *reduce* the fear.

(d) *It will probably be slightly easier the next time.*
**Correct.** It will not always be obvious right away, since there are bound to be ups and downs. But on the *average*, it will tend to get easier each time.

## HOW CAN AGORAPHOBIA BE TREATED? (II)

Practice in facing situations that have been avoided for a long time is often frightening. Therefore you will have to expect some fear and try to find ways to cope with it. This does not mean forcing yourself to the point of total panic all the time, but it does mean that the main point of practice is to experience *some* fear without overreacting and making it worse. Given time, and provided that you don't run away from it, the fear will always fade away.

When doing something difficult for the first time, it occasionally helps to take a tranquilizer (if one has been prescribed) just beforehand. However, it is usually better to manage without pills. If you do use them, it should be only the first time you tackle something that you have been avoiding.

Similarly, it is *not* a good idea to rely on help from others, if this means that they are doing things for you. This can only lead you to depend on them. Equally, well-meaning sympathy only encourages you to dwell on your problems. Instead, you must do something about them.

---

Before practicing you should:
   (a) Always take a tranquilizer.
   (b) Avoid taking a tranquilizer if possible; take it only when you have to practice something new or difficult.
   (c) Avoid tranquilizers completely.
   (d) Take a tranquilizer if you feel panicky when going out.

---

(a) *Always take a tranquilizer.*
No. If you take a tranquilizer every time, you will not learn to rely on yourself.

(b) *Avoid taking a tranquilizer if possible; take it only when you have to practice something new or difficult.*
**Correct.** A tranquilizer can help you tackle, for the first time, items that are particularly difficult. However, you should repeat the item without the aid of a tranquilizer as soon as possible.

(c) *Avoid tranquilizers completely.*
No. There are occasions when a tranquilizer can help you.

(d) *Take a tranquilizer if you feel panicky when going out.*
No. By then it is too late for it to have an effect. In any case, it is better for you to learn to cope with the anxiety in the way we explain later.

SUMMARY OF TREATMENT PLAN

1. Practice facing the feared situations every day.
2. Plan progress from easier to difficult situations.
3. Expect to experience *some* fear when practicing; the point of the exercise is to cope with the feelings instead of overreacting to them.
4. Use tranquilizers only when it is necessary to help with new and particularly difficult situations.
5. Avoid relying on others or dwelling on your own problems and symptoms. Concentrate on help that leads to doing things for yourself.

---

Which would be the *wrong* thing to recommend for someone with agoraphobia?
  (a) Doing things one step at a time.
  (b) Taking tranquilizers before occasional practice sessions.
  (c) Practicing going out every day.
  (d) Having help from others with things like shopping.

---

(a) *Doing things one step at a time.*
This is a *good* thing to recommend for someone with agoraphobia, as it builds up confidence for more difficult items. The question asked which was the wrong thing.

(b) *Taking tranquilizers before occasional practice sessions.*
This does help when particularly difficult items are practiced for the first time, so it cannot be the wrong thing to recommend.

(c) *Practicing going out every day.*
It is only by practice in facing the feared situations that the fear will be overcome, and it is important to get into the habit of doing this daily, so this *cannot* be wrong.

(d) *Having help from others with things like shopping.*
*Correct.* It is *not* helpful in the long run to get someone else to do the shopping. It simply makes it easy for you to stay at home and makes the habit of avoidance stronger.

## TREATMENT IN PRACTICE: STEP 1

To begin with, you will have to decide exactly what you are aiming for. In other words, what are the treatment *targets?*

This is not as easy as it sounds. It is no good saying something like "I just want to get better." You must decide on *specific* descriptions of *behavior.*

Examples could be "Going by myself to the supermarket for groceries," or "Going alone by bus to the school to meet the children."

Make a written list of all the things that you would like to do if you were completely recovered.

Do not forget difficult things (such as long trips) that you have avoided for many years. Anything you think you want to do someday and cannot do now because of your phobia can be put in the list as a long-term target.

Lastly, you must put all the items on the list in order, from the least difficult to the most difficult. Make a careful note of this order—you will be using it later.

---

Which of the following would be a useful description of a treatment target?

(a) Go out for a walk.

(b) Practice going out every day.

(c) Walk alone to the school.

(d) Try to keep calm when shopping in the supermarket.

---

(a) *Go out for a walk.*
This is not quite clear enough. How long should the walk last? How far should you go before you feel that you have succeeded?

(b) *Practice going out every day.*
Of course you should practice going out every day, but this is not really a treatment *target.* It is a habit that you want to adopt.

(c) *Walk alone to the school.*
**Correct.** This is a useful description of a treatment target. It is precise, so that you will know when you have successfully completed the item.

(d) *Try to keep calm when shopping in the supermarket.*
Telling yourself to "try to keep calm" isn't a useful description of a treatment target. It is too vague for you to know exactly what to *do.*

WHY ARE SPECIFIC DESCRIPTIONS OF BEHAVIOR IMPORTANT?

Agoraphobia cannot be treated like a physical disease. You have to change in the way you *behave*. You can think of the phobia as showing itself in three main ways: *feelings* (of fear); *thoughts* (about what awful things might happen); and *behavior* (avoiding things). Of course, these are all connected with each other, but the only way to start things moving in the right direction is by changing the *behavior*. This will lead to changes in thoughts and feelings later on.

It is because you have to change your behavior that you must have very specific descriptions of what it is you are to change. Your descriptions must be specific so that you avoid misunderstanding about what is to be practiced. And you must not be in doubt and must not be able to deceive yourself about whether something has been done successfully or not.

Provided your list includes enough specific behaviors, you will be able to use them to keep a careful track of your progress as treatment continues.

---

Which of the following would be the best target for an agoraphobic person?
  (a) Start practice in going shopping.
  (b) Go to the local supermarket alone on a Wednesday morning, when it is least crowded.
  (c) Find ways to make yourself feel differently about crowded stores.
  (d) None of these.

---

(a) *Start practice in going shopping.*
This is a good thing to do, but it is not specific enough.

(b) *Go to the local supermarket alone on a Wednesday morning, when it is least crowded.*
*Correct.* This target makes clear exactly what you have to do.

(c) *Find ways to make yourself feel differently about crowded stores.*
No. this is not a *behavioral* target. Of course, you want to feel differently, but you can achieve this only by practicing new behaviors.

(d) *None of these.*
No. One of these *would* be a good way to deal with a fear of crowded stores.

### TREATMENT IN PRACTICE: STEP 2 (I)

It is very important that you set aside adequate time for practice *every day.*

Start with the easiest item on the list that you *cannot* do at the moment. Let us suppose that this is "Walking alone to the supermarket for groceries." Begin practice in walking *toward* the supermarket every day. Never mind whether you actually get there or not at first. Make a careful note of how far you get each time.

It is not so very important to reach the supermarket right away. However, it is important to get into the habit of daily practice in *trying* to get there because this is the opposite of avoidance.

------------

Daily practice in learning to overcome avoidance is important because:
  (a) If several days go by without practice, it may get harder.
  (b) It builds confidence for harder items later.
  (c) With each practice, the fear will tend to get less.
  (d) All of these.

------------

(a) *If several days go by without practice, it may get harder.*
It is true that by not practicing for several days, you learn to avoid the feared situations, and this may increase the fear again. However, daily practice is also important for other reasons.

(b) *It builds confidence for harder items later.*
Success with easier items does build confidence for attempting more difficult ones later. Daily practice is the best way to achieve this, but increased confidence is not the only advantage of daily practice.

(c) *With each practice, the fear will tend to get less.*
Regular practice in going out will gradually reduce the fear you feel. However, daily practice is helpful in other ways as well.

(d) *All of these.*
**Correct.** All of these are reasons that you should practice daily.

TREATMENT IN PRACTICE: STEP 2 (II)

Repeat each exercise several times to find out if you can gradually do more each time. You must expect some ups and downs from day to day, depending on how you feel. So keep going for several days before deciding whether there are any signs of improvement. To know this, you will have to keep a careful check of how *far* you get and how *long* you are out.

If you succeed in completing the item, do not assume that it is finished. Try it a few more times to make sure.

If you continue to be successful, move on to the next, more difficult item. If you do not seem to be making any progress, despite honestly trying your hardest, you should move to Step 3 in these instructions.

---

If you succeed the first time you practice an item, you should:
  (a) Try it again tomorrow.
  (b) Try a more difficult one.
  (c) Try an easier one.
  (d) Congratulate yourself and have a well-earned rest.

---

(a) *Try it again tomorrow.*
**Correct.** Now that you have achieved the item once, you should repeat it a few times to check it and to increase your confidence.

(b) *Try a more difficult one.*
A single success does not mean that the item is finished. You should repeat it a few times to make sure.

(c) *Try an easier one.*
No. There would be no point in going back when you are winning.

(d) *Congratulate yourself and have a well-earned rest.*
No. By "resting" you are avoiding going out, and this is just what you must not do.

TREATMENT IN PRACTICE: STEP 3 (I)

If your progress has come to a halt, try to find out why. It may be that the item you have chosen is to difficult at the moment, or it may require too big a jump from what you have been doing.

First, check to see whether the original order of difficulty of your list has changed for some reason. You may find that some items that seemed very difficult at first are now easier than the one you have been attempting.

If you find that this is not the case and that the easiest item not yet done is still the one you have been trying, you will have to invent some practice items *in between* where you are now and the next target, to bridge the gap.

Suppose that after (1) "Walking alone to the supermarket" has been done successfully, the next one should be (2) "Going by bus to the school." Your job is to invent some items in between (1) and (2) in difficulty.

---

Which might bridge the gap between "Walking to the supermarket" and "Going alone by bus to the school"?

(a) Going with someone by bus to the school.

(b) Going alone for just one stop at first.

(c) Going alone, and being met at the other end.

(d) All of these.

---

(a) *Going with someone by bus to the school.*
This is one way of bridging the gap, but other items might be used as well.

(b) *Going alone for just one stop at first.*
Traveling for just one stop would be a useful in-between item, but it is not the only possibility.

(c) *Going alone, and being met at the other end.*
This item could be used, but it might be too difficult at first. Other, slightly easier items might be needed as well.

(d) *All of these.*
*Correct.* All of these would be ways of bridging the gap between the items, as they are more difficult than (1) but less difficult than (2).

## TREATMENT IN PRACTICE: STEP 3 (II)

These in-between items will not necessarily be useful for their own sake. It might not be useful, for example, to travel on a bus for just one stop. However, the point is, of course, that they build the confidence you need to practice later items (which are useful, and which will seem much too difficult at first).

It is obviously very important to choose in-between items carefully, as well as to decide how many might be needed and how many times to practice them. However, you will have to be prepared to be flexible about these items. If you experience persistent difficulty in making progress with the in-between items chosen at first, try alternatives.

Once the target item has been successfully completed a few times, it will probably not be necessary to practice the in-between items anymore. However, at regular intervals, the target item must be practiced. Better still make it a part of everyday life —a habit.

---

Practice items between target behaviors are useful because:
   (a) They are slightly easier than the last target item successfully practiced.
   (b) They build confidence.
   (c) They bridge any large gaps in difficulty between targets.
   (d) All of these.

---

(a) *They are slightly easier than the last target item successfully practiced.*
No. They should be slightly *more difficult* than the last target item successfully practiced.

(b) *They build confidence.*
It is true that practicing in-between targets builds confidence, but that is not an end in itself. There is a more specific reason for using them.

(c) *They bridge any large gaps in difficulty between targets.*
*Correct.* Because they bridge any large gaps in difficulty, smooth progress can be continued and confidence increases until it is time to try the next target.

(d) *All of these.*
No. Not all of the answers are correct.

TREATMENT IN PRACTICE: STEP 4

Suppose that progress seems to be held up because you are experiencing too much fear during practice or just before it. It may be useful to take a single dose of a tranquilizer (provided your doctor has prescribed one) shortly before the practice.

Find out when the medication seems to have the most effect (this might be anywhere from 10 minutes to a few hours after you have taken it). Note also when you generally feel most tense: before going, on the way, or coming back. Take the medication so that the maximum effect comes at the time when you are likely to feel at your worst.

*Don't* exceed the maximum dose recommended. Don't drink anything alcoholic. And look out for side effects like drowsiness. These might not matter, but drowsiness, for example, would be important if you were to do any driving.

Otherwise you can start with a reasonably large dose, and if this overcomes the problem, then you can gradually bring the dose down. You should ask your doctor if you are unsure about the dose to take.

---

Suppose you succeed with practice after taking several pills but then find that you cannot manage without any. You should:
(a) Go on to the next most difficult item.
(b) Repeat the same item several times.
(c) Stop practice for a while.
(d) Gradually reduce the dose while practicing the same item.

---

(a) *Go on to the next most difficult item.*
As a rule, you should not go on to a more difficult item until the current one has been successfully completed. Going on will only lead to more difficulties.

(b) *Repeat the same item several times.*
When an item has been achieved for the first time, it is useful to repeat it. However, when tranquilizers have been used, simply repeating the item with the same dose is not the most useful thing to do.

(c) *Stop practice for a while.*
No. There is no reason to think that this will help, and it may be more difficult to start again after a pause.

(d) *Gradually reduce the dose while practicing the same item.*
**Correct.** By repeating the item with a gradual reduction in dose, you should eventually be able to do it without any tranquilizers at all.

SUMMARY OF TREATMENT IN PRACTICE

1. Decide on target behaviors.
2. Start practicing with the least difficult items.
3. Repeat each item a few times; if successful, move on.
4. If progress stops, find some in-between items.
5. Use tranquilizers only for new or difficult items; then reduce the dose.
6. Try to establish the habit of practice every day.

———————————

Which is a correct description of treatment practice?
   (a) Try each item once; if successful, move on.
   (b) Decide on target behaviors, and practice one every day.
   (c) Start practicing with easier items, and progress to more difficult ones.
   (d) Use tranquilizers during all treatment practice sessions.

———————————

(a) *Try each item once; if successful, move on.*
No. Each item should be practiced more than once before you move on.

(b) *Decide on target behaviors, and practice one every day.*
It is essential to practice every day, but it is sometimes necessary to use items "in between" targets.

(c) *Start practicing with easier items, and progress to more difficult ones.*
*Correct.* It is important to move from less difficult to more difficult items as this method helps to build up confidence for the more difficult ones.

(d) *Use tranquilizers during all treatment practice sessions.*
Tranquilizers should be used only for difficult practice sessions, not for *all* sessions.

## COPING WITH FEELINGS OF PANIC (I)

As was mentioned earlier, panic feelings at the beginning of the phobia seem to come "out of the blue." Later on, panic is often triggered by the (conditioned) fear reaction to some places or situations. These reactions die down quite quickly—if they are allowed to. Usually they are kept going by the alarming thoughts they cause (fear of the feelings of fear) and by attempts at avoidance. The best advice—and the most difficult to follow—is "Let it happen and wait for it to pass."

Practicing in stages and the occasional use of tranquilizers make attacks of panic unlikely, but, of course, some fear must be expected. After all, everybody gets twinges of fear and other unpleasant feelings sometimes. More than this, it is part of recovery from agoraphobia to accept these unpleasant feelings for what they are and to cope with them—without running away or giving up.

---

Which of these is likely to cause or contribute to a panic attack?
   (a) The conditioned fear reaction to certain places.
   (b) Worry about strange feelings during practice.
   (c) Thinking that the fear is going to get out of control.
   (d) All of these.

---

(a) *The conditioned fear reaction to certain places.*
The conditioned fear reaction to certain places is likely to trigger panic feelings, but other things contribute as well.

(b) *Worry about strange feelings during practice.*
Worry about strange feelings often makes panic feelings worse, but other things are also involved.

(c) *Thinking that the fear is going to get out of control.*
Thinking that the fear will get out of control certainly does make panic feelings worse, although other things are also involved.

(d) *All of these.*
*Correct.* Each of the things described can play a part in bringing about a panic attack.

## COPING WITH FEELINGS OF PANIC (II)

At the beginning, agoraphobia was described as a fear of going out alone. Just as important, it is a fear that the symptoms of fear will themselves get out of control. For this reason, an essential part of practice must be to deliberately do things that produce *some* fear in order to practice coping with it. This does not mean getting into a total panic, but it does mean that the most useful practice involves doing things that bring on the feelings, coping with them, and going on. Practicing things that don't cause any fear at all—to make sure of them—is also helpful. However, this is not how real progress is made.

It is important to remember that one of the purposes of practice is to learn a new attitude of mind toward panic feelings. This attitude means no longer trying to avoid them at all costs, but going out to meet them. You must deal with these feelings as much as possible and also accept the remaining feelings as natural, if unpleasant, bodily feelings.

---

Which would you say indicates most progress?
(a) Doing something new without any trouble the first time.
(b) Trying something new even if you have to come back because of tension.
(c) Doing something new despite experiencing some panic at first.
(d) Doing something new but finishing in a total panic.

---

(a) *Doing something new without any trouble for the first time.*
This is obviously encouraging but does not necessarily mean that it will be as easy every time. Moreover, you may not be confident of it when not at your best.

(b) *Trying something new even if you have to come back because of tension.*
This is no indication of progress, since this was probably what happened when the agoraphobia was getting worse.

(c) *Doing something new despite experiencing some panic at first.*
*Correct.* When you can manage this, you know you are making progress both in what you can do and in coping with fear.

(d) *Doing something new but finishing in a total panic.*
This could be a step forward or a step back, depending on whether you can do it again soon with less panic. In general, you should avoid leaving off when still in a panic.

## COPING WITH FEELINGS OF PANIC (III)

Suppose you are out practicing when suddenly you feel frightened by a strange feeling. Do *not* immediately go home. Try to find somewhere to rest, sit down somewhere, walk back a little way—do anything that will help you *stay* in or near the place where the feeling started.

Remind yourself that these are just unpleasant bodily feelings that you had expected anyway. *They cannot harm you.* They do not mean that something awful will happen. It won't. Don't be fooled into thinking that way.

In time, the feelings will go down. Although you can then go back home, it would be better to go on practicing for a little while before doing so. Fortunately, once panic has come and gone, it is unlikely to come back again for a while. For this reason, you can sometimes make a panic attack an occasion for more progress.

The golden rule is to try never to leave a situation until the fear is going *down*.

------

If you become frightened in a store, it would be best to:
  (a) Try to snap out of it.
  (b) Get home as soon as possible.
  (c) Go to another store.
  (d) Stay until you feel better.

------

(a) *Try to snap out of it.*
Yes, of course you should, but the question was getting at something more specific.

(b) *Get home as soon as possible.*
Going home immediately might make avoidance more likely the next time, because you have "learned" that only after going home does the fear go down.

(c) *Go to another store.*
Going to another store might help, provided that it is nearby. There is a danger, however, that you will learn to be afraid of, and avoid, the first store.

(d) *Stay until you feel better.*
**Correct.** If it is possible to stay until the fear goes down, this might make it easier for you to cope next time.

When panic starts, sensible thinking stops. You cannot depend on being able to think very clearly at the time. For this reason, you should read through the 10 rules that follow very carefully before practicing, so that they are clear in your mind. When you feel panicky, run through them again. It is a good idea to make a copy of the shorter list below to carry with you to read at the time. If you find other ideas that help, add them to the list.

Below is a shortened version of the rules that follow. These are designed to act as reminders. First, read the rules in full, then read the shortened form and see if you can remember when using only the reminders to prompt you.

1. The feelings are normal bodily reactions.
2. They are not harmful.
3. Do not add frightening thoughts.
4. Describe what is happening.
5. Wait for fear to pass.
6. Notice when it fades.
7. It is an opportunity for progress.
8. Think of what you have done.
9. Plan what to do next.
10. Then start off slowly.

TEN RULES FOR COPING WITH PANIC

1. Remember that the feelings are nothing more than an exaggeration of the normal bodily reactions to stress.
2. They are not in the least harmful or dangerous—just unpleasant. Nothing worse will happen.
3. Stop adding to panic with frightening thoughts about what is happening and where it might lead.
4. Notice what is really happening in your body right now, not what you fear *might* happen.
5. Wait and give the fear time to pass. Do not fight it or run away from it. Just accept it.
6. Notice that once you stop adding to it with frightening thoughts, the fear starts to fade by itself.
7. Remember that the whole point of practice is to learn how to cope with fear—without avoiding it. So this is an opportunity to make progress.
8. Think about the progress you have made so far, despite all the difficulties. Think how pleased you will be when you succeed this time.
9. When you begin to feel better, look around you, and start to plan what to do next.
10. When you are ready to go on, start off in an easy, relaxed way. There is no need for effort or hurry.

SETBACKS

Hardly anyone recovers from agoraphobia without having at least one "setback." Feelings vary, sometimes from day to day, and what you did successfully yesterday may seem impossible today. Even then, you could make real progress. What counts is how you cope with whatever feelings you experience. So, a little done on a bad day can be worth more than a lot done on a good day.

Most people feel that they have their worst setbacks after severe panics, especially if they ran away before the fear started going down. If this happens and you feel that you are back to "square one," do not give up. Simply try again the next day, preferably after taking a tranquilizer. If you do this, you should find that the lost ground can be made up quite quickly. Provided that you do not give up when things look black, your chances of eventual recovery are very good indeed.

---

You are on a bus. In a panic, you find yourself getting off earlier than planned. You should:

(a) Force yourself to get on the next bus.

(b) Try again, soon, possibly after taking a tranquilizer.

(c) Try an easier "in-between" item.

(d) All of these.

---

(a) *Force yourself to get on the next bus.*
This sometimes works but has some dangers. If the same thing happens again, it might get more and more difficult to go on practicing.

(b) *Try again soon, possibly after taking a tranquilizer.*
Correct. You should, of course, try not to get off the bus in the first place. However, once this has happened, it would be best to try again when you are calmer.

(c) *Try an easier "in-between" item.*
This is one possibility, but there is something else that you could try first.

(d) *All of these.*
No. Some are not advisable.

SUMMARY: COPING WITH FEELINGS OF PANIC

1. Expect some fear, encourage it to happen sometimes, and learn ways of coping with it.
2. Try to stay in or near the place where it started. Rest somewhere, and wait for it to pass.
3. Go back slowly a short way if necessary, but don't rush away.
4. Remind yourself of the 10 rules for dealing with panic.
5. When the fear goes down, continue practice if possible.
6. If you have to return home before the fear dies away, try to go back soon.
7. Some setbacks are inevitable. Expect them and don't give up.

---

The best way to cope with panic during practice is to:
   (a) Continue practice without stopping.
   (b) Let it happen and wait for it to pass.
   (c) Go home and relax.
   (d) Take a tranquilizer as soon as possible.

---

(a) *Continue practice without stopping.*
This might work, but there is a risk that the panic will increase until it is impossible to do anything except go home.

(b) *Let it happen and wait for it to pass.*
*Correct.* This is always the best course, although it will need persistent practice to learn how to do it.

(c) *Go home and relax.*
No. This should be avoided if at all possible. If you go home, you will probably need to repeat the practice soon with a tranquilizer.

(d) *Take a tranquilizer as soon as possible.*
This is unlikely to work fast enough to help right away, although it could be used before the next practice.

## PLANNING FOR THE LONG RUN

Many people find that their difficulties in going out have progressively cut them off from friends, social activities, and other outings that they used to enjoy. For this reason, they settle into a routine that centers on the home, leaving no time for anything else. An essential part of recovery is to change this routine completely and to make time for developing interests outside your home. You must start to visit friends, join clubs or classes, and, best of all, find a job. These are not things to do later on; they are important ways of helping yourself *now*. They provide regular opportunities for practice in going out and meeting people, quite apart from the satisfaction that they will give you in themselves.

Always try to use visits or outings as practice, by varying and extending what you do. You may do anything from going to a further store to going off alone when out on a trip with others. Once going out has changed from something to be avoided to an opportunity to practice, you have taken the most important step toward recovery.

---

A job or outside interest is important because:
  (a) It provides regular practice in going out.
  (b) It is a source of satisfaction away from home.
  (c) Meeting new situations and people helps break the habit of avoidance.
  (d) All of these.

---

(a) *It provides regular practice in going out.*
This is one of the main reasons, although there are others.

(b) *It is a source of satisfaction away from home.*
This is an important aspect of a job or outside interest, but there are other more direct effects that are just as important.

(c) *Meeting new situations and people helps break the habit of avoidance.*
This is one of the important advantages of a job or outside interest, although there are other important aspects.

(d) *All of these.*
**Correct.** Several different reasons add together to make getting a job and developing outside interests important aims.

## SUMMARY OF TREATMENT

1. Practice in facing the situations you fear will help you to regain your lost confidence. It is important for you to practice regularly, even if only for short periods at a time.

2. Start practicing with the easiest situations on the list of things that you are avoiding at the moment. Move on to the next situation when you have completed the first one successfully.

3. Feelings of panic may occur from time to time, but it is important that you face them without running away. Remember that learning to cope with fear, rather than just avoiding it, is the main aim of treatment.

4. At times, it may seem that you are not progressing as fast as you would like. You may even experience occasional setbacks. Don't worry—with regular practice you are bound to overcome your difficulties in the long run.

# Appendix 2.
# Programmed Practice: Partners' Manual

## INTRODUCTION

This booklet is designed as a guide for the relative or friend of someone suffering from the problem called *agoraphobia*.[1] Although agoraphobics can do a great deal to help themselves, the right kind of support and encouragement from others is extremely valuable. For this reason, you may well be in a position to help a great deal. To understand the nature of the problem you must first read Appendix 1, that is, the booklet that the agoraphobic person has received. You should then go on to this booklet for details of what you can do to help.

Because most, although by no means all, agoraphobics are married, this part is addressed mainly to spouses. However, it could be just as useful to any friend or relative of a person who has the problem. Remember to try to answer the questions at the bottom of each page before you turn over. Always check your answer.[2]

## CONTENTS

1. These self-help instructions are intended for use by professionals or under their direct guidance. The authors strongly recommend against their unsupervised applications and assume no responsibility for any effects resulting from such use.
2. This appendix is available as a separate offprint for partners. Because it is not desirable for partners to have the answers on the same page as text and questions, the answers in that version will appear on the next page.

## WHY YOUR HELP IS NEEDED

What you have already read in Appendix 1 could all be done by the agoraphobic person. You may think that if any extra help is needed, it should be given by qualified people, such as doctors or social workers. This is not true. In the long run, it is the people who are close to an agoraphobic who can help most.

Often there are special difficulties connected with, say, journeys from home that you know about, but other people do not. When treatment is done away from home (e.g., at a hospital), any improvement may disappear when the person returns home.

You may feel that advice from doctors would carry more weight. However, the way in which people behave and feel is influenced most by the people who are close to them. Because we are treating agoraphobia as a learned emotional reaction rather than as a *disease*, your influence is most important.

---

Your help is important because:
- (a) You know more about special problems.
- (b) Practice is best done from home.
- (c) Your influence counts more in the long run.
- (d) All of these.

---

(a) *You know more about special problems.*
This is one reason that your help is important, but there are others.

(b) *Practice is best done from home.*
Practice is best done from the home, because that is where the learning took place, but there are other ways in which your help is important.

(c) *Your influence is most important in the long run.*
Your influence is very important, and you are with the agoraphobic person much more than any doctor could be. However, your help is also important in other ways.

(d) *All of these.*
**Correct.** All of these are ways in which your help is important.

HOW OTHER PEOPLE BECOME INVOLVED

Unlike a disease, agoraphobia always depends in part on things that other people do, often with the best of intentions. For example, people with agoraphobia often depend a lot for getting out on another person who comes with them. The trouble is that depending on others in this way tends to become a habit.

It can be very difficult to discourage this dependence. For example, if a husband worries about his wife's health, he might think of her as an invalid who needs to be looked after and kept at home. Sometimes it can be rather reassuring to know that a person depends on you to get out at all. Or it might be quite convenient for the family for one person to stay at home all day.

There are many other ways in which people can encourage agoraphobics to depend on them, without realizing it. In this way, these people help to keep the problem going.

_____

Agoraphobics tend to depend on others because:
  (a) They feel safer with familiar people.
  (b) Other people don't always encourage self-help and independence.
  (c) It is one way of avoiding the most frightening situations.
  (d) All of these.

_____

(a) *They feel safer with other people.*
Yes, this is one reason that dependence develops, but there are other reasons as well.

(b) *Other people don't always encourage self-help and independence.*
This is often why agoraphobics find it difficult to stop being dependent. However, dependence develops for other reasons as well.

(c) *It is one way of avoiding the most frightening situations.*
Yes, depending on others does mean that going out alone is avoided. However, this is not a complete explanation.

(d) *All of these.*
**Correct.** At different times in different people, all of these things can play a part in making agoraphobics become dependent on others.

GIVING THE RIGHT KIND OF HELP

Many of the things that people do to be helpful, such as doing the shopping because the agoraphobic finds it frightening, don't really help at all in the long run. Making it easier for the agoraphobic to stay at home just makes the habit of avoidance, and the fear, grow stronger. To be really helpful, you have to find ways of helping the person make efforts at getting out—even if the change seems to come slowly.

It is easy to feel impatient if things seem to be moving slowly and even more so after a setback. But that is just when your encouragement will be most needed. Understanding and sympathy are important, too, but that does not mean that it helps to talk too much about the agoraphobic person's unpleasant feelings, since that may only keep them going. Praise for the agoraphobic's own efforts and reassurance that nothing too awful can happen are much more important.

But even more important than talking about practice is doing it—and as often as possible.

———————————

If the agoraphobic almost managed to get to a store that has been avoided, you should:
 (a) Say how pleased you are and suggest another try.
 (b) Tell the person not to make a fuss until he/she has succeeded.
 (c) Find out whether the agoraphobic has felt any strange, panicky feelings.
 (d) Advise a rest from trying that store for a while.

———————————

(a) *Say how pleased you are and suggest another try.*
*Correct.* It is important to encourage every effort, and several attempts may be necessary before success is seen.

(b) *Tell the person not to make a fuss until he/she has succeeded.*
He/she may not have succeeded in getting there, but the attempt has been made and it should be praised.

(c) *Find out whether the agoraphobic felt any strange, panicky feelings.*
No, as this will only cause the person to think about any unpleasant feelings that may have arisen and keep them going.

(d) *Advise a rest from trying that store for a while.*
Avoiding the shop again may increase the agoraphobic's fear of it. It certainly won't make it any easier the next time.

### WORKING TOGETHER TO OVERCOME THE PROBLEM (I)

In the rest of this manual, we refer to the agoraphobic person you are helping as your partner. At each step in the plan described earlier, there are some particular points where your help may be very important.

Before deciding on treatment targets, discussion may help in finding items that you both agree would be useful. You may be able to suggest targets that have been avoided so long that they are being overlooked. But remember that in the end, your partner must choose the targets him/herself.

Find out which target seems right to begin practicing on. Do this from what you know, and from how your partner feels about it. It should not be too easy (i.e., not something your partner can do already), nor too difficult (something your partner doesn't feel ready to try yet). It should be somewhere between.

If it is something you can do together, then it may be a good idea to start that way and gradually move your partner toward doing it alone (see "Suggestions for Practice Items" at the end of this booklet).

Every day, ask what practice has been done and make a point of showing that you are pleased with the effort your partner is making.

---

Which would be the *wrong* thing to recommend for someone with agoraphobia?

(a) Doing things one step at a time.

(b) Having someone help by doing the shopping.

(c) Practicing going out every day.

(d) Having firm encouragement from others.

---

(a) *Doing things one step at a time.*
This is a *good* thing to recommend for someone with agoraphobia, as it builds up confidence for more difficult items.

(b) *Having someone help by doing the shopping.*
**Correct.** It is *not* helpful in the long run to do shopping for an agoraphobic. It simply makes it easier for the person to stay at home, and it makes the habit of avoidance stronger.

(c) *Practicing going out every day.*
It is only by practice in facing the feared situations that the fear will be overcome. It is important to get into the habit of doing this daily, so this cannot be *wrong*.

(d) *Having firm encouragement from others.*
This is important, as practice can often be difficult and boring. Encouragement helps the agoraphobic to keep trying, so this cannot be the *wrong* thing to do.

WORKING TOGETHER TO OVERCOME THE PROBLEM (II)

To keep you in touch with the practice that your partner does alone, it is very important to ask him/her to keep a diary (if this is not being done already). Also ask your partner to note down every day the length of any journeys and the destination. If you keep a list of agreed practice targets, then you can check each of them off every time the diary record shows that it has been achieved. Once your partner has managed a target several times, you could ask whether he/she feels ready to try something more (don't forget to congratulate your partner at the same time!).

Try not to complain or show impatience if progress is slow or variable. Remember that the first aim of practice for an agoraphobic is to learn how to cope with the unpleasant feelings that keep it going. Remember also that these alter from day to day. Pay no special attention to failures other than encouraging your partner to try again in a slightly different way, perhaps with your help or after taking a tranquilizer. However, never forget to praise, either for carrying on despite feeling tense, or for doing something that was avoided before.

---

If your partner succeeds the first time that an item is practiced, you should:
  (a) Suggest that it be tried again tomorrow.
  (b) Advise the trial of a more difficult item.
  (c) Point out how your partner exaggerates the difficulties.
  (d) Congratulate your partner and suggest taking a rest.

---

(a) *Suggest that it be tried again tomorrow.*
**Correct.** Now that the item has been achieved once, it should be repeated a few times to check it and to increase your partner's confidence.

(b) *Advise the trial of a more difficult item.*
A single success does not mean that the item is finished; it should be repeated a few times to make sure.

(c) *Point out how your partner exaggerates the difficulties.*
It is not going to help to say that your partner exaggerates the difficulties every time an item is completed. In fact, this is likely to discourage him/her from trying in the future.

(d) *Congratulate your partner and suggest taking a rest.*
You should congratulate your partner, of course, but suggesting a rest is not the right thing to do. By "resting," the agoraphobic is avoiding going out, and this is just what he/she must not do.

## WHAT TO DO ABOUT PANIC (I)

Suppose you are out together when suddenly your partner says that he/she feels frightened by some strange feeling.

Do *not* immediately take your partner home. Try to find somewhere to rest, sit down somewhere, walk back a little way—or do anything that will help him/her to stay in or near the place where the feelings started.

Do *not* keep asking how your partner feels. Do not get involved in lengthy discussions of the panic feelings, since these might make them worse. Find something else to talk about until you judge that your partner is feeling better. Judge this from how he/she looks and behaves.

In time, the feelings will subside. Although you can then go home, it would be better to go on practicing for a little while first. Fortunately, once panic has come and gone, it is unlikely to come back again for a while. You can sometimes use this fact to push on a little further.

The golden rule is "Try not to leave a situation until the fear is going *down.*"

---

If your partner becomes frightened in a store it would be best to:
   (a) Tell your partner to snap out of it.
   (b) Help him/her to get home as soon as possible.
   (c) Go to another store.
   (d) Help your partner to stay until he/she feels better.

---

(a) *Tell your partner to snap out of it.*
Telling your partner to snap out of it will have no effect. If this were possible, he/she would have done it already.

(b) *Help him/her to get home as soon as possible.*
"Helping" him/her to get home immediately might make avoidance more likely the next time, because an agoraphobic quickly learns that only when he/she goes home does the fear go down.

(c) *Go to another store.*
Going to another store might help, provided that it is nearby. There is a danger however that the person will learn to be afraid of, and avoid, the first store.

(d) *Help your partner to stay until he/she feels better.*
**Correct.** If it is possible to help your partner stay until the fear goes down, this might make it easier for him/her to cope the next time.

## WHAT TO DO ABOUT PANIC (II)

Sometimes it may be impossible to stay somewhere long enough for the fear to die down. If the panic happens when your partner is alone, then it may be possible to overcome the problem by asking him/her to go back with you to the same place as soon as possible. If you were together, you should arrange for a return visit as soon as possible. If it is not possible to get back again soon, you may notice a "setback," that is, that item or others like it seem more difficult again.

There is no need for alarm; simply back up a bit and arrange practice with some easier in-between items. If this is done without delay, the lost ground will be made up again quite quickly.

Very occasionally, you may have more than one setback with the same item. This probably means that the item is more difficult than you realized, and it may be better to go on and bypass that particular item.

---

You are on a bus together when, in a panic, your partner insists on getting off earlier than planned. You should:
- (a) Insist that your partner get on the next bus.
- (b) Try again soon when anxiety is less.
- (c) Ask your partner to try it alone next time.
- (d) All of these.

---

(a) *Insist that your partner get on the next bus.*
This sometimes works but has some dangers: your partner might be very upset and refuse to attempt it, so the only result might be an argument. It is best if he/she can be persuaded not to get off in the first place; once that has happened you might as well wait for anxiety to subside.

(b) *Try again soon when anxiety is less.*
**Correct.** You should, of course, try to persuade your partner not to get off the bus in the first place. However, once this has happened, it would be best to try again when anxiety has subsided somewhat.

(c) *Ask your partner to try it alone next time.*
No. Doing it alone would probably be even more difficult and will not succeed.

(d) *All of these.*
No. Some of the answere are not advisable.

## ENCOURAGEMENT FROM OTHERS (I)

To get the habit of regular practice started, and to keep it going, the most important thing is constant encouragement from other people, especially close relatives and friends. To understand this, remember that practice is likely to be frightening at times, boring and hard work at others. In other words, most of the effects of practice on an agoraphobic have become unpleasant or even punishing. Obviously this makes it easy to think, "It's just not worth the effort," and to stop trying. If this happens, the battle is lost.

To stop this, you have to arrange things so that efforts to practice and get back to normal are encouraged and rewarded. Strengthening the pleasant associations of new behavior in this way is called *reinforcing* it.

---

To help in establishing the habit of regular practice, it is best to reinforce it by:
  (a) Praising your partner more often.
  (b) Praising your partner when he/she has done well in practice.
  (c) Criticizing your partner when he/she has not done any practice.
  (d) None of these.

---

(a) *Praising your partner more often.*
It is not always necessary to praise your partner more often. You reinforce something by *timing* your praise correctly.

*(b) Praising your partner when he/she has done well in practice.*
**Correct.** You reinforce behavior by giving a reward immediately after it has happened, rather than at any other time.

(c) *Criticizing your partner when he/she has not done any practice.*
Criticism is the wrong thing. It can have many other effects apart from the one you want; for example, your partner might resent it and do the opposite.

(d) *None of these.*
No. One of the other answers *is* correct.

## ENCOURAGEMENT FROM OTHERS (II)

1. Remember to ask how practice has gone every day. It *does not* help to criticize lack of progress. However, genuine praise for the efforts made is important. Discuss progress regularly and try to suggest ways around difficulties.

2. Make sure that other people know about the problem—the more help the better. Remember that "help" by doing things for your partner isn't really help at all. However, you can encourage him/her to do things independently.

3. Make a point of giving a small gift (it doesn't have to be expensive) whenever a landmark is passed in practice. If you already are in the habit of giving your partner gifts at times, from now on you must give something only when it follows progress in practice.

---

Reinforcing efforts by praise or presents is an important part of treatment because it:
  (a) Makes your partner more cheerful generally.
  (b) Strengthens the connection between your partner's efforts and pleasant things.
  (c) Shows your partner that you care about him/her.
  (d) Will make your partner do things that he/she wouldn't have bothered to do otherwise.

---

(a) *Makes your partner more cheerful generally.*
If you are encouraging progress, your partner may well feel more cheerful. However, feeling more cheerful does not, *by itself*, always lead to more efforts to overcome the problem by practice.

(b) *Strengthens the connection between your partner's efforts and pleasant things.*
**Correct.** The point of reinforcement is to build positive associations with practice efforts, which will make it easier for your partner to make practice a habit.

(c) *Shows your partner that you care about him/her.*
Of course, one reason for giving is that you care. However, to reinforce your partner's efforts, you must give praise or presents at the *right time*. You could care a lot but still give them at the wrong time, which would not help the practice.

(d) *Will make your partner do things that he/she wouldn't have bothered to do otherwise.*
No. You will not *make* your partner do anything, and it is not that he/she cannot be bothered. More likely, the associations with practice have been *unpleasant* in the past. Reinforcement will make it easier for your partner to practice once he/she has decided to try.

## ENCOURAGEMENT FROM OTHERS (III)

4. As far as possible, try to stop anything coming into the house that your partner might be able to go out and get. Postpone all but the most essential purchases until you can arrange a shopping expedition as part of practice and buy them then. This is helpful both because it "reinforces" the successful practice, and because it gives a reason for doing that practice item.

5. Whenever you are planning to buy something at all expensive that your partner wants, or something for the family, try to arrange it so that the timing depends on progress. A good idea is to count one "point" every time a new item has been done, and to buy the item when a previously agreed-on number of points has been earned —not before. Apart from buying things, your partner might prefer to "earn" time off from some everyday chore, or to use the points to "buy" your time to do something for her/him.

---

Reinforcing practice efforts will mean:
 (a) Buying more things.
 (b) Giving something when your partner least expects it.
 (c) Buying the same things but timing the purchases differently.
 (d) All of these.

---

(a) *Buying many more things.*
No. You will not necessarily have to buy anything more. Reinforcement involves deciding *when* something is given, rather than *whether* it is given.

(b) *Giving something when your partner least expects it.*
This may be a nice surprise, but it doesn't really matter if your partner is expecting it or not. The important thing is that it be associated with practice efforts.

(c) *Buying the same things but timing the purchases differently.*
**Correct.** Giving the same things at the *right time* (that is, after successful practice) is important.

(d) *All of these.*
No. Not all of the answers are correct.

## ENCOURAGEMENT FROM OTHERS (IV)

6. Many agoraphobic people are housewives who do not have another job outside the house. In this case, one of the best ways to make progress is for them to find a regular job outside the home. Obviously a paid job may seem a good idea; the extra money is bound to come in handy, and it can be saved to buy special rewards that would be difficult to afford otherwise. If a paid job is not possible, it is worth think-ing about voluntary work, or some other outside interest, such as a social group, a club, or an evening class. Visits to friends are obviously valuable as well. These things help because they involve practice in getting to the place and meeting people. And they may be a source of satisfaction in themselves. It is not usually a good idea to wait until your partner is better before thinking of a job. The sooner it is done, the better.

7. You may be able to think of other ways to encourage practice. Whatever you use, some form of reinforcement is essential for success.

---

A job or outside interest will help because:
   (a) The money will be useful.
   (b) It reinforces self-discipline.
   (c) It will enable your partner to be financially independent.
   (d) It is a source of reinforcement away from home.

---

(a) *The money will be useful.*
Obviously, extra money is useful, but money *in itself* does not necessarily help treat-ment. There are other ways in which jobs or outside interests help.

(b) *It reinforces self-discipline.*
Yes, but if you describe self-discipline in terms of *specific behavior*, it means some-thing like "behaving in a more organized way." The question is: How can a job help an agoraphobic to behave differently?

(c) *It will enable your partner to be financially independent.*
It might help financial independence, but this would not necessarily help progress in treatment.

(d) *It is a source of reinforcement away from home.*
*Correct.* A job or interest can provide reinforcement for developing activities away from home. In this way, it helps to overcome the agoraphobia.

## NOTES FOR TREATMENT IN PRACTICE

When you are ready to start practice, read through the suggestions given here for *before* practice, as well as *during* practice. If the things you will be doing come under walking, stores, buses, trains, movie houses, or eating places, then you should read that particular section before you start. Others, such as being alone at home, are not covered because they usually disappear once the problems of going out are overcome.

### BEFORE PRACTICE

1. When you judge that your partner is ready to start a new practice item, take the initiative and make *a firm* suggestion about what he/she might do. Don't let your partner do the same thing *too* many times before you suggest moving on.

2. However, always let your partner make the final decision. You cannot make someone do something unless that person is really prepared to try. Remember that your partner's feelings will vary from day to day. If practice is to succeed, you must both agree about the decision.

3. Your partner is in a better position than you to know which items are more difficult than others. Make suggestions, but don't assume that you know the answers.

4. When your partner is hesitating about something, get agreement to *try* it. Reassure your partner by making several alternative arrangements to fall back on in case of difficulty. Things will, of course, usually turn out better than he/she expects.

5. Try to include some items that your partner can practice alone, even if you have to be "around" (near at hand, or by a phone). This helps to prevent your partner from being too dependent on your actually being present.

6. Watch out for "excuses" to put off practice—housework that has to be done, letters to write, headaches, etc. This may be true, but firmly suggest that your partner try something anyway; however, don't make an issue of it.

7. Your partner may complain that practice causes feelings of exhaustion afterwards. This is not surprising, since he/she is probably out of practice at walking. You could encourage your partner to do regular exercises to help this. Many "symptoms" experienced during the early stages of practice may be due to being out of condition.

### DURING PRACTICE

1. If you notice that your partner behaves in special ways when he/she is tense (e.g., rushing ahead too fast, talking or breathing too quickly), encourage slowing down and acting more naturally by giving praise when this is done.

2. Talk about things that you know might interest your partner when you are out together, and encourage an interest in the things around you, such as displays in shop windows. Remember *not* to talk about feelings more than you have to.

3. Although you should have discussed and planned most practice sessions in advance, if things go well you can take the opportunity of suggesting something more difficult while you are out. Sometimes new things can be done more easily on impulse.

4. If it is necessary to repeat an item several times, you can still change it in small ways. For example, you can alter the route or the time of day, so that your partner gets used to slightly different conditions.

5. When planning visits to meet other people, making appointments at the hairdresser, dentist, etc., or just calling on friends, it often helps if these people are told in advance that your partner might feel unwell and wish to leave. If agoraphobics know that they *can* leave if necessary, they are less likely to feel trapped and therefore less likely to *want* to leave.

6. If your partner has taken any medication, remember that tranquilizers and alcohol don't mix. If, for some reason, both *have* been taken together, he/she should *never* drive afterwards.

7. Always try to have arrangements agreed on in case something goes wrong. Being available on the phone is often useful, and so is some other method of contact with you or another person. If you have arranged to meet somewhere, decide what each should do in case one misses the other—it does happen occasionally.

## SUGGESTIONS FOR PRACTICE ITEMS

The remaining pages cover common practice situations such as *walking, stores, buses, trains, movie houses, and eating places.*

In each, suggestions are made for practice items, arranged roughly in order of difficulty. If you are looking for practice items between targets, then you should read through the appropriate sections.

Obviously, these are only suggestions. You should use what you need, but add to them or leave out what you don't want.

### WALKING

It often happens that walking with someone is easier than walking alone. In this case, you can use the following items:

1. Walking together to the furthest point from home that your partner can manage. (Stay for a short while if possible before going back.)
2. Repeat (1), with you following a short distance behind.

3. Walk around in a circle, going in opposite directions so that you pass in the middle.

4. Walk separately to an agreed place (make sure you both know where it is) by different routes, meeting at the furthest point from home. You should be there *first*.

5. Your partner sets off first, and you meet later at an agreed-on place and *time* (make sure that this is understood, and *never* frighten your partner by failing to do as you say you will).

6. Walking alone, with you at home (increasing distances).

7. Walking alone when you are away from home (increasing distances).

Other things apart from your presence may be important: how crowded it is, what the weather is like, and so on. Particular places on roads, open spaces, bridges, etc., may be especially difficult. Look out for these, and arrange practice items for them in a similar way.

STORES

Large, crowded stores or supermarkets are usually the most difficult. If this is the case, use the following items:

1. Go together to the target store at a quiet time.

2. Go in together, but split up inside for a while.

3. Wait outside (staying in sight) while your partner shops inside.

4. Go somewhere else for an agreed-on length of time while your partner stays in the store.

5. Gradually increase the time that your partner is alone before you meet again.

6. Your partner goes alone for shopping and back (make sure that he/she is able to go into all different parts of the store).

7. Repeat these exercises at a busy time (Friday afternoon or Saturday morning).

Again, there might be special individual difficulties to watch out for: lines, basements, escalators, and so on. Special practice items will be needed for these.

BUSES

Many people find buses difficult but think that they need not bother with them, especially if they have a car. It is important to overcome the fear of buses; and your partner may need to use them one day. If in doubt, include them.

If going alone is the most difficult, try the following items:

1. Walk to and wait at the bus stop (without getting on).
2. Go together on a very short trip (two or three stops).

*If there is a car available:*

3. Your partner goes on the bus, and you follow closely in the car, picking him/her up at the destination.
4. Your partner goes by bus and you go separately by car: you meet at an agreed-on stop.

*If there is no car available:*

5. Get on the bus together but sit separately (if possible out of sight of each other).
6. Your partner goes alone by bus, and you go on ahead (by foot or by an earlier bus); you meet at the agreed-on stop.
7. Your partner goes by bus and returns alone (you could be "around" or near a phone).
8. Gradually extend bus trips alone for longer distances.

TRAINS

Similar to buses. Examples include:

1. Go together on a train one station and back.
2. Go together, but sit in separate cars.
3. Travel separately (you go ahead by train or car), and meet at the station.
4. Your partner goes both ways alone.
5. Gradually extend trips alone to longer distances.

MOVIE HOUSES (AND THEATERS, SHOWS, MEETINGS,
CHURCH ATTENDANCE, ETC.)

When these are a target, let your partner choose the film or meeting that he/she would enjoy most. Avoid delays before going in if possible.

1. Go together and sit where your partner can leave easily (back of the house, end of a row). Go at a quiet time.
2. If your partner is embarrassed about the possibility of leaving, get him/her to go out briefly and come in again, just for practice.
3. Gradually move toward the center of the row, the front of house, etc. In a movie house, this could be done in the intermission between films.
4. Repeat when more crowded (e.g., Saturday evening).

EATING PLACES

These are useful places to go as a rest during other practice. Arrange practice in similar ways to those outlined under "Movie Houses." Let your partner choose a place that he/she likes, and preferably avoid places where you have to wait.

1. Go together and have something that need not be finished (e.g., coffee). Self-service may be easier at first, especially at a quiet time.

2. You leave, and return after a few minutes.

3. Your partner can also practice leaving and coming back.

4. Your partner goes in first, alone; you arrive later.

5. Practice for your partner alone, extending to busier and more crowded places, meals, etc.

# *Appendix 3.*
# Summary and Checklist
# for Therapists

SUMMARY OF FIRST VISIT (allow about 1¼ hours)

1. Explain the purpose of the visit and set an agenda.
2. See that the manuals have been read and are understood.
3. Review the treatment approach:
   a. The self-help nature of the method.
   b. Practice as the real treatment.
   c. Panic-management methods.
   d. The importance of firm encouragement from others.
4. Negotiate a treatment contract.
5. Help the couple to select targets.
6. Discuss the importance of daily records (diary and target sheet).
7. Arrange a meeting place and a target for the next session.

SUMMARY OF SECOND VISIT (practice session: allow ¾ hour)

1. Accompany the client and partner during exposure:
   a. Encourage them to take responsibility for practice.
   b. Praise achievement and coping behavior.
2. Observe the behavior of both client and partner:
   a. Model appropriate behavior if a panic occurs.
   b. Prompt the partner to reinforce the client's achievements.
   c. Suggest further practice.
3. See that diaries are being used correctly and arrange the next visit.

## SUMMARY OF SUBSEQUENT VISITS (each about ½ hour)

1. Set an agenda for the visit.
2. Check diaries and target sheet.
3. Discuss the importance of regular practice, prompting reinforcement and feedback.
4. Discuss any specific difficulties encountered by the couple during practice, and encourage efforts at problem solving.
5. Discuss long-term plans:
   a. Continuing practice.
   b. Setting new targets.
   c. Increasing social activities.
   d. Anticipating setbacks.
   e. Rereading manuals to help solve problems.
6. Arrange further appointments.

## SUMMARY OF FOLLOW-UP VISITS (about ½ hour)

1. Discuss any problems that have arisen during practice.
2. Give support and encouragement for achievements so far.
3. Encourage the client and partner to set targets that are outside the client's daily routine (e.g., shopping in large towns, long-distance trips, vacations).
4. Emphasize the need for continuing practice and the involvement of the family.
5. Make the next appointment and discuss the procedure for making any extra appointments in case of difficulty.

# *Appendix 4.*
# Assessment Materials

Behavioral Diary

| Date | Time | | Medication | Anxiety (0-10) | Destination and/or purpose of trip (with approximate distance from home) | Accompanied | Met | Alone | Transport | | | |
| | Out | Back | | | | | | | Walk | Car | Bus | Other |
|---|---|---|---|---|---|---|---|---|---|---|---|---|
| | | | | | | | | | | | | |
| | | | | | | | | | | | | |
| | | | | | | | | | | | | |
| | | | | | | | | | | | | |
| | | | | | | | | | | | | |
| | | | | | | | | | | | | |

Target Sheet. ($\times$ entered on successful completion of target. Progress should lead to the chart's being completed along a diagonal increasing from left to right.)

10

9

8

7

6

| Target items (start with least difficult at bottom) | Week 1 | | | | | | | Week 2 | | | | | | | Week 3 | | | | | | | Week 4 | | | | | | |
|---|---|---|---|---|---|---|---|---|---|---|---|---|---|---|---|---|---|---|---|---|---|---|---|---|---|---|---|---|
| | 1 | 2 | 3 | 4 | 5 | 6 | 7 | 1 | 2 | 3 | 4 | 5 | 6 | 7 | 1 | 2 | 3 | 4 | 5 | 6 | 7 | 1 | 2 | 3 | 4 | 5 | 6 | 7 |
| 1 | | | | | | | | | | | | | | | | | | | | | | | | | | | | |
| 2 | | | | | | | | | | | | | | | | | | | | | | | | | | | | |
| 3 | | | | | | | | | | | | | | | | | | | | | | | | | | | | |
| 4 | | | | | | | | | | | | | | | | | | | | | | | | | | | | |
| 5 | | | | | | | | | | | | | | | | | | | | | | | | | | | | |
| Reinforcement for achieving target ×3 | ( | ) | ( | ) | ( | ) | ( | ) | | | | | | | | | | | | | | | | | | | | |

Fear Questionnaire

Name .......................... Age .... Sex ... Date ..........

Choose a number from the scale below to show how much you would avoid each of the situations listed below because of fear or other unpleasant feelings. Then write the number you chose in the box opposite each situation.

| 0 | 1 | 2 | 3 | 4 | 5 | 6 | 7 | 8 |
|---|---|---|---|---|---|---|---|---|

| *Would not avoid it* | *Slightly avoid it* | *Definitely avoid it* | *Markedly avoid it* | *Always avoid it* |
|---|---|---|---|---|

1.  Main phobia you want treated (describe in your own words)
    ...................................................................... □
2.  Injections or minor surgery ......................... □
3.  Eating or drinking with other people .................. □
4.  Hospitals ....................................... □
5.  Traveling alone by bus or coach .................. □
6.  Walking alone in busy streets .................... □
7.  Being watched or stared at ......................... □
8.  Going into crowded shops ....................... □
9.  Talking to people in authority ....................... □
10. Sight of blood .................................... □
11. Being criticized .................................. □
12. Going alone far from home ...................... □
13. Thought of injury or illness ........................ □
14. Speaking or acting to an audience ................... □
15. Large open spaces ............................. □
16. Going to the dentist ............................ □
17. Other situations (describe) ....................................... □

leave blank → □□□   □

Ag+Bl+Soc = Total
2-16

Fear Questionnaire *(continued)*

Now choose a number from the scale below to show how much you are troubled by each problem listed, and write the number in the box opposite.

| 0 | 1 | 2 | 3 | 4 | 5 | 6 | 7 | 8 |
|---|---|---|---|---|---|---|---|---|

| *Hardly at all* | *Slightly troublesome* | *Definitely troublesome* | *Markedly troublesome* | *Very severely troublesome* |
|---|---|---|---|---|

18. Feeling miserable or depressed .................. ☐
19. Feeling irritable or angry ...................... ☐
20. Feeling tense or panicky ...................... ☐
21. Upsetting thoughts coming into your mind ......... ☐
22. Feeling you or your surroundings are strange or unreal ☐
23. Other feelings (describe) ........................................ ☐

☐ Total

How would you rate the present state of your phobic symptoms on the scale below?

| 0 | 1 | 2 | 3 | 4 | 5 | 6 | 7 | 8 |
|---|---|---|---|---|---|---|---|---|

| *No phobias present* | *Slightly disturbing/ not really disabling* | *Definitely disturbing/ disabling* | *Markedly disturbing/ disabling* | *Very severely disturbing/ disabling* |
|---|---|---|---|---|

Please circle one number between 0 and 8.

Three phobia subscores can be derived, each from the sum of five items, score range 0–40 (Ag: agoraphobia, from items 5, 6, 8, 12, 15; Bl: blood-injury, from items 2, 4, 10, 13, 16; Soc: social, from items 3, 7, 9, 11, 14). From I. M. Marks and A. M. Mathews, *Behaviour Research and Therapy*, 1979, *17*, 264. Copyright 1979 by Pergamon Press, Ltd. Reprinted by permission.

# References

Agras, W. S., Chapin, H. N., & Oliveau, D. C. The natural history of phobia. *Archives of General Psychiatry*, 1972, *26*, 315–317.

Agras, W. S., Leitenberg, H., & Barlow, D. H. Social reinforcement in the modification of agoraphobia. *Archives of General Psychiatry*, 1968, *19*, 423–427.

Agras, W. S., Sylvester, D., & Oliveau, D. The epidemiology of common fears and phobias. *Comprehensive Psychiatry*, 1969, *10*, 151–156.

Agulnik, P. The spouse of the phobic patient. *British Journal of Psychiatry*, 1970, *117*, 59–67.

Akiskal, H. S., & McKinney, W. T. Depressive disorders: Toward a unified hypothesis. *Science*, 1973, *182*, 20–28.

Andrews, J. D. W. Psychotherapy of phobias. *Psychological Bulletin*, 1966, *66*, 455–480.

Arieti, S. New views on the psychodynamics of phobias. *American Journal of Psychotherapy*, 1979, *33*, 82–95.

Averill, J. R. Personal control over aversive stimuli and its relationship to stress. *Psychological Bulletin*, 1973, *80*, 286–303.

Bandura, A. Self-efficacy: Toward a unifying theory of behavioral change. *Psychological Review*, 1977, *84*, 191–215.

Bandura, A., Blanchard, E. B., & Ritter, B. Relative efficacy of desensitization and modeling approaches for inducing behavioral, affective and attitudinal changes. *Journal of Personality and Social Psychology*, 1969, *13*, 173–199.

Barlow, D. H., & Mavissakalian, M. Directions in the assessment and treatment of phobia: The next decade. In M. Mavissakalian & D. H. Barlow (Eds.), *Phobia: Psychological and pharmacological treatment*. New York: Guilford Press, 1981.

Baum, M. Extinction of avoidance responding through response prevention (flooding). *Psychological Bulletin*, 1970, *74*, 276–284.

Beaumont, G. A large open multicentre trial of clomipramine (anafranil) in the management of phobic disorders. *Journal of International Medical Research*, 1977, *5*, Supplement (5), 116–123.

Beck, A. T., & Rush, A. J. A cognitive model of anxiety formation and anxiety resolution. In I. Sarason & C. Spielberger (Eds.), *Stress and anxiety* (Vol. 2). New York: Halsted Press, 1975.

Becker, M. H., & Maiman, L. A. Sociobehavioral determinants of compliance with health and medical care recommendations. *Medical Care*, 1975, *13*, 10–24.

Benedikt, V. "Über Platzschwindel." *Allgemeine Wiener Medizinische Zeitung*, 1870, *15*, 488.

Betts, T. A., Clayton, A. B., & Mackay, G. M. Effects of four commonly-used tranquilizers on low speed driving performance tests. *British Medical Journal*, 1972, *4*, 580–584.

Borkovec, T. D. Self-efficacy: Cause or reflection of behavioral change? *Advances in Behavior Therapy*, 1978, *1*, 163–170.

Bowen, R. D. The relationship between agoraphobia and primary affective disorders. *Canadian Journal of Psychiatry*, 1979, *24*, 317–322.

Bridges, P. K., & Bartlett, J. R. Psychosurgery: Yesterday and today. *British Journal of Psychiatry*, 1977, *131*, 249–260.

Buglass, D., Clarke, J., Henderson, A. S., Kreitman, N., & Presley, A. S. A study of agoraphobic housewives. *Psychological Medicine*, 1977, *7*, 73–86.

Burns, L. E., & Thorpe, G. L. The epidemiology of fears and phobias with particular reference to the national survey of agoraphobics. *Journal of International Medical Research*, 1977, *5*, Supplement (5), 1–7.(a)

Burns, L. E., & Thorpe, G. L. Fears and clinical phobias: Epidemiological aspects and the national survey of agoraphobics. *Journal of International Medical Research*, 1977, *5*, Supplement (1), 132–139.(b)

Chambless, D. L., Foa, E. B., Groves, G. A., & Goldstein, A. J. Flooding with Brevital in the treatment of agoraphobia: Countereffective? *Behaviour Research and Therapy*, 1979, *17*, 243–251.

Cole, A. *Predicting spouse co-operation in treatment of agoraphobia.* Paper delivered at BABP conference, July 1978.

Committee on the Review of Medicines. Systematic review of the benzodiazepines. *British Medical Journal*, 1980, *1*, 910–912.

Cooper, J. E. A study of behaviour therapy in thirty psychiatric patients. *The Lancet*, 1963, *1*, 411–415.

Cooper, J. E., Gelder, M. G., & Marks, I. M. Results of behaviour therapy in 77 psychiatric patients. *British Medical Journal*, 1965, *1*, 1222–1225.

Cordes, E. Die Platzangst (Agoraphobie): Symptom einer Erschöpfungsparese. *Archiv für Psychiatrie und Nervenkrankheiten*, 1871, *3*, 521–524.

Crowe, M. J., Marks, I. M., Agras, W. S., & Leitenberg, H. Time-limited desensitization, implosion and shaping for phobic patients: A crossover study. *Behaviour Research and Therapy*, 1972, *10*, 319–328.

Dixon, J. J., de Monchaux, C., & Sandler, J. Patterns of anxiety: The phobias. *British Journal of Medical Psychology*, 1957, *30*, 34–40.

Emmelkamp, P. M. G. The behavioral study of clinical phobias. In M. Hersen, R. M. Eisler, & P. M. Miller (Eds.), *Progress in behavior modification* (Vol. 8). New York: Academic Press, 1979.

Emmelkamp, P. M. G. Anxiety and fear. In A. Bellack, M. Hersen, & A. Kazdin (Eds.), *International handbook of behavior modification*. New York: Plenum Press, 1980.

Emmelkamp, P. M. G., & Cohen-Kettenis, P. T. Relationship of locus of control to phobic anxiety and depression. *Psychological Reports*, 1975, *36*, 390–391.

Emmelkamp, P. M. G., & Emmelkamp-Benner, A. Effects of historically portrayed modeling and group treatment on self-observation: A comparison with agoraphobics. *Behaviour Research and Therapy*, 1975, *13*, 135–139.

Emmelkamp, P. M. G., & Kuipers, A. C. M. Agoraphobia: A follow-up study four years after treatment. *British Journal of Psychiatry*, 1979, *134*, 352–355.

Emmelkamp, P. M. G., Kuipers, A. C. M., & Eggeraat, J. B. Cognitive modification versus prolonged exposure in vivo: A comparison with agoraphobics as subjects. *Behaviour Research and Therapy*, 1978, *16*, 33-41.

Emmelkamp, P. M. G., & Ultee, K. A. A comparison of "successive approximation" and "self-observation" in the treatment of agoraphobia. *Behavior Therapy*, 1974, *5*, 606-613.

Emmelkamp, P. M. G., & Wessels, H. Flooding in imagination vs. flooding in vivo: A comparison with agoraphobics. *Behaviour Research and Therapy*, 1975, *13*, 7-15.

Epstein, L. H. Psychophysiological measurement in assessment. In M. Hersen & A. S. Bellack (Eds.), *Behavioral assessment: A practical handbook*. Oxford: Pergamon Press, 1976.

Errera, P., & Coleman, J. V. A long-term follow-up study of neurotic phobic patients in a psychiatric clinic. *Journal of Nervous and Mental Disorders*, 1963, *136*, 267-271.

Ey, H., Bernard, P., & Brisset, C. *Manuel de psychiatrie*. Masson: Paris, 1974.

Eysenck, H. J. Correspondence on behaviour therapy. *British Journal of Psychiatry*, 1965, *111*, 1007-1013.

Eysenck, H. J. The learning theory model of neurosis—New approach. *Behaviour Research and Therapy*, 1976, *14*, 251-267.

Eysenck, H. J., & Rachman, S. *Causes and cures of neurosis*. London: Routledge & Kegan Paul, 1965.

Fenichel, O. *Psychoanalytic theory of neurosis*. New York: Norton, 1945.

Frankl, V. E. (Ed.). *Psychotherapy and existentialism: Selected papers on logotherapy*. New York: Souvenir Press, 1970.

Freud, S. Obsessions and phobias. Reprinted as Chapter 7 in *Collected papers* (Vol. 1). London: Hogarth Press, 1924.(a) (Originally published, 1919.)

Freud, S. Turnings in the ways of psychoanalytic therapy. Reprinted as Chapter 34 in *Collected papers* (Vol. 2). London: Hogarth Press, 1924.(b) (Originally published 1919.)

Freud, S. Analysis of a phobia in a 5-year-old boy. In *Collected papers* (Vol. 3). London: Hogarth Press, 1925. (Originally published 1909.)

Friedman, D. E. L. A new technique for the systematic desensitisation of phobic symptoms. *Behaviour Research and Therapy*, 1966, 4, 139-140.

Friedman, D. E. L., & Silverstone, J. T. Treatment of phobic patients by systematic desensitisation. *The Lancet*, 1967, *1*, 470-472.

Friedman, J. H. Short term psychotherapy of a "phobia of travel." *American Journal of Psychotherapy*, 1950, *4*, 259-278.

Friedman, P., & Goldstein, J. Phobic reactions. In S. Arieti & E. G. Brodie (Eds.), *American handbook of psychiatry* (2nd ed.). New York: Basic Books, 1974.

Gelder, M. G., Bancroft, J. H. J., Gath, D. H., Johnston, D. W., Mathews, A. M., & Shaw, P. M. Specific and non-specific factors in behaviour therapy. *British Journal of Psychiatry*, 1973, *123*, 445-462.

Gelder, M. G., & Marks, I. M. Severe agoraphobia: A controlled prospective trial of behaviour therapy. *British Journal of Psychiatry*, 1966, *112*, 309-319.

Gelder, M. G., & Marks, I. M. Desensitisation and phobias: A crossover study. *British Journal of Psychiatry*, 1968, *114*, 323-328.

Gelder, M. G., Marks, I. M., & Wolff, H. H. Desensitisation and psychotherapy in the treatment of phobic states: A controlled clinical inquiry. *British Journal of Psychiatry*, 1967, *113*, 53-73.

Gertz, H. O. Experience with the logotherapeutic technique of paradoxical intention in the treatment of phobic and obsessive–compulsive patients. *American Journal of Psychiatry*, 1967, *123*, 548-558.

Gertz, H. O. The treatment of the phobic and the obsessional patient using paradoxical intention. In V. E. Frankl (Ed.), *Psychotherapy and existentialism: Selected papers on logotherapy*. New York: Souvenir Press, 1970.

Gill, M. M., & Brenman, M. Treatment of a case of anxiety hysteria by a hypnotic technique employing psychoanalytic principles. *Bulletin of the Menninger Clinic*, 1943, *1*, 163-171.

Gillan, P., & Rachman, S. An experimental investigation of desensitisation in phobic patients. *British Journal of Psychiatry*, 1974, *124*, 392-401.

Goldstein, A. J., & Chambless, D. L. A reanalysis of agoraphobia. *Behavior Therapy*, 1978, *9*, 47-59.

Goldstein-Foder, I. G. The phobic syndrome in women. In V. Franks & V. Burtle (Eds.), *Women in therapy*. New York: Brunner/Mazel, 1974.

Gray, J. A. *The psychology of fear and stress*. London: Weidenfeld & Nicholson, 1971.

Greer, S. The prognosis of anxiety states. In M. H. Lader (Ed.), *Studies of anxiety*. British *Journal of Psychiatry*, Special Publication No. 3, 1969.

Hafner, R. J. Fresh symptom emergence after intensive behaviour therapy. *British Journal of Psychiatry*, 1976, *129*, 378-383.

Hafner, R. J. The husbands of agoraphobic women and their influence on treatment outcome. *British Journal of Psychiatry*, 1977, *131*, 289-294.(a)

Hafner, R. J. The husbands of agoraphobic women: Assortative mating or pathogenic interaction. *British Journal of Psychiatry*, 1977, *130*, 233-239.(b)

Hafner, J., & Marks, I. Exposure in vivo of agoraphobics: Contributions of diazepam, group exposure and anxiety evocation. *Psychological Medicine*, 1976, *6*, 71-88.

Hafner, J., & Milton, F. The influence of propranolol on the exposure in vivo of agoraphobics. *Psychological Medicine*, 1977, *7*, 419-425.

Hagnell, O., & Kreitman, N. Mental illness in married pairs in a total population. *British Journal of Psychiatry*, 1974, *125*, 293-302.

Haley, J. *Strategies of psychotherapy*. New York: Grune & Stratton, 1963.

Hallam, R. S. Agoraphobia: A critical review of the concept. *British Journal of Psychiatry*, 1978, *133*, 314-319.

Hallam, R. S., & Hafner, R. J. Fears of phobic patients: Factor analyses of self-report data. *Behaviour Research and Therapy*, 1978, *16*, 1-6.

Hand, I., Lamontagne, Y., & Marks, I. M. Group exposure (flooding) in vivo for agoraphobics. *British Journal of Psychiatry*, 1974, *124*, 588-602.

Harper, M., & Roth, M. Temporal lobe epilepsy and the phobic anxiety depersonalization syndrome. *Comprehensive Psychiatry*, 1962, *3*, 129-151.

Heiser, J. F., & Defrancisco, D. The treatment of pathological panic states with propranolol. *American Journal of Psychiatry*, 1976, *133*, 1389-1394.

Herrnstein, R. J. Method and theory in the study of avoidance. *Psychological Review*, 1969, *76*, 49-69.

Hersen, M. Self assessment of fear. *Behavior Therapy*, 1973, *4*, 241-257.

Hersen, M., & Bellack, A. S. (Eds.). *Behavioral assessment: A practical handbook*. Oxford: Pergamon Press, 1976.

Hollingshead, A. B., & Redlich, F. C. *Social class and mental illness*. New York: Wiley, 1958.

Hussain, M. Z. Desensitization and flooding (implosion) in treatment of phobias. *American Journal of Psychiatry,* 1971, *127,* 1509–1514.

Ivey, E. P. Recent advances in the psychiatric diagnosis and treatment of phobias. *American Journal of Psychotherapy,* 1959, *13,* 35–50.

Jacobson, E. *Progressive relaxation.* Chicago: University of Chicago Press, 1938.

Jacobson, E. *Anxiety and tension control.* Philadelphia: Lippincott, 1964.

Jannoun, L., Munby, M., Catalan, J., & Gelder, M. A home-based treatment programme for agoraphobia: Replication and controlled evaluation. *Behavior Therapy,* 1980, *11,* 294–305.

Johnston, D., & Gath, D. Arousal levels and attribution effects in diazepam-assisted flooding. *British Journal of Psychiatry,* 1973, *123,* 463–466.

Johnston, D. W., Lancashire, M., Mathews, A. M., Munby, M., Shaw, P. M., & Gelder, M. G. Imaginal flooding and exposure to real phobic situations: Changes during treatment. *British Journal of Psychiatry,* 1976, *129,* 372–377.

Kelly, D., Guirguis, W., Frommer, E., Mitchell-Heggs, N., & Sargant, W. Treatment of phobic states with antidepressants: A retrospective study of 246 patients. *British Journal of Psychiatry,* 1970, *116,* 387–398.

Kelly, D., Walter, C. J. S., & Sargant, W. Modified leucotomy assessed by forearm blood flow and other measurements. *British Journal of Psychiatry,* 1966, *112,* 871–881.

King, A. Phenelzine treatment of Roth's calamity syndrome. *Medical Journal of Australia,* 1962, *1,* 879–883.

King, A., & Little, J. C. Thiopentone treatment of the phobic-anxiety-depersonalization syndrome: A preliminary report. *Proceedings of the Royal Society of Medicine,* 1959, *52,* 595–596.

Klein, D. F. Delineation of two drug responsive anxiety syndromes. *Psychopharmacologia (Berlin),* 1964, *5,* 397–408.

Klein, D. F., Zitrin, C. M., & Woerner, M. Anti-depressants, anxiety, panic and phobia. In M. Lipton, A. DiMascio, & K. F. Killam (Eds.), *Psychopharmacology: A generation of progress.* New York: Raven Press, 1978.

Lader, M. H., & Mathews, A. M. A physiological model of phobic anxiety and desensitisation. *Behaviour Research and Therapy,* 1968, *6,* 411–421.

Lang, P. The application of psychophysiological methods to the study of psychotherapy and behaviour modification. In A. E. Bergin & S. L. Garfield (Eds.), *Handbook of psychotherapy and behavior change: An empirical analysis.* New York: Wiley, 1971.

Langer, T. S., & Michael, S. T. *Life stress and mental health.* New York: Macmillan, 1963.

Laughlin, H. P. *The neuroses in clinical practice.* London: W. B. Saunders, 1956.

Legrand du Saule, H. De l'agoraphobie. *Practicien,* 1885, *8,* 208–210.

Leitenberg, H., Agras, W. S., Allen, R., Butz, R., & Edwards, J. Feedback and therapist praise during treatment of phobia. *Journal of Consulting and Clinical Psychology,* 1975, *43,* 396–404.

Lemkau, P., Tietze, C., & Cooper, M. Mental hygiene problems in an urban district. *Mental Hygiene,* 1942, *26,* 100–119.

Levis, D. J., & Boyd, T. L. Symptom maintenance: An infrahuman analysis and extention of the conservation of anxiety principle. *Journal of Abnormal Psychology,* 1979, *88,* 107–120.

Lick, J., & Bootzin, R. Expectancy factors in the treatment of fear: Methodological and theoretical issues. *Psychological Bulletin,* 1975, *82,* 917–931.

Lipsedge, M., Hajioff, J., Huggins, P., Napier, L., Pearce, J., Pike, D. J., & Rich, M. The management of severe agoraphobia: A comparison of iproniazid and systematic desensitisation. *Psychopharmacologia*, 1973, *32*, 67–80.

Lopez-Ibor, J. Anxiety states and their treatment by intravenous acetylcholine. *Proceedings of the Royal Society of Medicine*, 1952, *45*, 511–516.

Luthe, W., & Schultz, J. *Autogenic therapy*. Vol. 3: *Applications in psychotherapy*. New York: Grune & Stratton, 1969.

Marks, I. M. Components and correlates of psychiatric questionnaires. *British Journal of Medical Psychology*, 1967, *40*, 261–271.

Marks, I. M. *Fears and phobias*. London: Heinemann, 1969.

Marks, I. M. Agoraphobic syndrome (phobic anxiety state). *Archives of General Psychiatry*, 1970, *23*, 538–553.

Marks, I. M. Phobic disorders four years after treatment: A prospective follow-up. *British Journal of Psychiatry*, 1971, *118*, 683–688.

Marks, I. M., Birley, J. L. T., & Gelder, M. G. Modified leucotomy in severe agoraphobia: A controlled serial inquiry. *British Journal of Psychiatry*, 1966, *112*, 757–769.

Marks, I. M., Boulougouris, J., & Marset, P. Flooding versus desensitisation in the treatment of phobic patients: A cross-over study. *British Journal of Psychiatry*, 1971, *119*, 353–375.

Marks, I. M., & Gelder, M. G. A controlled retrospective study of behaviour therapy in phobic patients. *British Journal of Psychiatry*, 1965, *111*, 561–573.

Marks, I. M., & Gelder, M. G. Different ages of onset in varieties of phobia. *American Journal of Psychiatry*, 1966, *123*, 218–221.

Marks, I. M., Gelder, M. G., & Edwards, G. Hypnosis and desensitisation for phobias: A controlled prospective trial. *British Journal of Psychiatry*, 1968, *114*, 1263–1274.

Marks, I. M., & Herst, E. R. A survey of 1,200 agoraphobics in Britain. *Social Psychiatry*, 1970, *5*, 16–24.

Marks, I. M., Marset, P., Boulougouris, J., & Huson, J. Physiological accompaniments of neutral and phobic imagery. *Psychological Medicine*, 1971, *1*, 299–307.

Marks, I. M., & Mathews, A. M. Brief standard self-rating for phobic patients. *Behaviour Research and Therapy*, 1979, *17*, 263–267.

Marks, I. M., Viswanathan, R., Lipsedge, M. S., & Gardner, R. Enhanced relief of phobias by flooding during waning diazepam effect. *British Journal of Psychiatry*, 1972, *121*, 493–505.

Marshall, W. L., Gauthier, J., & Gordon, A. The current status of flooding therapy. *Progress in Behavior Modification*, 1979, *7*, 205–275.

Mathews, A. M. Recent developments in the treatment of agoraphobia. *Behavioral Analysis and Modification*, 1977, *2*, 64–75.

Mathews, A. M. Fear-reduction research and clinical phobias. *Psychological Bulletin*, 1978, *85*, 390–404.

Mathews, A. M., Johnston, D. W., Lancashire, M., Munby, M., Shaw, P. M., & Gelder, M. G. Imaginal flooding and exposure to real phobic situations: Treatment outcome with agoraphobic patients. *British Journal of Psychiatry*, 1976, *129*. 362–371.

Mathews, A. M., Johnston, D. W., Shaw, P. M., & Gelder, M. G. Process variables and the prediction of outcome in behaviour therapy. *British Journal of Psychiatry*, 1974, *125*, 256–264.

Mathews, A. M., & Munby, M. Home-based treatment of agoraphobic clients without direct therapist contact. In preparation.

Mathews, A. M., Teasdale, J., Munby, M., Johnston, D., & Shaw, P. A home-based treatment program for agoraphobia. *Behavior Therapy*, 1977, *8*, 915-924.

Mawson, A. B. Methohexitone-assisted desensitisation in treatment of phobias. *The Lancet*, 1970, *1*, 1084-1086.

McDonald, R., Sartory, G., Grey, S. J., Cobb, J., Stern, R., & Marks, I. The effects of self-exposure instructions on agoraphobic outpatients. *Behaviour Research and Therapy*, 1979, *17*, 83-85.

McGennis, A., Nolan, G., & Hartman, M. The role of a self-help associations in agoraphobia: One year's experience with "out and about." *Irish Medical Journal*, 1977, *70*, 10-13.

McNair, D. M., & Lorr, M. An analysis of mood in neurotics. *Journal of Abnormal and Social Psychology*, 1964, *69*, 620-627.

McPherson, F. M., Brougham, L., & McLaren, S. Maintenance of improvement in agoraphobic patients treated by behavioural methods—A four-year follow-up. *Behaviour Research and Therapy*, 1980, *18*, 150-152.

Mendel, J. G. C., & Klein, D. F. Anxiety attacks with subsequent agoraphobia. *Comprehensive Psychiatry*, 1969, *10*, 190-195.

Meyer, V., & Gelder, M. G. Behaviour therapy and phobic disorders. *British Journal of Psychiatry*, 1963, *109*, 19-28.

Milton, F., & Hafner, J. The outcome of behavior therapy for agoraphobia in relation to marital adjustment. *Archives of General Psychiatry*, 1979, *36*, 807-811.

Mineka, S. The role of fear in theories of avoidance, learning, flooding and extinction. *Psychological Bulletin*, 1979, *86*, 958-1010.

Mischel, W. *Personality and assessment*. New York: Wiley, 1968.

Mitchell-Heggs, N., Kelly, D., & Richardson, A. Stereotactic limbic leucotomy—A follow-up at 16 months. *British Journal of Psychiatry*, 1976, *128*, 226-240.

Moll, A. *Hypnotism*. London: Walter Scott, 1891. (English translation of *Der Hypnotismus*, Berlin, 1889.)

Mountjoy, C. Q., Roth, M., Garside, R. F., & Leitch, I. M. A clinical trial of phenelzine in anxiety depressive and phobic neuroses. *British Journal of Psychiatry*, 1977, *131*, 486-492.

Mullaney, J. A., & Trippett, C. J. Alcohol dependence and phobias. *British Journal of Psychiatry*, 1979, *135*, 565-573.

Munby, M., & Johnston, D. W. Agoraphobia: The long term follow-up of behavioural treatment. *British Journal of Psychiatry*, 1980, *137*, 418-427.

Nisbett, R. E., & Wilson, T. P. Telling more than we know: Verbal reports on mental processes. *Psychological Review*, 1977, *84*, 231-279.

Öhman, A., Fredrikson, M., & Hugdahl, K. Towards an experimental model for simple phobic reactions. *Behavioral Analysis and Modification*, 1978, *2*, 97-114.

Oliveau, D. C., Agras, W. S., Leitenberg, H., Moore, R. C., & Wright, D. E. Systematic desensitisation, therapeutically oriented instructions and selective positive reinforcement. *Behaviour Research and Therapy*, 1969, *7*, 27-33.

Parker, G. Reported parental characteristics of agoraphobics and social phobics. *British Journal of Psychiatry*, 1979, *135*, 555-560.

Paul, G. L. *Insight vs. desensitization in psychotherapy.* Stanford, Calif.: Stanford University Press, 1966.

Phillips, R. M., & Hutchinson, J. T. Intravenous acetylcholine in the treatment of the neuroses. *British Medical Journal,* 1954, *1,* 1468-1470.

Quitkin, F. M., & Rifkin, A., Kaplan, J., & Klein, D. F. Phobic anxiety syndrome complicated by drug dependence and addiction, a treatable form of drug abuse. *Archives of General Psychiatry,* 1972, *27,* 159-162.

Rachman, S. The conditioning theory of fear acquisition: A critical examination. *Behaviour Research and Therapy,* 1977, *15,* 375-387.

Roberts, A. H. Housebound housewives—A follow-up study of a phobic anxiety state. *British Journal of Psychiatry,* 1964, *110,* 191-197.

Robinson, D., & Henry, S. *Self-help and health: Mutual aid for modern problems.* London: Martin Robinson & Co., 1977.

Rock, M. H., & Goldberger, L. Relationships between agoraphobia and field dependence. *Journal of Nervous and Mental Disease,* 1978, *166,* 781-786.

Roth, M. The phobic anxiety depersonalization syndrome. *Proceedings of the Royal Society of Medicine,* 1959, *52,* 587-595.

Roth, M., Garside, R. F., & Kerr, T. A. Studies in classification of affective disorders. *British Journal of Psychiatry,* 1972, *121,* 147-161.

Rutter, M., Tizard, J., & Whitmore, K. *Education, health and behaviour.* London: Longman, 1968.

Sargant, W., & Dally, P. Treatment of anxiety states by antidepressant drugs. *British Medical Journal,* 1962, *1,* 6-9.

Schilder, P. *The nature of hypnosis.* New York: International Universities Press, 1956.

Seligman, M., & Johnston, J. A cognitive theory of avoidance learning. In F. McGuigan & D. Lumsden (Eds.), *Contemporary approaches to conditioning and learning.* New York: Academic Press, 1973.

Sergeant, H. G. S., & Yorkston, N. J. Some complications of using methohexitone to relax anxious patients. *The Lancet,* 1968, *2,* 653-655.

Shafar, S. Aspects of phobic illness—A study of 90 personal cases. *British Journal of Medical Psychology,* 1976, *49,* 211-236.

Shapira, K., Kerr, T. A., & Roth, M. Phobias and affective illness. *British Journal of Psychiatry,* 1970, *117,* 25-32.

Sherman, A. R. Real life exposure as a primary therapeutic factor in the desensitization treatment of fear. *Journal of Abnormal Psychology,* 1972, *79,* 19-28.

Sim, M., & Houghton, H. Phobic anxiety and its treatment. *Journal of Nervous and Mental Disease,* 1966, *143,* 484-491.

Slater, E., & Shields, J. Genetical aspect of anxiety. In M. Lader (Ed.), *Studies of anxiety. British Journal of Psychiatry,* Special Publication No. 3, 1969.

Slovic, P., Fishoff, B., & Lichtenstein, S. Behavioral decision theory. *Annual Review of Psychology,* 1977, *28,* 1-40.

Snaith, R. A clinical investigation of phobias. *British Journal of Psychiatry,* 1968, *114,* 673-697.

Solyom, L., Beck, P., Solyom, C., & Hugel, R. Some etiological factors in phobic neurosis. *Canadian Psychiatric Association Journal,* 1974, *19,* 69-77.

Solyom, L., Heseltine, G. F. D., McClure, D. J., Solyom, C., Ledwidge, B., & Steinberg, G.

Behaviour therapy versus drug therapy in the treatment of phobic neurosis. *Canadian Psychiatric Association Journal*, 1973, *18*, 25-32.

Solyom, L., McClure, D. J., Heseltine, G. F. D., Ledwidge, B., & Solyom, C. Variables in the aversion relief therapy of phobics. *Behavior Therapy*, 1972, *3*, 21-28.

Solyom, L., Silberfeld, M., & Solyom, C. Maternal overprotection in the etiology of agoraphobia. *Canadian Psychiatric Association Journal*, 1976, *21*, 109-113.

Stampfl, T. G., & Levis, D. J. Essentials of implosion therapy, a learning-theory-based psychodynamic behavioural therapy. *Journal of Abnormal Psychology*, 1967, *72*, 496-503.

Stern, R., & Marks, I. Brief and prolonged flooding. *Archives of General Psychiatry*, 1973, *28*, 270-276.

Teasdale, J. D., Walsh, P. A., Lancashire, M., & Mathews, A. M. Group exposure for agoraphobics: A replication study. *British Journal of Psychiatry*, 1977, *130*, 186-193.

Terhune, W. B. The phobic syndrome: A study of eighty-six patients with phobic reactions. *Archives of Neurology and Psychiatry*, 1949, *62*, 162-172.

Torgersen, S. The nature and origin of common phobic fears. *British Journal of Psychiatry*, 1979, *134*, 343-351.

Tucker, W. I., Diagnosis and treatment of the phobic reaction. *American Journal of Psychiatry*, 1956, *112*, 825-830.

Tversky, A., & Kahneman, D. Judgment under uncertainty: Heuristics and biases in judgments reveal some heuristics of thinking under uncertainty. *Science*, 1974, *185*, 1124-1131.

Tyrer, P. *The role of bodily symptoms in anxiety* (Maudsley Monograph No. 23). Oxford: Oxford University Press, 1976.

Tyrer, P., Candy, J., & Kelly, D. Phenelzine in phobic anxiety: A controlled trial. *Psychological Medicine*, 1973, *3*, 120-124.(a)

Tyrer, P., Candy, J., & Kelly, D. A study of the clinical effects of phenelzine and placebo in the treatment of phobic anxiety. *Psychopharmacologia (Berlin)*, 1973, *32*, 237-254.(b)

Tyrer, P., & Steinberg, D. Symptomatic treatment of agoraphobia and social phobias: A follow-up study. *British Journal of Psychiatry*, 1975, *127*, 163-168.

Ullrich, R., Ullrich de Muynck, G., Crombach, G., & Peikert, V. Three flooding procedures in the treatment of agoraphobia. In J. C. Brendelmann, J. T. Quinn, P. J. Grahaam, J. J. M. Harbison, & H. McAllister (Eds.), *Progress in behavioral therapy*. Berlin: Springer-Verlag, 1975.

Watson, J. P., Gaind, R., & Marks, I. M. Prolonged exposure: A rapid treatment for phobias. *British Medical Journal*, 1971, *1*, 13-15.

Watson, J. P., & Marks, I. M. Relevant and irrelevant fear in flooding—A crossover study of phobic patients. *Behavior Therapy*, 1971, *2*, 275-293.

Watson, J. P., Mullett, G. E., & Pillay, H. The effects of prolonged exposure to phobic situations upon agoraphobic patients treated in groups. *Behaviour Research and Therapy*, 1973, *11*, 531-545.

Webster, A. S. The development of phobias in married women. *Psychological Monographs*, 1953, *67*, No. 367.

Weekes, C. A practical treatment of agoraphobia. *British Medical Journal*, 1973, *2*, 469-471.

Westphal, C. Die Agoraphobie: Eine neuropathische Erscheinung. *Archiv für Psychiatrie und Nervenkrankheiten*, 1871, *3*, 138-161.

Winokur, G., & Holeman, E. Chronic anxiety neurosis: Clinical and sexual aspects. *Acta Psychiatrica Scandinavica*, 1963, *39*, 384-412.

Wolberg, L. R. *The techniques of psychotherapy* (3rd ed., Vol. 2). New York: Grune & Stratton, 1977.

Wolpe, J. *Psychotherapy by reciprocal inhibition*. Stanford, Calif.: Stanford University Press, 1958.

Wolpe, J., & Lang, P. S. A fear survey schedule for use in behaviour therapy. *Behaviour Research and Therapy*, 1964, *2*, 27-30.

Yorkston, N. J., Sergeant, H. G. S., & Rachman, S. Methohexitone relaxation for desensitising agoraphobic patients. *The Lancet*, 1968, *2*, 651-655.

Zitrin, C. M. Combined pharmacological and psychological treatment of phobias. In M. Mavissakalian & D. H. Barlow (Eds.), *Phobia: Psychological and pharmacological treatment*. New York: Guilford Press, 1981.

Zitrin, C. M., Klein, D. F., Lindemann, C., Tobak, P., Rock, M., Kaplan, J. H., & Ganz, V. H. Comparison of short-term treatment regimens in phobic patients: A preliminary report. In R. L. Spitzer & D. F. Klein (Ed.), *Evaluation of psychological therapies*. Baltimore: Johns Hopkins University Press, 1976.

Zitrin, C. M., Klein, D. F., & Woerner, M. G. Behavior therapy, supportive psychotherapy, imipramine and phobias. *Archives of General Psychiatry*, 1978, *35*, 307-316.

Zitrin, C. M., Klein, D. F., & Woerner, M. G. Treatment of agoraphobia with group exposure *in vivo* and imipramine. *Archives of General Psychiatry*, 1980, *37*, 63-72.

# Index

Italicized page numbers indicate material in figures and tables.

Acetylcholine, 52
Adultery, 64
Aggression, 63
  repression of, 64
Agras, W. S., 9, 12, 14, 85, 99, *100*,
    *101*, 214*n*., 215*n*., 218*n*., 220*n*.
Agulnik, P., 16, 214*n*.
Akiskal, H. S., 32, 214*n*.
Alcoholics Anonymous, 103
Alcoholism, 2, 8, 10
Alertness, 8
Allen, R., 99, *101*, 218*n*.
Alprenolol, 97
Amines
  pressor, 53
  sympathomimetic, 53
Amitriptyline, 53
Analogue fears, 28
"Analysis of a Phobia in a 5-Year-Old
    Boy" (Freud), 40
Andrews, J. D. W., 35, 40, 66, 70,
    214*n*.
Anesthetics, 53
Anticipatory anxiety, 2, 4, 5, 49, 67,
    152 (*see also* Anxiety)
Antidepressants, 62, 69, 156
  MAO inhibitor type, 52–56, 62
  tricyclic, 34, 53, 57–59, 62
Anxiety, 1–5, 21, 31, 39, 41, 45, 48,
    *60*, 110, 111, *126*, 143, *145*,
    154, 156–159, *156*
  in activity schedule, *26*, *27*
  anticipatory, 2, 4, 5, 49, 67, 151

autonomous, 51, 56, 97, 150
and avoidance, 4
and behavioral treatment, *76*, 78,
    79, 81, 83, *84*, 85, *86*, 88, 91,
    94, 96–98
components of, 18
and drugs, 51, 54, 55, 59
and exposure, 147–153
free-floating, 9
generalized, 5, 6, 7, 9, 10, 34, 122,
    123, 139, 155
and modes of onset, 13
neurosis, *36*, 44–46, 48
and panic, 42, 196
and programmed practice, 117–119
and psychotherapy, 63
scale rating of, 24, 25, *137*
self-rating of, *140*, 142
separation, 37
situational relief of, *5*
situational provocations of, 3, 4, *4*
and social influences, 103, *105*, 108
somatic, 20
and stimuli, 44
subjective experience of, 23
trait, 33, 34, 47, *47*
and treatment follow-up, *138*
Anxiolytics, 50–52, 62, 110
Arieti, S., 41, 214*n*.
Arousal, psychophysiological, 29
Assessment, 18–31
  behavioral testing, 21–28, *24*, 30
    activity schedule on, *26*, *27*, 28

225

Chlordiazepoxide, 53, 54
Clarke, J., 7, 215n.
Clayton, A. B., 51, 215n.
Clients' manual for programmed practice, 160-187
Cluster analysis, 3
Cobb, J., 90, 220n.
Cognition and phobias, 2, 6, 45, 46
  and autonomic-behavioral association, 148, 149
  cognitive modification, 155
  restructuring, 155
Cohen-Kettenis, P. T., 35, 215n.
Cole, A., 124, 215n.
Coleman, J. V., 12, 14, 216n.
Committee on the Review of Medicines, 51
Conditioning, 39, 164, 165, 167
  of autonomic responses, 148
  of avoidance, 147, 148
  classical, 43
  of fear, 42, 43, 148
Contracts, therapeutic, 115, 116
Cooper, J. E., 72, 215n.
Cooper, M., 12, 218n.
Cordes, E., 2, 215n.
Cornell Medical Index, 143
Crombach, G., 97, 222n.
Crowe, M. J., 85, 215n.

Dally, P., 52, 221n.
Death, fears of, 2, 6
Defrancisco, D., 51, 217n.
Dependency, 8, 35, 36, 37, 47, 65, 66, 158, 191
Depersonalization, 5, 6, 7, 11, 51, 54
Depression, 5, 7, 9-11, 21, 60, 122, 139
  and behavioral treatment, 76
  and drugs, 53, 57-59
  etiology of, 32
  inventory on, 139
  measures of, 139
  neurosis, 54
  self-rating of, 139, 140, 141, 142
  symptoms of, 6
Desensitization, 29, 68, 69, 135
  nonspecific, 130
  simple, 75, 76, 76, 78-81, 82, 83, 83
  systematic, 55, 57, 58, 71, 73, 76-79, 76, 77, 84, 85, 91, 93, 94, 99, 139, 141

Diabetes, 51
Diary records, 118, 120, 123, 154, 206, 207, 208-211
Diazepam, 54, 55, 95, 96
Disability, defined, 12
Displacement, 40, 41, 63, 64
Dixon, J. J., 9, 215n.
Dizziness, 1, 2, 4
Dream analysis, 64
Driving and drugs, 51
Drug treatment, 1, 10, 50-62, 132, 159, 202 (see also Antidepressants; Anxiolytics; Barbiturates; Tranquilizers)
  and anxiety, 51, 54, 55, 59
  and behavioral treatment, 93-97
  conclusion on, 62
  dependency on, 8
  and depression, 53, 57-59
  and driving, 51
  leukotomy, 59-62, 60
  MAO inhibitors, 52-56, 62

Eating places, practice situations in, 205
Edwards, G., 68, 76, 219n.
Edwards, J., 99, 101, 218n.
Eggeraat, J. B., 22, 216n.
Ego, strengthening of, 64
Embedded-figures test, 34
Emmelkamp, P. M. G., 22, 28, 34, 35, 87-89, 88, 100, 107, 135, 136, 139, 142, 143, 155, 156, 215n., 216n.
Emmelkamp-Benner, A., 22, 107, 215n.
Epidemiology, 11, 12
Epilepsy, 2
  temporal lobe, 11
Epstein, L. H., 28, 216n.
Errera, P., 12, 14, 216n.
Etiology
  and classification, 34
  cognition in, 46
  and depression, 32
  and family, 38
  models for, 40-49, 157
Exhibitionism, 41, 64
Existential reorientation, 67
Expectations and treatment, 143, 144, 156
Exposure, 147-154

McGennis, A., 103, 220*n*.
McKinney, W. T., 32, 214*n*.
McNair, D. M., 81, 139, 220*n*.
McPherson, F. M., 135, 136, 139,
    142, 220*n*.
Mendel, J. G. C., 10, 57, 220*n*.
Meperidine, 53
Methohexital sodium (Brevital), 93, 94
Methyldopa, 53
Meyer, V., 71, 220*n*.
Michael, S. T., 12, 218*n*.
Micropsia, 11
Middlesex Hospital Questionnaire, 61,
    132
Milton, F., 39, 42, 96, 97, 217*n*.,
    220*n*.
Mineka, S., 147, 148, 220*n*.
Mischel, W., 37, 220*n*.
Mitchell-Heggs, N., 53, 61, 218*n*.,
    220*n*.
Modeling, symbolic, 85
Moll, A., 68, 220*n*.
Monchaux, C. de, 9, 215*n*.
Monoamine oxidase (MAO) inhibitors,
    52–56, 62
Mood, 81
    and behavior therapy, 139
Mood Scale, 139
Moore, R. C., 99, 220*n*.
Mountjoy, C. Q., 54, 220*n*.
Mullaney, J. A., 8, 220*n*.
Mullett, G. E., 85, 222*n*.
Munby, M., 10, 19, 23, 30, 85, *87*,
    *124*, *125*, 127, *129*, 131, *132*,
    136, *137*, *138*, 139, *140*, 218*n*.-
    220*n*.
Muscle relaxation, 93

Napier, L., 55, 219*n*.
Natural history of agoraphobia, 13–15
Nausea, 2
Neurosis, 33, 34, 39, 64
    and anxiety, *36*, 44–46, 48
    and depression, 54
    incidence of, *32–34*
    in marriage, 16
    symptoms of, 2
Nisbett, R. E., 43, 220*n*.
Nolan, G., 103, 220*n*.

Obsessions, 5, 6, 7, 11, 143
Öhman, A., 43, 220*n*.

Olfactory hallucinations, 11
Oliveau, D. C., 9, 14, 99, 214*n*., 220*n*.
Open Door, 103
Opiates, 53
Out and About, 103
Overarousal, 47
Overprotection, maternal, 35, *36*, 37

Palpitations, 2
Panic attacks, 6, 10, 13, 34, 39, 42,
    44, 45, 48, 49, 53, 54, 57, 97,
    110, 111, 120, 148, 149, 156,
    157, 161–163, 166, 167, 180–
    185, 195, 196
Paradoxical intention, 66, 67
Parker, G., *36*, 37, 220*n*., 221*n*.
Partners
    manual for, 188–205
    in treatment, 109
Passivity (*see* Dependency)
Paul, G. L., 80, 221*n*.
Pearce, J., 55, 219*n*.
Peikert, V., 97, 222*n*.
Persistence, 134–146
Personality, 34–38, *36*
    of agoraphobic patients, 8
    and psychotherapy, 66
Phenelzine, 53–56
Phillips, R. M., 52, 221*n*.
Phobias, general, 1–18, 4–7
    assessment of, 18–31, *24*, *26*, *27*,
        *209–213*
    behavioral treatment of, 71–98, *73*,
        *74*, *76*, *77*, *82–84*, *86*, *88*, 134–
        146, *137*, *138*, *140*, *145*
    and drugs, 50–62, *60*
    and exposure, 99–108, *100*, *101*,
        *105*, *106*
    and programmed practice, 109–133,
        *124–126*, *129*, *130*, *132*, 160–
        205
    and psychotherapy, 63–70
    summary/checklist for, 206, 207
    theoretical aspects, 32–49, *36*, *47*,
        147–159, *156*
    and trait anxiety, 47
Phobic-anxiety depersonalization syn-
    drome, 11 (*see also* Anxiety)
Phobic Society, 103
Phobic Trust, 103
Pike, D. J., 55, 219*n*.
Pillay, H., 85, 222*n*.